JEWISH IDENTITY IN AMERICA

The Susan and David Wilstein Institute of Jewish Policy Studies is an international research and policy studies center based at the University of Judaism in Los Angeles. The Institute was established to conduct Jewish policy analysis and to disseminate its findings throughout the community. The aim of the Institute is not merely to gather information and analyze it, but also to stimulate creative thinking about pivotal issues facing American Jews, and to formulate strategies and become an instrument for change and growth in Jewish life.

JEWISH IDENTITY IN AMERICA

edited by
David M. Gordis
and
Yoav Ben-Horin

THE SUSAN AND DAVID WILSTEIN INSTITUTE OF JEWISH POLICY STUDIES
University of Judaism
Los Angeles, California

Typeworks for KTAV Publishing Co.
Disk No. 2
Input Date:
Job Name: 129a
Ft A
Ft B times roman
Ft C
Ft D

Library of Congress Cataloging-in-Publication

Jewish Identity in America / edited by David M. Gordis and Yoav Ben
-Horin.
    p.   cm.
   ISBN 0-88125-365-0. — ISBN 0-88125-366-9 (pbk.)
   1. Jews—United States—Identity—Congresses. 2. Jews—United
States—Intellectual life—Congresses. 3. United States—Ethnic
   relations—Congresses. I. Gordis, David M. II. Ben-Horin, Yoav.
   E184.J5J557   1990
   305.892'4073—dc20   90-23610
                                                               CIP

Copyright © 1991
Wilstein Institute

Manufacturered in the United States of America

Contents

Preface	David Gordis and Yoav Ben-Horin	vii
Introduction	Seymour Martin Lipset	xiii

I. Defining Jewish Identity

Sociological Analysis of Jewish Identity	Bruce A. Phillips	3
Response	Stephen M. Cohen	27
The Psychology of Identity Formation	Perry London and Allissa Hirschfeld	31
Responses	Irving White	51
	Chaim Seidler-Feller	61

II. The American Jewish Experience

The American Component of American Jewish Identity	Henry Feingold	69
Response	Howard I. Friedman	81
Jewish Identity in the Changing World of American Religion	Jonathan D. Sarna	91
Responses	David Ellenson	105
	Steven Bayme	111

III. American Jews and Israel

Israel in the Jewish Identity of American Jews: A Study in Dualities and Contrasts	Steven M. Cohen	119
Response	Howard Miller	137

American Jews and Israel in the Bush Era	Stuart E. Eizenstat	139

IV. Religion, Education, and Culture

Panel Discussion: The Role of the Synagogue in Jewish Identity	Harold M. Schulweis	159
	Richard N. Levy	167
	Daniel Landes	173
An Agenda for the Study of Jewish Identity and Denominationalism Among Children	Daniel Steinmetz	181
Responses	Hanan Alexander	187
	William Cutter	191
Jewish Studies in the University	Bernard D. Cooperman	195
Responses	Arnold J. Band	207
	Steven T. Zipperstein	211
Popular Fiction and the Shaping of Jewish Identity	Arnold J. Band	215
Job's Children: Post-Holocaust Jewish Identity in Second-Generation Literature	Alan L. Berger	227

V. The Economics of Jewish Identity

Keeping the Cost of Living Jewishly Affordable	J. Alan Winter	253
Responses	Deborah E. Lipstadt	267
	Russell D. Roberts	271

VI. Creating a Policy Research Agenda

Jewish Identity and Policy Research	David Rosenhan	279
Response	Roy Feldman	283
Reflections on the Establishment of the Wilstein Institute	Marshall Sklare	287
Contributors		295

Preface

DAVID GORDIS and YOAV BEN-HORIN

Historians, theologians, and sociologists have tried without success to describe Jews by means of one or another of the conventional sociological categories: religion, nationality, or ethnic group. Though religion, for example, has been an important component of Jewish life, it is clearly inadequate to describe Jews as simply a religious group. The same can be said for the ethnic, cultural, and national elements of Jewishness. The difficulty in describing Jews as a group is quite naturally reflected in the parallel difficulty of describing Jewish identity, by and large a personal phenomenon. Everyone seems to sense what Jewish identity is; no satisfactory definition has as yet gained wide acceptance.

The difficulty of defining Jewish identity is compounded in modern, pluralist America, where new modes have evolved for Jews to connect Jewishly, often radically different from earlier ones and quite detached from them. In our times, assimilation, intermarriage, and indifference have become palpable realities, and yet there also appear to be some significant signs of Jewish renewal. It was to reflect on the nature of Jewish identity, methods of assessing and measuring it, and the possibility of nurturing it in this American environment that the Wilstein Institute of Jewish Policy Studies convened a national conference on "Jewish Identity in America," in June of 1989. This book represents the edited proceedings of that conference.

The conference was not designed to survey the subject of Jewish identity comprehensively. It had a more modest goal: to assist the new Wilstein Institute in shaping a research agenda in this area. Though the conference developed into a broader approach to the topic than was originally planned, this book does not pretend to "cover the field." Important areas are either not treated or inadequately covered. A far more extensive treatment of the religious and cultural dimensions, for example, would be part of a complete review of Jewish identity. Perhaps the single clearest addition to a revised conference agenda would be that of the changing perceptions and roles of women in American Jewish life, a complex and dynamic process of potentially enormous significance, though as yet only partially understood, let alone worked out. The application of the growing research corpus on identity generally to the area of Jewish identity is only touched upon in this volume. This requires further elaboration and is part of the Wilstein Institute's research agenda. But the conference brought together some of the most attentive and thoughtful observers from a number of areas, scholars, lay and professional Jewish leaders, and stimulated some fresh approaches. This book reflects their thinking and summarizes those approaches, and, we believe, makes a significant contribution to the field.

A major unresolved issue dealt with by a number of the contributors to this book concerns "measuring" Jewish identity. The analyses by *Bruce Phillips* and by *Perry London* and *Alissa Hirshfeld* share a common social scientific premise that for Jewish identity to be studied and its fortunes in America evaluated, it has to be itself "identified," that is, defined by and related to certain concretely observable criteria or indicators. And indeed, particularly in a diverse and voluntaristic environment, the community needs a sense of how it is doing in maintaining the "connectedness" of its constituents. Since one of the fundamental objectives of the Jewish community is to nurture Jewish identity, it requires criteria to evaluate the effectiveness of specific programs and approaches and to make programmatic and budgetary decisions on the basis of these evaluations.

But the field of measurement confronts a number of problems. One is the lack of standardization of measuring instruments. More profound is the issue of what it is that we are measuring. The common approach involves the selection of a set of behaviors, expressed attitudes, and beliefs which are considered by knowledgeable students of Jewish life to be good indicators of Jewish identity. Though these identity scales differ, they invariably include such items as lighting Sabbath candles, having a "special meal" on Passover, joining a synagogue, supporting Jewish community institutions, contributing to Israel, and reading a Jewish publication. Establishing these scales allows quantification and comparisons between, for example, different generational groups and groups with different educational backgrounds.

Identity studies based on instruments of this kind are useful and interesting. But their critics point to a number of fundamental shortcomings. First, they measure attitudinal and behavioral manifestations of identity, not identity itself. They shed no light on the question of whether there is a psycho-cognitive reality underlying these manifestations. They assume that the items chosen for the identity scales are both accurate and desirable. Second, they tell us very little about the Jewishness or potential Jewishness of those who score low on the scale. Absent a consensus on what we mean by Jewish identity, and on what characteristics we wish to nurture when we talk of enhancing Jewish identity, the relationship of the items on any of these identity scales to the desirable objective remains problematic. The role of philosophers, theologians, ethicists, and ideologists in suggesting the purpose of Jewish existence and the quality of life toward which Jewishness and Judaism should lead is excluded from the process, with the result that our apparent successes with those who score high on these scales may be misleading.

This concern is present in several of the papers in the present collection, including those by Phillips and by London and Hirshfeld, as well as in the responses to them by *Steven M. Cohen* and *Irving White*. Throughout the conference there lingered a sense of unease about the content of the identity of those who by current measures would rate as highly identified. Are the behaviors and expressed attitudes which rate high scores on a Jewish identity scale of any real relevance to what have been termed "inner-meaning" issues, that is, issues relating to the individual's responses to core questions of life and death, relationships to others, and the values by which one makes life's fundamental decisions? Are these behaviors and attitudes of genuine importance to individuals, and are they sufficiently durable to be of significance in assessing the future of the community? These measures appear to be, at best, incomplete, and if they are, how can the underlying psychodynamic reality, which may relate more to inner-meaning issues, be studied?

Most of the contributors to this volume agree that the American Jewish experience is in many ways unique in Jewish history. This uniqueness carries with it both promise and threat. *Henry Feingold* discusses the American component of American Jewish identity. He traces in particular the evolving contrast and complementarity between the historical Jewish and American notions of liberty and equality. In his response *Howard Friedman* elaborates on the promise of modern Jewish life in a context that is as dynamic and inviting as present American society and culture, and on the challenges of creativity and purposefulness that are implicit in this historical opportunity. In a less upbeat vein, *Jonathan Sarna* examines what he considers to be the deteriorating strategic position of American Jews in the context of a changing pattern of American religious life. Focusing in particular on the rapid rise of Islam in this country, Sarna forcasts the erosion of the current "Protestant-Catholic-Jewish" paradigm, and with it increasing threats to the status, interests, and power of American Jewry. His respondents, *David Ellenson* and *Steven Bayme,* argue in effect that Sarna underestimates the complex and peculiarly potent affinity of character and ethos between the Jewish community and experience and that of the broader American society.

Israel and its fortunes constitute central issues in American Jewish organizational life and public behavior. How does it relate to Jewish identity, and what are the implications of apparently changing realities of American Jewish–Israeli relationships? Steven M. Cohen draws a sharp distinction between the powerful symbolic role that Israel plays in American Jewish identity and its limited substantive dimension. He argues that the attachment of American Jews to Israel is actually quite superficial, and may be waning. Cohen points out that commitment to Israel is dominated by fear, is a political issue that rarely touches the private sphere, and is not translated into familiarity with Israel's society and culture. *Howard Miller,* in response to Cohen, interprets some of the same data very differently: whatever their specific, detailed familiarity and involvement with things Israeli, Miller finds that an extraordinary number of American Jews define their self-image by the way Israel behaves at any given moment. He finds such identification dangerous insofar as it tends to confuse individual morality with the requirements of statecraft. Interestingly, from their different vantage points both Cohen and Miller conclude that it is incumbent upon American Jews to focus on and come to grips with the differences between American and Israeli Jewish life. *Stuart E. Eizenstat* attempts to do this and to develop some norms of both attachment and dissent. His paper is the text of a public address he delivered at the conference.

Religion, education, and culture are essential building blocks of Jewish identity. Consideration of fundamental issues about the existence of an American Jewish culture and the prognosis for its development would constitute excellent agendas for several conferences and could cover the pages of many books. Although very much of concern to the Wilstein Institute, no attempt was made at this conference to deal with the subject exhaustively. Instead, a number of related issues were addressed. Rabbis *Daniel Landes* (Orthodox), *Richard Levy* (Reform), and *Harold Schulweis* (Conservative) consider the contemporary American synagogue in its relationship to Jewish identity. In different ways and perhaps to different degrees, all three rabbis warn against the temptation to use the synagogue as a crutch and even as a substitute for a genuinely personal Jewish engagement. Schulweis decries the gap between the public and private spheres of Jewish life in America, and the increasing willingness of individual Jews to relegate and confine their Jewishness to the synagogue. Levy, too, challenges the common view of the synagogue as primarily an instrument for individuals to find or fulfill their Jewish identity, because this attitude places social needs over deeper religious ones. By contrast, Landes reports on the dynamism and enthusiasm within the Orthodox community. But he too voices a certain concern that the quest for "authenticity" that appears to have replaced the previously predominant preoccupation with the fusion of modernity with tradition should endanger individual and communal creativity, which is another part of authentic Jewish life.

Daniel Steinmetz reports and *William Cutter* and *Hanan Alexander* critique a Wilstein Institute project on the role of Jewish schools in shaping attitudes of children to Jews of other denominations. Bernard Cooperman writes about the good news and the misleading news of the recent rapid development of Jewish studies on the American campus. *Steven Zipperstein* responds to the Cooperman paper, as does *Arnold Band*, who also contributes a paper on Jewish identity as reflected in American-Jewish popular literature. Alan Berger writes of Jewish identity in the fiction of American-Jewish Holocaust survivors.

Discussion of a very different kind of subject took place at the conference with the paper of *J. Alan Winter*. He deals with the costs and affordability of Jewish affiliation. Along with responses by *Deborah Lipstadt* and *Russell Roberts*, this paper represents another area which requires a good deal of further study. Here, too, a line of research for the Wilstein Institute and for others was suggested.

Finally, the conference concluded with prescriptive analyses by *David Rosenhan* and *Roy Feldman*, who sought to synthesize the papers and discussions and draw from them implications for policy research. Also included in this section of the book are the reflections by *Marshall Sklare*, scholar-in-residence at the conference, on the establishment of the Wilstein Institute as a new policy research entity for the Jewish community. It was useful for those responsible for the Wilstein Institute to hear the perspectives of a major figure in American Jewish studies who had not been closely involved with its establishment. Though some of Sklare's comments are of broad application rather than specifically directed at the Institute as it has been structured, his overall suggestions and caveats are important and highly constructive and supportive. A substantive introduction to the book was written by our other scholar-in-residence at the conference, *Seymour Martin Lipset*, who serves as senior scholar at the Institute.

We wish to acknowledge with thanks the efforts of Dr. Fredelle Spiegel, who served as fellow of the Wilstein Institute and conference program coordinator, and of Gail Schwartz, who served as research assistant at the Institute during the 1988–89 academic year. It is no exaggeration to say that neither the conference nor these proceedings would have been possible without the extraordinary talents, efforts, and dedication of the Institute's administrative assistant, Martha Davis. The smooth functioning of the conference and of the Institute itself are in no small measure a reflection of her remarkable abilities. In the preparation of the manuscript she was assisted ably by Julie Lodgen, who serves as secretary of the Institute. We are very grateful to all of these colleagues.

The conference whose written results are presented here drew heavily on the social sciences. In at least two important ways, however, it was not a scientific conference. First, it brought together scientists and nonscientists, academics and lay people, and so the articulation of even sophisticated and technical ideas avoided recourse to technical jargon accessible only to select initiates. Second, and more important, the conference did not bring together detached, strictly "objective" observers of the Jewish community. Rather, those who participated, though diverse in disciplines, training, and political, religious, and ideological views, were united in their commitment to contentful Jewish continuity. It is our hope and intention that the Wilstein Institute will continue to bring together talented and committed individuals of diverse views to consider matters of profound importance to Jewish life. There is much that trained, thoughtful minds can contribute to shaping that life. This book is offered in the context of that conviction, that commitment, and that hope.

Introduction

SEYMOUR MARTIN LIPSET

This book is about Jewish identity as analyzed by social scientists. Efforts to define what it means to be a Jew go back over three millennia. Religious practitioners and theologians have been concerned with the issue since biblical times. Historians have reported on Jewish behavior for at least two thousand years. The writings of non-Jews describing ways their Jewish contemporaries act also came down to us for the same period of time. They describe a stubborn people, insistent on maintaining their religious laws, their Sabbath, their dietary practices, the purity of their bloodlines.

There has been a Jewish Diaspora since the days of ancient Egypt, of Hebrews living among Gentiles, and the situation has always posed problems for the host communities and the children of Israel. Some of the traits distinguishing Jews and the reactions of the dominant peoples have been somewhat similar over time. Thus Diaspora Jews have always been among the more learned, reflecting the injunction that all males must study the Bible, and have been found disproportionately among the trading strata and the more well-to-do, perhaps a result of the advantages "outsiders" have in economic relationships, but also of the emphasis in their religious outlook on rationality and work.

In recent decades, social scientists, anthropologists, psychologists, and sociologists, as well as students of literature, have attempted to define or describe Jews, using their empirical research techniques—participant observation, interviews, questionnaires, attitude and personality scales, and analyses of written materials. A goodly sample of the most recent and best of this work is presented in the chapters which follow.

The need to move beyond religion-bound sources and factors to understand Jewish identity is inherent in the fact that although many millions of people continue to think of themselves as Jews, only a minority the world over adhere to Orthodox or traditional Judaism, while a larger proportion are basically irreligious, and a substantial number are the offspring of religiously mixed marriages. It is impossible to provide precise hard numbers for these generalizations. But considering that eight to ten of the fourteen to seventeen million Jews in the world are in the United States and the Soviet Union, of whom 10 to 15 percent in the former and almost none in the latter are Orthodox, the weakness of traditional Jewish religious identification is obvious. If to these figures are added the four million in Israel, of whom no more than 25 percent are Orthodox, the need to define Judaism in ways other than what is specified in the Bible and the Talmud is clear.

In the United States, the arena which almost totally concerns the authors of the essays in this book, fully one out of four of those randomly selected for the 1988 *Los Angeles Times* national survey, the best extent sample of American Jews, said that though born Jews, they did not see themselves as Jews. Another 25 percent identified, but had no affiliation with any Jewish group or institution and did not contribute to any communal or overseas cause. Some of these were willing, however, to describe themselves as Conservative or Reform, more the latter than the former.

Perhaps the most dramatic statistics attesting to the fall-off from traditional beliefs and values of American Jews are the intermarriage rates. They vary across age groups and communities. But among young people, those under thirty, they appear to be between 40 and 50 percent. These figures are not as surprising as they seem. They derive from three major factors. First is the decline and even lack of binding religiosity among most American Jews; second is the extent to which American non-Jews accept their fellows of Jewish origin economically and socially; and third the propensity of almost all Jewish young people, 90 percent, to spend the four to six years in which they are most likely to develop a romantic relationship in the most universalistic institution in the country—in higher education, colleges and universities—whose norms negate emphasis on religion as a barrier to dating and marrying.

Given the evidence that as we approach the beginning of the twenty-first century of the common era the Jewish community in the United States is probably the least committed, the least involved, it has ever been in Jewish religious belief, practice, and ritual, the subject of Jewish identity, or rather identities—what they are, how they are maintained, which aspects are likely to continue—must be of major interest to anyone concerned with Jewish continuity. Will there be a significant community a century from now, given the propensity to assimilate and the extremely low birthrate?

There is a great deal of evidence that Jews react and behave differently from other Americans, even those Jews who do not identify, are not affiliated, or are intermarried in families in which no conversion has occurred. Most prominent is their support for Israel. For one thing, even nonidentified Jews know more about the Middle East situation and are more favorable to Israel than non-Jews, though their degree of commitment is lower than that of other Jews. Second, most Jews, roughly three-quarters of them, feel that the threat of anti-Semitism is serious; the nonidentified also are concerned, although again less so. Third, Jews are politically much more liberal than other Americans, although the Orthodox are conservative. The nonidentified are as liberal as the identified. Fourth, as noted, Jews continue to be among the most affluent, best educated, and of highest occupational status of identifiable ethno-religious groups; and nonidentified do as well. Jews work hard, contribute heavily to charitable causes, are major consumers of expensive goods, buy more books and serious magazines, take more vacations abroad, etc. They outdo non-Jews in these qualities, even those at similar income levels. Jews are less likely to be caught doing illegal or deviant acts, they are less alcoholic and divorce less than others at their station or income level. There is little evidence as to the internal variations among them in these aspects.

While there are reliable data as to a great deal of the above, we know little as to what sustains these patterns, particularly among the weakly identified. Jean-Paul Sartre once noted that very assimilated, even self-hating Jews tend to associate with each others, that they do not escape into the larger community.

The whole issue of continuity, of what keeps Jews Jewish, is something that the community and social science know little about. It is surprising, given the billions of dollars raised for Israel and American communal activities, how little is spent on research to specify the traits of diverse strata of Jews and to identify the factors related to different degrees of involvement. Jewish educational systems, from preschool to university programs like Hillel, have never been systematically evaluated, although large sums are spent on them.

The articles in this book represent an important contribution to the larger objective of teaching American Jewry about itself. Although except for Steven Cohen's chapter, which is derived in part from national surveys, they are based on limited data, they do suggest hypotheses as to the nature and sources of Jewish identity. The conference held by the Wilstein Institute at which they were presented was designed to encourage more systematic and elaborate research, by reviewing what we know. The task is admirably accomplished in this volume. It teaches us much we must know, but as importantly, it sets the stage for further exploration.

PART I
Defining Jewish Identity

Sociological Analysis of Jewish Identity

BRUCE A. PHILLIPS

Introduction

The sociological study of Jewish identity is framed within but stands against the larger treatment of ethnic identity by American sociology. The dominant sociological stance has been exemplified (as well as influenced) by the work of Milton Gordon. In his classic work *Assimilation in American Life* (1964) Gordon presented ethnic identity as a stage in the process of an inevitable assimilation.

Gordon conceptually divided assimilation into a number of smaller processes of which cultural and structural assimilation are the two major components. Cultural assimilation is the process of minority adaptation to the culture of the dominant group. Structural assimilation is the movement of the minority into the social structure of the majority society. The movement of Jews into executive positions in corporations and into the professions would be an example of structural assimilation.

In addition, Gordon sets forth five other processes of assimilation. "Attitude Receptional" and "Behavioral Receptional" are the diminution of prejudice and discrimination (respectively). Civic assimilation is the ability of the minority to take positions of responsibility (elected or appointed) in the civic or governmental structure. The final stages Gordon called "marital assimilation," or the willingness of the majority group to marry with members of the minority, and "identificational assimilation," where the minority group ceases to identify as a separate entity.

The assumption that only social structural conditions imposed by the majority stand in the way of a minority's assimilation continues to be central to most of current sociology. The most recent example is the popularity of the "middleman minority" approach (Bonacich 1973), which explains Jewish distinctiveness in terms of the traditional Jewish position as an economic middleman.

Jewish persistence is problematic for the mainstream of ethnic sociology, which would have predicted Jewish disappearance on the basis of the Jews' economic success. Gordon, for example, found Jews to be culturally but not structurally assimilated and attributed this lack of structural assimilation to an "enthnocentrism" born of discrimination.

In reviewing *Assimilation in American Life,* Marshall Sklare (1965) objected that Gordon had missed a critical point about Jewish self-esteem: seeing oneself as part of a "long and proud" tradition is not ethnocentrism—it is a culturally valid worldview. On the other hand, when Jewish sociologists concentrate on Jewish persistence, they target a subject that is of little interest to sociology in general. The problem, explained Sklare (1982, p. 268), pertains to the "yardstick" used.

> [A] question which must be faced by the analyst is whether to place Jewish life in a unique or special framework, or whether to place it in some larger framework—to view Jewish life as an instance of minority group behavior and measure the extent to which it parallels the behavior of other groups. The natural inclination of the social scientist is to use a general yardstick rather than a Jewish one. Using a general yardstick has the advantage of making one's work relevant to all social science. Using a Jewish yardstick has the disadvantage that one's work may interest primarily those concerned with Jewish studies.

Waxman (1977/78) has introduced the terms "assimilationists" and "survivalists" to contrast those who measure Jews by the "general yardstick" with those who study Jews from the perspective of Jewish continuity. Assimilationist sociologists such as Gordon take for granted that ethnic minorities (including Jews) will disappear when circumstances warrant. Although American Jews retain a distinctive identity, it is only a matter of time until they will eventually act on the basis of their recently consolidated position in the American mainstream. To the assimilationists, American Jews are like the character Wylie Coyote in the old "Road Runner" cartoons: If they remain identifying Jews it is because they have not yet realized that they have already run beyond the edge of the cliff.

The main difference between the assimilationists and the survivalists is their starting assumption. It may also be where they would like to see the minority end up. Because they are committed to the idea of Jewish survival, survivalist sociologists seek to identify and strengthen the mechanisms of Jewish group continuity.

The Study of Jewish Identity

The sociological study of Jewish identity begins with suburbanization after the Second World War. Prior to this point the sociology of American

Jewry concentrated on the monumental demographic changes taking place within American Jewry, such as occupational and geographic mobility. It was not until the sixties that Jewish identity first became a specific focus for sociologists, as Jews began to enter what Sklare at the time called the "Suburban Frontier."

The studies examined here are the major empirical studies of Jewish identity, all produced during and after the period of suburbanization

1. Marshall Sklare, *Jewish Identity on the Suburban Frontier*. A study of a midwestern suburb of a major Jewish community conducted in the 1960s.
2. Sidney Goldstein and Calvin Goldscheider, *Jewish Americans: Three Generations in a Jewish Community*. A study of Providence, Rhode Island, conducted in 1963 and published in 1968.
3. Arnold Dashevsky and Howard Shapiro, a study of St. Paul conducted in the early 1970s.
4. Geoffrey Bock, "The Jewish Schooling of American Jews: A Study of Non-Cognitive Educational Effects." dissertation using data from the National Jewish Population Study, a survey of American Jewry conducted in 1970–71.
5. Steven M. Cohen, *American Modernity and Jewish Identity*. Uses data from the 1965 and 1975 Boston Jewish Population studies.
6. Calvin Goldscheider, *Jewish Continuity and Change*. Based on the 1975 Boston Jewish Population study.
7. Steven M. Cohen, *American Assimilation or Jewish Revival?* Based on the 1981 New York Jewish Population study
8. Neil Sandberg, *Jewish Life in Los Angeles: A Window to Tomorrow*. Based on a study conducted in Los Angeles in 1976–77.
9. Simon Herman, *Jewish Identity: A Social Psychological Perspective*. Based on research conducted in the 1960s through the early 1970s.

This paper is organized around three questions:

1. How has Jewish identity been conceptualized and measured in studies of change in identity?
2. What has been learned about Jewish identity from these change models, and how is this affected by the measures and conceptualizations used?
3. What new directions are and should be emerging in the sociological study of Jewish identity?

The sociological study of Jewish identity takes one of two forms: an emphasis on studying the changing level of Jewish identity over time or an emphasis on the content of Jewish identity. These two perspectives are not mutually exclusive, but the major empirical studies of Jewish identity tend to fall into either one mode or the other, with the most recent studies falling into the "change" camp.

How Jewish Identity Has Been Conceptualized and Measured by Change-Oriented Models

Sociologists interested in studying change in Jewish identity use scales and indexes which can summarize "levels" of Jewish identification in either behavioral or attitudinal terms.

Behavioral Measures of Change

Because they are the easiest to identify and are the clearest in their meaning, the behavioral measures are the most widely used. The behavioral measures consist of ritual observances and communal affiliations. They are summarized in Table 1.

Jewish observance. Some kind of Sabbath observance is included on everybody's list but not always in the same way. Lighting candles on the Sabbath is the only Sabbath observance asked about by everybody. Sklare and Dashevsky also ask about a "special" or "Sabbath" meal on Friday nights. Dashevsky included a rather vague question about "observance of the Sabbath," while Cohen specifically asks about an Orthodox observance: "carries no money on the Sabbath." Having or attending a seder on Passover is also on every list. Sklare adds "no bread eaten," and Dashevsky includes "special food." Fasting on Yom Kippur is the third observance found on every list. Lighting Chanukah candles is on every list but the Boston study (used by Cohen). Thus, there is general uniformity about what observances to include as indicators of Jewish identity, along with some variations.

Formal and informal ties. Various attachments to other Jews form the second behavioral dimension. Synagogue membership is included on every list, and synagogue attendance is part of every study but one (Goldstein and Goldscheider). Jewish organizational memberships are included in every study either as a dichotomous variable (belongs/does not belong) or as a count of organizational memberships. Bock includes the degree of participation in Jewish organizations as a measure of the intensity of involvement. In this respect it is a kind of parallel to synagogue attendance. In both his studies of Jewish identity Cohen adds Jewish giving to the list of formal affiliations. Jewish friendships are used

Table 1
Jewish Observances

Jewish observances	Author
Sabbath	
Light Sabbath candles	Sklare 1967; Cohen 1983, 1988; Goldstein and Goldscheider 1968; Bock 1976
Special/Sabbath meal on Friday night	Sklare 1967; Dashevsky and Shapiro
Kiddush on Friday night	Sklare 1967; Bock 1976
No smoking allowed in house on Sabbath	Sklare 1967
Carries no money on the Sabbath	Cohen 1988
"Observed the Sabbath"	Dashevsky and Shapiro
Kashruth	
Bacon or ham never served	Sklare 1967
"Kosher meat bought regularly"/ "kosher meat"	Sklare 1967; Goldstein and Goldscheider
Kasher the meat	Sklare 1967
Has two sets of dishes for meat and dairy/separate dishes	Cohen 1988; Goldstein and Goldscheider
Kept kosher	Cohen 1983; Dashevsky and Shapiro
Passover	
Seder on Passover/attends Passover seder/seder	Sklare 1967; Cohen 1983, 1988; Dashevsky and Shapiro; Goldstein and Goldscheider
No bread eaten in home on Passover/ate only special food on Passover	Sklare 1967; Dashevsky and Shapiro
Yom Kippur	
Either or both parents fast on Yom Kippur/fasts-fasted on Yom Kippur	Sklare 1967; Cohen 1983, 1988; Dashevsky and Shapiro
Hanukah	
Candles lit/lights hanukah candles	Sklare 1967; Cohen 1988; Goldstein and Goldscheider

as a measure of informal attachment to the Jewish community in every study but one (Goldstein and Goldscheider).

Jewish education is used only once as a behavioral indicator of Jewish identity. Dashevsky and Shapiro ask about a number of Jewish study activities. These include the study of Hebrew, Yiddish, sacred texts, Jewish history, and Jewish customs and ceremonies. Goldstein and Goldscheider have a question on whether the respondent received a Jewish education as a child. This is confusing since it is really more of an antecedent variable than a measure of Jewish identification.

Israel is another important dimension to Jewish identity, and it has both behavioral and attitudinal components. Since we have an excellent paper on the Israeli component of American Jewish identity, I need not dwell on it other than to note that there has been considerable variety on the Israel questions, from having considered aliyah to dancing Israeli dances to seeing Israel as a threat to American Jewish standing in Gentile eyes.

Intermarriage is included in every study of Jewish identity, usually as a separate topic. Intermarriage is among the (if not the most) profound changes in the American Jewish population, and is most often used as a measure of Jewish decline rather than a subject for investigation in its own right. In the Boston study, for example, Cohen uses intermarriage as a dichotomous variable in his list of Jewish identifications. Making intermarriage a measure of Jewish identity is problematic, however, because it cannot be both a consequence and a measure of Jewish identity. The use of intermarriage as a behavioral measure of Jewish identity assumes that a person who is married to a non-Jew has a weaker Jewish identity than one who has married another Jew. Making this assumption precludes an important and much-needed direction for Jewish research: the relationship between Jewish identity and intermarriage, and the Jewish identity of intermarried Jews.

The theoretical assumption behind the behavioral measures is that more strongly identified Jews will do a greater number of Jewish things. There is potential bias, however, inherent in such indexes. The same items which might be used to differentiate among classes of observant Jews (between the Hassidim and the modern Orthodox, for example) tip the scales in favor of stronger identities for more traditional Jews because there will be more items which apply to "observant" Jews. While I do not find this to be a problem in the studies discussed here, neither is it raised as an issue of concern. Since so much of Jewish identity research depends on behavioral measures, some attention should be paid to the potential artifice introduced by potentially "lopsided" scales. By the same token, the emphasis on traditional observances has obscured the possible use of nontraditional observances among more secular Jews. For example, refraining from going to work on Yom Kippur might be an observance which still has symbolic meaning as an attachment to the Jewish group among Jews who do not attend synagogue.

Attitudinal Measures of Change

Attitudinal scales of Jewish identity have not been used to the same extent as behavioral measures. This is probably because most Jewish research is sponsored by local federations doing planning studies. Attitudinal items about Jewish identity must compete with more applied planning data for inclusion in the survey. Of the five studies discussed here which included attitudinal items, only one was sponsored by a local federation (Dashevsky and Shapiro).

Dashevsky and Shapiro. Dashevsky and Shapiro originally included thirty-one attitudinal items in their questionnaire. They performed a factor analysis and found only seven items that were statistically intercorrelated (i.e., loaded heavily on the first factor). They call these seven items their "Jewish Identity," or "JI," scale. Six of the seven items involve some kind of word signifying "attachment" to other Jews. I have highlighted these words below:

1. I feel an *attachment* to the local Jewish community.
2. I feel an *attachment* to American Jewry.
3. Of all foreign countries, I feel the strongest *ties* to Israel.
4. I feel a strong *attachment* to Jewish life.
5. My general outlook has been affected by my *sharing* in the Jewish culture.
6. I think it is important to know the fundamentals of Judaism.
7. [I] feel a *close kinship* to the Jewish people throughout the world.

Bock. In 1970–71 the Council of Jewish Federations sponsored the first national study of American Jews. Included in the schedule of the National Jewish Population Study were a number of attitudinal items on Jewish identity. These were analyzed by Geoffrey Bock in 1976 as part of a dissertation studying the effects of Jewish schooling. Like Dashevsky and Shapiro, Bock performed a factor analysis on the attitudinal items to create Jewish identity subscales on the basis of the highest interitem correlations (pp. 74–75). Bock presents the raw factor loadings, and the pattern of intercorrelation among the subscale items is striking, but the interpretation of the underlying "common dimension" of these items must be examined. Bock calls the four factors identified by the factor analysis "Jewish Self Esteem," "Cultural Familiarity," "Social Networks," and "Jewish Survival." He also uses an Israel support scale (not discussed here) which he constructed without a factor analysis. It consists of both behavioral and attitudinal items that were part of the NJPS schedule.

Most of the self-esteem items are positive affirmations about being Jewish, such as "I am happy to be Jewish" and "It is important that there should always be a Jewish people." The Cultural Familiarity subscale asks about knowledge of Jewish history, culture, ethics, and other aspects of Jewish culture. The Social Networks scale includes both behavioral and attitudinal items. The behavioral items have already been cited in the previous section and are included again here. The three Jewish Survival questions tap anxieties about Jewish survival, and begin with "There is a good chance that . . ."

Jewish Self-Esteem
  1. I believe in the Jewish religion.
  2. I live in a very Jewish home.
  3. I am happy to be Jewish.
  5. Being Jewish means something very definite to me.
  6. Jewish people everywhere have important things in common.
  7. It is important that there should always be a Jewish people.
  8. Jewish children must have a Jewish education.
  9. If a Jew marries a non-Jew, his children must be brought up as Jews.

Cultural Familiarity
  10. I have Jewish books in the home.
  11. I know Jewish history.
  12. I know Jewish culture.
  13. I know Jewish ethics.
  14. I know Jewish religious teachings.
  15. I enjoy Jewish music.
  16. I enjoy Jewish literature.

Social Networks
  17. Being Jewish affects my choice of personal friends.
  18. Being Jewish affects my choice of a place to live.
  19. It is alright for Jews to marry non-Jews.
  20. It is alright for Jews to date non-Jews.
  21. Among my friends, [all or almost all/most/some/few/none] are Jewish.
  22. Among people in my neighborhood [all or almost all/most/some/few/none] are Jewish.

Jewish Survival
23. There is a good chance that drifting away from Jewish values will cause the Jewish people to disappear.
24. There is a good chance that drifting away from Jewish observances will cause the Jewish people to disappear.
25. There is a good chance that intermarriage will cause the Jewish people to disappear.

Sandberg. Sandberg created a thirty-item scale in which he divides Jewish identity into cultural, national, religious-communal, and religious-devotional dimensions. The cultural items are affirmations of the importance of Jewish culture; for example, "We need to know the history of the Jewish people." The "National" scale consists of questions related to the concept of peoplehood, such as: "I feel an obligation to help Jews anywhere in the world who are in need." The "Religious-Communal" scale contains statements of positive feelings toward the synagogue and Jewish observance; for example, "I enjoy participating in synagogue programs." These latter two dimensions parallel the synagogue membership and ritual observance dimensions of the behavioral scales discussed above. The difference is that Sandberg tends to use affective attitudes about synagogue and Jewish observance rather than behaviors.

Unlike Bock and Dashevsky and Shapiro, who constructed their dimensions of Jewish identity according to statistical intercorrelations among items grouped by factor analysis, Sandberg composes his scales by question content alone. He does not demonstrate that the items in the subscales of Jewish identity are reliable (i.e., consistent) scales in the statistical sense, and it is not clear why some statements belong in one subscale as opposed to another. For example the statement "Pesach seders are important to me" is included in the Religious-Communal dimension, while a parallel statement about the High Holidays is included in the "Religious-Devotional" subscale: "Attending services on the High Holy Days is important for me."

Cultural Items
1. The public schools should teach more about the contribution of Jews to America.
2. Organizations which carry on the Jewish culture are not very important.
3. Los Angeles newspapers should feature more news about Jewish community life.
4. We need to know the history of the Jewish people.
5. We should be willing to give money to preserve our Jewish heritage.

6. It is too bad that the Jewish tradition is not being carried on by more of our young people.
7. Jews should read Jewish periodicals and books.
8. I like to listen to Jewish music.
9. Jewish education is essential for Jewish survival.
10. It is important for American Jews to learn Hebrew.

National
11. A Jewish neighborhood is a friendlier place to live.
12. It is all right to change your name.
13. I feel more comfortable with Jewish people.
14. It is better for a Jew to marry someone who is Jewish.
15. I feel an obligation to help Jews anywhere in the world who are in need.
16. You can be for your own people first and still be a good American.
17. It is not important for Jews to continue as a people.
18. It is important to encourage a sense of Jewish identification in our children.
19. I am glad I was born a Jew.
20. I feel no special bonds to the State of Israel.

Religious-Communal
21. It is important for me to contribute my time and resources to a synagogue or temple.
22. I like attending religious services to be with other Jews.
23. I enjoy participating in synagogue programs.
24. Pesach Seders are important to me.
25. Our religious tradition helps to bring Jewish people closer together.

Religious-Devotional
26. Attending services on the High Holy Days is important for me.
27. Jewish prayers help me when I am troubled.
28. I feel good when the Sabbath candles are lighted.
29. I am moved when I hear the Shofar (ram's horn).
30. The Jewish faith is a source of real strength to me.

Summary. Whereas there was considerable overlap among the behavioral items used to measure Jewish identity, there is almost no consistency found among the attitudinal items used to study change, other than broad measures of "attachment" to other Jews or "affirmations" of Jewish life and culture.

Findings About Jewish Identity

The "generational change" researchers use either one of two statistical techniques. The most common is the simple comparison of "levels" of

Jewish identity over generations and time. The second is a statistically sophisticated causal analysis of factors that "predict" Jewish identity. The conclusions reached and the discussion generated by the "change" studies have defined the central ground for the current sociological debate about the health of American Jewry. The causal analysis has for the most part been without impact on contemporary Jewish policy discussion.

Causal or Regression Models of Jewish Identity

Regression models are causal models. They explain or predict a dependent variable (in this case Jewish identity) in terms of causal or predictor variables. The relative importance of each of the independent variables is calculated as part of the regression equation, so that one can say that one variable causes or predicts Jewish identity more than another. There have been two studies of the "predictors" of Jewish identity, Dashevsky and Shapiro, and Bock.

Dashevsky and Shapiro divide their predictor variables into two groups: socialization variables and structural variables. The socialization variables which most affect Jewish identity (as measured by the JI scale presented above) are, in order of influence: father's religiosity, friends' expectations (i.e., peer influence), Jewish education, and other family factors. The structural factors include socioeconomic status (occupation, income, and education), residence (in a Jewish area and the proportion of neighbors who are Jewish), and religiosity (synagogue attendance, synagogue membership).

Dashevsky and Shapiro conclude that "Jewish identification is *determined* [emphasis added] by a complex array of factors" (p. 78). Because the structural factors have the highest correlations with the JI scale when simultaneously controlling for all the other factors, they conclude that "[socialization] variables operate for the most part indirectly through their effect on current structural factors that in turn influence Jewish identification" (p. 78) and that their regression model suggests "the primacy of structural factors over socialization effects" (p. 79).

This conclusion is highly problematic because it reverses cause and effect in concluding that synagogue membership and living in a Jewish neighborhood "cause" Jewish identity. If anything, one would think that Jewish identity would precede affiliation with a synagogue and the choice of neighborhood.

The Dashevsky and Shapiro study has not turned out to have been particularly influential, in part because regression analysis is not easily

Table 2
Religious Affiliation

Nature of affiliation	Author
Synagogue membership	Cohen 1983, 1988; Goldstein and Goldscheider; Dashevsky and Shapiro; Sklare 1967
Attendance at services	
"Service attended?"	Cohen 1983
Attends(ed) services on High Holidays	Cohen 1988; Sklare 1967; Dashevsky and Shapiro
Attended services on Sabbath	Dashevsky and Shapiro
Attended services on other occasions	Dashevsky and Shapiro
Attends services monthly or more	Cohen 1988
Denomination	Cohen 1988; Goldstein and Goldscheider; Sklare 1967
Jewish study/Jewish education	
Received Jewish education	Goldstein and Goldscheider
Attended Jewish camp	Dashevsky and Shapiro
Discussed topics with Jewish themes	Dashevsky and Shapiro
Studied Hebrew	Dashevsky and Shapiro
Studied Yiddish	Dashevsky and Shapiro
Studied Jewish sacred texts	Dashevsky and Shapiro
Studied Jewish history	Dashevsky and Shapiro
Studied Jewish customs and ceremonies	Dashevsky and Shapiro
Detailed chapter on Jewish education	Sklare 1967
Reads Jewish newspaper	Cohen 1988
Jewish organizational and communal memberships	
Member of/belongs to Jewish organization	Cohen 1983, 1988; Goldstein and Goldscheider; Dashevsky and Shapiro; Sklare 1967
Jewish giving	Cohen 1983, 1988
Nonsectarian organization member	Cohen 1983
Nonsectarian giving	Cohen 1983
Has Jewish friends	Cohen 1983, 1988; Dashevsky and Shapiro; Sklare 1967
Israel	
Has considered aliyah	Cohen 1988
Has visited Israel	Cohen 1988; Dashevsky and Shapiro
Studied in Israel	Dashevsky and Shapiro
Danced Israeli dances	Dashevsky and Shapiro
Intermarriage	
Couple is intermarried	Cohen 1983

read by the lay public, and in part because their analysis is confined to the discussion of their regression equation. The analysis is so influenced by the choice of statistical model that much of the content and implications of the "findings" are ignored. In other words, the statistical analysis is far removed from the texture of Jewish life. In the conclusion of the paper I will suggest that this is increasingly seen as a problem in Jewish identity research.

Bock divides his Jewish identity indicators into Personal and Public Jewishness. Personal Jewishness consists of the self-esteem, home observance, social networks, and cultural perceptions scales (described above). The Public Jewishness dimensions consist of synagogue activities, organizational activities, and the Israel Support Scale. Other than a few attitudinal items on Israel, Public Jewishness consists of behaviors.

Using a multiple-regression model, Bock found that home environment factors (including generation) had a greater impact than Jewish schooling on the various dimensions of Personal Jewishness (pp. 144 ff.). Bock found that Jewish schooling had a greater impact on public Jewishness that did generation and other home environmental factors (pp. 156 ff.).

The Bock study, although never formally published in its entirety (there were some short summaries published by the American Jewish Committee and the Council of Jewish Federations) has been much discussed in the field of Jewish education because of the controversial finding that a minimum of one thousand hours of Jewish education is needed to have a significant impact on Jewish identity. (The conclusion that supplementary education is without value has recently been challenged by Cohen [1988, pp. 83–95]). The rest of the regression analysis (more thorough and better thought out than Dashevsky and Shapiro's) has largely been ignored. This is in part because Bock himself chose to emphasize the policy-relevant findings, and in part because regression models are not consonant with the larger theoretical framework in which Jewish identity is viewed: assimilation. Regression models try to "explain" the variance in a single dependent variable (in this case, Jewish identity), using a variety of independent or "predictor" variables. The primary interest in ethnic identity, Jews included, is in its erosion over generations and over time. Bock, in fact, had some interesting findings in this regard (to be discussed later), but because they are buried in regression terminology and not cast by Bock in terms of the assimilation model, they have been ignored.

Generational Change and Assimilation

The majority of Jewish identity studies have focused on the impact of generational change. There has been remarkable consistency over the past twenty years about the scope and direction of that change. During the last few years, however, sociologists have reached divergent conclusions about the meaning of that change.

Sklare. Although I group Sklare with the "content"-oriented researchers (discussed later), his landmark study of Lakeville included an important discussion of generational change. Sklare included not only generation in his analysis of "The Lakeville Jew and Religion" (pp. 78 ff.), but the impact of being from German, Eastern European, or mixed descent as well. He concluded that "generational position has dynamic religious effects. With descent, parents' observance level, and life cycle controlled, a persuasive case can be made for the influence of generational status" (p. 87). To interpret the meaning of this generational decline, Sklare puts it in the context of the rapid upward social mobility experienced by third-generation Lakeville Jews and finds that "the more advanced generations maintain a higher observance level, despite the fact that their educational achievement is considerable" (p. 87). At the same time he cautions that "sacramentalism [i.e., Jewish observance] in Lakeville is in crisis" (p. 87).

Goldstein and Goldscheider. The Providence study, conducted in 1963, was for over a decade the principal source of demographic information about American Jewry because of the care and precision with which it was conducted, and the prominence of its co-authors in Jewish demography. It is an empirical study of assimilation based on the Gordon model from *Assimilation in American Life*. Goldstein and Goldscheider emphasize generational change over a number of dimensions, including ideological, ritualistic, organizational, and cultural dimensions of Jewish identity.

By the early sixties the movement toward Reform was already underway. Even though the Conservative movement remains the largest, Reform had grown from 12 percent to 35 percent over three generations (p. 77). Two distinct patterns emerge with regard to ritual: "On the one hand, always lighting candles Friday evening and adhering to kashrut (both purchasing kosher meat and keeping separate dishes) have minimal adherence and their practice has radically declined in three generations. On the other hand, attending a Seder on Passover and lighting Chanuka candles are very popular, with little or no change by generation" (pp. 201–202). (This trend would later become the center of much of the "quality of Jewish life" debate of the 1980s.) They also discovered a decrease in Jewish organizational membership over three generations, but felt that Jewish education played a role in strengthening Jewish identity among their adult respondents. Their overall conclusion—and one that would be expanded upon by Calvin Goldscheider two decades later—is that "traditional concepts of religiousness" have been rejected and: "There has instead been an over-all development of new forms of Jewish identity and expression, with an emphasis on those aspects that are congruent with Americanization" (pp. 228, 229).

Steven M. Cohen—Boston. Steven M. Cohen's book *American Modernity and Jewish Identity* uses the broadest data available on generational change. By combining the 1965 and 1975 Boston Jewish population surveys, Cohen is able to examine change *within generation, over time*, as well as *by generation, over time*. His findings about Boston (in contrast with his later thinking) border on pessimism.

Like Goldstein and Goldscheider and Sklare, Cohen notes a decrease in ritual observance. He, too, finds that keeping kosher at home has decreased the most and attending a seder has decreased the least. Overall he notes that the erosion of ritual activity took place in stages: dietary ritual "decayed first and fastest," while other, less demanding and less segregation-inducing rituals eroded more slowly, Passover had held more or less steady (p. 9).

Cohen found lower rates of Jewish, but not general, affiliation among the third generation, indicating a "diminished attachment to Jewish life" not explained by weaker institutional attachments over all (p. 60). Cohen concludes that "rather than stabilizing, Jewish identification continued to decline into the third generation." Continuing his analysis into the fourth generation, Cohen similarly predicts that "we can expect continued erosion of Jewish ritual practice as younger, more assimilated birth cohorts replace their more identified elders" (p. 62).

As did Goldstein and Goldscheider almost two decades earlier, Cohen discovered a dramatic shift toward the Reform movement among third- and fourth-generation Jews. He further found that the shift to Reform was accompanied by a continued erosion of ritual observance: in 1975 the proportion of Reform Jews who lit Sabbath candles, attend services, belong to Jewish organizations, or were Jewish givers had "declined deeply since 1965" (p. 73). Cohen cautions that these declines must be seen in the context of the rapid change that has taken place both among Jews and within American society, but he concludes his study by questioning the ability of American Jews to cope with that change. "Inevitable changes in the larger society and in many of the Jews' fundamental social characteristics will continue to test and challenge Jewish religious and ethnic ingenuity. Whether—and how many—American Jews will meet those challenges or even care enough to try, remains to be seen" (p. 179).

Goldscheider—Boston. Calvin Goldscheider has also analyzed the 1975 Boston Jewish population study, but with different conclusions than Cohen's. Cohen saw the effect of social and demographic change as "eroding" Jewish identification. Goldscheider, by contrast, finds Jewish continuity within change. Rather than discuss identity per se, Goldscheider examines sources of "cohesion" among American Jews and finds them in residential concentration, distinctive patterns of family formation, household configuration, class homogeneity, and persistence of distinctive occupational patterns. Even among the mixed-marrieds Goldscheider finds room for optimism, noting a convergence toward more conventional Jewish patterns among younger mixed-marrieds.

Goldscheider concludes on an upbeat note.

> Nevertheless, the response to modernization as threatening, as the road to total assimilation and the end of the Jewish people, is not consistent with the evidence. The Jewish community in America has changed; indeed has been transformed. But in that process, it has emerged as a dynamic source of networks and resources binding together family, friends, and neighbors, ethnically and religiously. As a community, Jews are surviving in America, even as some individuals enter and leave the community. Indeed, in every way the American Jewish community represents for Jews and other ethnic minorities a paradigm of continuity and change in modern pluralistic society. (p. 184)

Steven M. Cohen—New York. Goldscheider's bold statement in *Jewish Continuity and Change* influenced Steven M. Cohen's subsequent analysis of his own New York data (collected in 1981). The approach Cohen takes is of special interest because New York Jews constitute a third of American Jewry, and his are the only data from the 1980s published so far.

Cohen differentiates between the "assimilationists," who tend to be pessimistic about chances for Jewish survival, and the "transformationists," who agree that Jews have changed, but not that they are assimilating. He examines the New York data from both the assimilationist and the transformationist point of view. In the chapter on "Generational Changes in Jewish Identification," Cohen again finds continuing signs of erosion, but this time he focuses more on the continuities that are also present in the data. For example, he notes that Jewish practices which were unpopular among the parents' generation became even more unpopular with the children. At the same time, those which were popular with the parents' generation have been sustained (p. 45). While conceding that "large numbers of American Jews have indeed abandoned many traditional practices," it is still true "that almost all later generation Jews sustain some sorts of participation in some sorts of holiday celebration" (p. 9). Similarly, while the exclusivity of Jewish friends declines, having Jewish friends remains the dominant pattern (at least among New York City Jews) (p. 3).

Cohen concludes that there are signs both of assimilation and continuity.

> Thus it is true that third generation Jews less often undertake traditional activities, but the vast majority continue to undertake the more popular although perhaps less intensive religious activities (such as Passover Seder or High Holiday Worship) just as often as earlier generations. They adopt less traditional denominational preferences, but they maintain some denominational identification no less than the early generations. (p. 55)

Sandberg. The most optimistic conclusions about generational change come from the place where one would least expect them: Los Angeles. Sandberg found that while "the analysis of the data shows a more or less straight line decline of Jewish identity among Los Angeles Jews from the first through the third generations ... There is, however, a leveling off of the decline and some upturn of identity from the third to the fourth generations" (p. 107). This resurgence of fourth-generation identity takes place in the national identity (peoplehood) scale, followed closely by the cultural identity scale. The religious identity scale levels off in the fourth generation, again a trend toward stabilization (pp. 107–111).

What to make of this depends on what one makes of the scale items used to measure identity. I have already suggested that these attitudinal dimensions do not have the kind of statistical underpinnings that went into the creation of the Dashevsky-Shapiro and the Bock scales. On the other hand, the individual affirmations of Jewish life contained in these scales are pretty clear, and thus the fourth generation's endorsement of them is intriguing. Further, Sandberg's findings echo similar findings in Bock's NJPS analysis. With regard to personal religious observance, Bock observed that the decline in observance from the second to the third generation is not as sharp as from the first to the second, and that there is even a slight reversal from the third to the fourth generation (p. 149). He reports a similar observation about Jewish friendships: the decline between the second and third generations is not as sharp as between the first and second, and there is even a slight reversal evident in the fourth generation (p. 52).

Charles Liebman stands out as one of the few dissenters in what has come to be called the "quality of Jewish life" debate. While a short statement here does not do justice to the richness of his work, a recent essay produced for the American Jewish Committee on this question (1989) summarizes the "loyal opposition." I stress the word "loyal" because, as Liebman himself takes pains to point out, he does not count himself among those sociologists who see assimilation as inevitable. On the other hand, he cautions that "the recent celebratory mood of the American Jewish community invites reminders of some bitter truths" (p. 3).

Liebman flags what he sees as four signs of serious erosion in American Jewish life: the rising rates of mixed marriage, which will substantially alter the character of the Jewish family; Jewish education, which has become increasingly weakened; decreasing commitment to synagogue life; the watering down of the content of Jewish cultural life.

The Content of Jewish Identity

The working assumption of the change studies is that ritual observance retains a consistent meaning over time. On the other hand, the behavioral and attitudinal measures are removed from the fabric of Jewish life, and even sociologists who work within the generational-change paradigm admit that they are uncomfortable working with this degree of abstraction.

At the conclusion of *American Assimilation or Jewish Revival,* Cohen suggests that only qualitative research can shed further light on the meaning of the changes taking place among American Jews.

> The moderate version of transformationism—the view that Jewish expression may be changing qualitatively but not quantitatively—the one I believe is best supported by the data at hand. The only way to fully describe the nature of qualitative change is through careful qualitative observation of a kind that ought to supplement and complement quantitative research. (p. 125)

Goldscheider, too, ends his analysis with an acknowledgment of the limits of the available data to answer questions about the qualitative content of American Jewish life (1986, p. 183).

> Are the new forms of ethnicity able to balance secularization? Will the "return" to Judaism or the development of creative expressions of Jewish

religious fellowship become the new core of generational continuity? These questions emerge from our study, although they cannot be addressed with any data available.

The studies that come closest to dealing with the "content" of Jewish identity are twenty years old. Simon Herman's work builds on a theoretical understanding of the content of Jewish identity. Marshall Sklare's Lakeville study is theoretically based, but presents detailed analyses of what I call here the content of Jewish identity.

Simon Herman

The work on Jewish identity of the Israeli–South African social psychologist Simon Herman derives from Kurt Lewin's notions of field theory (1952) and studies of Jewish identity (1948). Herman begins with the assumption that nothing is so practical as a good theory and lays out the dimensions of Jewish identity in a work entitled *Jewish Identity: A Social Psychological Perspective* (1977), which summarizes his earlier research and thinking.

The essence of ethnic identity, argues Herman, is the group members' perception of group membership versus membership in the majority society. First, members of a minority group must see themselves as "marked-off" (either on their own or through discrimination) from the majority society. Second, members must see themselves as "aligned" with other members of the minority group with a sense of interdependence. This alignment can take place over time as well as over space.

Herman insists that ethnic identity must have a specific content, for "an ethnic identity implies more than the mere fact of affiliation with the group" (p. 49). Its content has a cognitive level, an affective level, and a behavioral level. At the cognitive level, the researcher must ask: How does the individual perceive the attributes of the group, and which of these attributes does he see as inhering in himself? At the affective level, the researcher must ask: How does he feel about the group, its members, and its attributes? At the behavioral level, the researcher asks: To what extent does he adopt its norms? (p. 49).

Herman also uses field theory notions of life-space to introduce two dimensions to identity: valence and salience. "Valence" pertains to how the individual feels about the group, and "salience" describes the prominence (or lack thereof) of membership in the group in the day-to-day consciousness of the individual. Like Liebman, Herman emphasizes the importance of distinctiveness in the content of identity: to what extent do members of the minority group perceive themselves as different from the majority and approve of that difference? Other than studying American Jewish students in Israel, Herman's work has not been applied to American Jews. In fact, the major American application of his work in the United States was to the ethnic identity of third-generation Japanese Americans (Israeli, 1975)

Marshall Sklare

Marshall Sklare's pioneering study of suburban Lakeville, entitled *Jewish Identity on the Suburban Frontier,* examines change over generations (as discussed above) but also grapples with the content of the Jewish identity to be found there. Sklare measures Jewish identity in much the same way as do Cohen, Dashevsky, Goldstein, and Goldscheider (or perhaps it should be the other way around, since the Sklare study came before the others). Sklare measures Jewish observance, having Jewish friends, synagogue membership, and Jewish organizational membership. But instead of using these factors simply as measures, he seeks to learn more about their meaning to the Jews of Lakeville.

For example, Sklare counts the number of ritual practices, but also inquires about how "adequate" people feel about their level of Jewish observance. While using the number of Jewish friends as an indicator of group attachment, he also looks at patterns of intergroup friendships over the life course. In a particularly interesting chapter on the synagogues of Lakeville, Sklare examines the meaning of synagogue membership for members, and touches upon the interrelationship between the Jewish individual and the Jewish institution. He asks about attachment to Israel, but he also asked why the respondents feel the way they do.

I see Sklare's "Image of the Good Jew" scale as very much content-oriented. He asked his Lakeville respondents what they felt was required of a "good Jew," and found that affirming one's Jewishness and general morality were most important. Sklare did not find this a hopeful sign, and expressed his doubts, as Liebman has most recently, that there was sufficient content in this identity for Jewish survival.

Back to the Future: New Directions for Identity Research

The three sociologists who have contributed the most to the framing of the "quality of Jewish life" debate are Steven M. Cohen, Calvin Goldscheider, and Charles Liebman. Goldscheider has suggested that Jewish sociologists have lagged behind the transformations taking place among American Jews by asking old questions of new realities. Cohen has specifically called for qualitative research in order to investigate questions that have thus far eluded quantitative research. For example, what does attending a seder mean to American Jews? Is it just a family dinner, or is it Jewishly meaningful to them, and in what terms? Liebman, who draws pessimistic conclusions about the prospects for American Jewish continuity, does so based on his assessment of the *content* of Jewish life.

Intermarriage is a good example of the importance of paying more attention to the content of Jewish life. Cohen uses it as a direct (negative) measure of Jewish identity, and Liebman cites it as an example of decline. And yet, the very data about intermarriage come from households which answered "yes" to the screening question, "Is there anyone Jewish living in this household?" The respondent thought he or she was affirming at least some kind of Jewish identity, but that very affirmation is used as a measure of "low" Jewish identity.

I would recommend that we turn our attention to those groups which have been interpreted as signifying a Jewish decline: Reform Jews, mixed-marriage couples, and young unaffiliated Jews. I would also recommend that we adopt some of the methodological approach associated with California: "ethnomethodology" and the "new ethnography." These approaches emphasize understanding the meaning systems developed by the participants themselves. We might begin by asking such questions as what being a Reform Jew means to Reform Jews or how Jews and non-Jews in mixed-marriages see themselves in relation to the rest of Jewry (and American society) and how they make decisions regarding how to raise their children. Whether qualitative or quantitative research is undertaken, the study of these subgroups has an economic advantage in that we do not have to conduct random samples of the entire community to find them—at least on an exploratory basis.

The Lakeville study is a good model for the way in which it combined qualitative interviewing with survey research. I also think that Simon Herman's work and Charles Liebman's remarks have continuing value in pointing us toward the question of what makes Jews distinct. Goldscheider has looked at these objectively observable measures of Jewish difference in his analysis of cohesion. We could also investigate "subjectively" on the part of Jews themselves: in what ways and to what extent do they see Jews as different from other Americans? As an experiment in this direction, I included some questions along these lines in a study of the leadership of the Reform movement (Winer 1987). The results were not examined beyond mere frequency distributions, but some of them were promising.

The concentrated study of Jewish identity began in the 1950s, after tremendous demographic changes had taken place. Since then new changes have taken place, and we ask the same question: are American Jews assimilating? Perhaps a new question is in order for the 1990s: how is it that American Jews have not assimilated yet?

References

Bock, Geoffrey. 1976. "The Jewish Schooling of American Jews: A Study of Non-Cognitive Educational Effects." Ph.D. diss., Harvard University.

Bonacich, Edna. 1973. "A Theory of Middleman Minorities." *American Sociological Review*, 38 (October); pp. 583–594.

Cohen, Steven M. 1983. *American Modernity and Jewish Identity*. New York: Tavistock.

———. 1988. *American Assimilation or Jewish Revival?* Bloomington: Indiana University Press.

Dashevsky, Arnold, and Howard Shapiro. *Ethnic Identification among American Jews*, Lexington, Mass.: Lexington Books.

Goldscheider, Calvin. 1986. *Jewish Continuity and Change*. Bloomington: Indiana University Press.

Goldstein, Sidney, and Calvin Goldscheider. 1968. *Jewish Americans: Three Generations in a Jewish Community*. Englewood Cliffs, N.J.: Prentice-Hall.

Gordon, Milton. 1964. *Assimilation in American Life*. New York: Oxford University Press.

Herman, Simon N. 1977. *Jewish Identity: A Social Psychological Perspective*. Beverly Hills: Sage.

Israeli, Hila Kuttenplan. 1975. "An Exploration into Ethnic Identity: The Case of Third-Generation Japanese Americans." Ph.D. diss., University of California, Los Angeles.

Lewin, Kurt. 1952. *Field Theory in Social Science*, London: Tavistock.

Lewin, Kurt. 1948. *Resolving Social Conflicts*. New York: Harper.

Liebman, Charles. 1989. "The Quality of American Jewish Life: A Grim Outlook." In *Facing the Future: Essays on Contemporary Jewish Life*, ed. Steven Bayme. New York: KTAV and American Jewish Committee.

Sandberg, Neil. 1986. *Jewish Life in Los Angeles, A Window to Tomorrow*. New York: University Press of America.

Sklare, Marshall. 1965. "Assimilation and the Sociologists." *Commentary*, 39, 5 (May) pp. 63–67.

Sklare, Marshall. 1967. *Jewish Identity on the Suburban Frontier*. New York, Basic Books.

Sklare, Marshall. 1982. "On the Preparation of a Sociology of American Jewry" in Marshall Sklare (ed.) *Understanding American Jewry*. New Brunswick: Transaction Books.

Winer, Mark L., P. Sanford Seltzer, and Steven J. Schwager. 1987. *Leaders of Reform Judaism, a Study of Jewish Identity, Religious Practices and Beliefs, and Marriage Patterns*. New York: Union of American Hebrew Congregations.

Response to Bruce Phillips

STEVEN M. COHEN

I want to take Bruce's fine paper and use it as a jumping-off point for a number of issues. What I tried to get across was that the two-camp distinction between optimists and pessimists is inadequate. I want to emphasize here that the two-camp distinction is simply wrong, that there is a vast middle between the two poles. I suppose my view can be compared to that of Richard Nixon, who often said, "Well, some folks think we should nuke Hanoi and others believe in abject surrender; but here's my policy." Well, there's a lot of room between nuking Hanoi and abject surrender. And there's also a lot of room between perceiving rapid assimilation and declaring that the glory days of Jewish survival are here again. My own point of view is somewhere in the middle.

Let me try to make that very clear. In a pamphlet entitled *The Quality of Jewish Life: Two Views,* Charles Liebman states, in effect, that American Jewish life is typically vacuous and empty and very far removed from tradition. He is cast as the pessimist. In the same pamphlet, my supposedly optimistic paper essentially boils down to the projection that we're not getting any worse. So that makes me an optimist and him a pessimist.

One issue in this debate is that the choice of measures of Jewish vitality is problematic; moreover, the choice of measures partially determines our answers. I would go further: the choice of measures is ideologically charged. The Reconstructionist and Reform Jews love Charles Silberman's optimistic *A Certain People* because it implicitly recognizes almost anything as Jewish. Whatever distinctive things Jews do are certifiably Jewish. At the other extreme, there is the very traditionalist notion of what constitutes Judaism: such things as reverence for ancient texts, faith in an active and personal God, and commitment to commandments and law. By those standards, today's Jews aren't very Jewish. So the answer to the question "How are Jews doing?" revolves around the standards you use. Depending on which standards you pick, you're going to come up with different answers.

The debate about the American Jewish future is not merely an intellectual exercise. It has policy implications for what the Jewish community does. If one believes that the Jewish community is rapidly going down the drain, then one will tend to fund things like *ba'alei teshuvah* yeshivas on the one hand, or B'nai B'rith dances on the other. If, on the other hand, we are reasonably secure about the Jewish future, then we are more likely to support institutions that promise slow but steady educational growth.

There is general agreement or concession, if you will, by the pessimists that the top quarter or half (in terms of intensity) is doing better than it once did. Most observers think that Jewish life, for the more Jewish Jew, is better than it was. The argument over the Jewish future, then, turns on the middle or the bottom third of the spectrum of involvement. The argument about the bottom third is basically over what happens to people who intermarry, or what happens to their children. The data we have on these individuals really are conflicting. About the middle group—mostly in-married, but not very intensive Jews—we know very little. This is why I'm suggesting that the next line of inquiry in our research focus on the Jewish middle, which we do not yet understand very well. It so happens that everybody who studies Jewish life for a living comes from the more intensive part of the Jewish spectrum. Every Jewish sociologist has spent a considerable amount of time in Israel; many teach at Jewish institutions. Thus most come from a background rich in Jewish content and identity. Therefore, we generally lack (from our own personal experience) the understanding of what it is that makes "middle Jews" Jewish.

Finally, I want to take the last minute or two to present some early findings from a survey of such Jews which I recently did for the American Jewish Committee. I just want to give you a sense, a feel, for these middle Jews. What do they do? They celebrate Passover, Hanukkah, and the High Holidays. They send their kids to Jewish school; they join a synagogue when they are parents; they have mostly Jewish friends; and most are married to other Jews. What are their important Judaic symbols? God, Torah, anti-Semitism, and the Holocaust. Paradoxically, the vast majority of middle-American Jews believe in God but only a small minority believes that God does anything. In their view, He is there, a force for good in the world. But He doesn't reward or punish us or answer our prayers.

The Jews in the middle feel proud to be Jewish. They feel close to Jews. Family is very important to them. They like tradition and heritage, but they are resentful of the Orthodox. They are voluntaristic. As Charles Liebman notes, most Jews in America are voluntarists: they believe that whatever a Jews does is okay; they resent the notion of being commanded. They're universalists. They believe that nothing about being Jewish separates them from being American. They are moralists; they are antiritualists. For them, performing rituals is not important; what's important is to get to their essence, which is a certain ethical and moral lesson. To these Jews, Israel is on the secondary level, not the primary level, of concern. They are not seriously committed to the study of texts or intensive Jewish education.

My last point is to call for more qualitative research. The debate over the Jewish future is essentially a debate over the quality and durability of middle Jews' group identity. Only qualitative research can probe this issue with the subtlety and nuance it demands.

The Psychology of Identity Formation

PERRY LONDON and ALISSA HIRSHFELD

This paper comments on four aspects of identity: what the term "identity" means; how identity forms and develops; how the psychology of identity is studied and measured; and how these topics apply to Jewish identity and identity education.

The present state of knowledge of all these topics is sometimes vague and always fragmentary. My remarks, therefore, are necessarily less an integrated perspective on them than a hopefully coherent set of notes about them.

First, the term "identity" lacks precise definition, and distinctions need to be made among the many terms for it in the literature. By and large, we can distinguish two kinds of identity which we may call "social" and "personal."

Second, little has been detailed about the psychological processes by which social and personal identity are formed and maintained or about the psychological functions that identities serve in people's lives, the conditions that motivate them, or the needs that their successful achievement fulfill. It is even uncertain whether having a positive social identity is "good for you" psychologically, in terms of personal adjustment or mental hygiene or ability to do well in school. In most respects, identity theory outdistances empirical knowledge by a great deal, though much of theory is itself incomplete or unclear. And empirical research on the subject gives only limited insight into the psychology of identity development in young children, in adolescents, and in adults.

Third, systematic study of identity has been inhibited by a lack of common or comparable instruments usable across different populations, a situation now changing for the better.

Fourth, much of what is known from other groups does not apply easily to Jewish identity, and psychological studies of Jewish identity are, thus far, few in number.

Even with these reservations in place, however, there is some interesting psychological theory of identity and some agreement within it, and some interesting empirical research has been done on identity. None of it answers fully the main questions of this topic, but it supplies clues to a

Social Identity and Personal Identity

The psychology of identity refers to the mental and interpersonal processes which motivate and shape the thoughts, feelings, attitudes, and actions which connect an individual to a reference group and give a person the sense of having "a self." Study of these processes is part of personality and developmental psychology, of social psychology, of sociology, and of anthropology, all of which have contributed to their understanding. No one discipline has a special claim on the theoretical or empirical turf of identity.

Surprisingly, however, no one has produced a single accepted definition of the concept. As the late Harold Isaacs noted, even "Erik Erikson, who has taken out a kind of international copyright on the very word identity," never bothered defining it in much more than a "blur" (1974, p. 19). Social psychologist Roger Brown goes even further to say that "identity is a concept no one has defined with precision, but it seems we can move ahead anyway because everyone roughly understands what is meant" (1986, p. 551).

The rough understanding of what is meant is not smoothed by the abundance of identity terms in the scholarly literature, such as "social identity," "group identity," "reference group identity," "ethnic identity," "personal identity," and "core identity." The same general idea as "identity" is also conveyed by the term "self," with all its attendant attributes—"existential," "categorical," "private," "public," and so forth.

Despite the variety of terminology, and with some variations in meaning among scholars, *all* the ideas of identity or self in the literature seem reducible to two general themes. One is the notion of identity as a person's *entire sense of self or ego*. At one extreme of self-perception or self-awareness or self-preoccupation, the internally aimed aspect of this total identity may subjectively seem like a near existential absolute—one feels as if his or her self existed all by itself, as one's perceptions, thoughts, feelings, and actions, without reference to a *social* or other external source or object of expression.

This self-contained self is the meaning of identity which Erikson thinks William James meant by the term "character": "A man's character is discernible in the mental or moral attitude in which, when it came upon him, he felt himself most deeply and intensely active and alive. At such moments there is a voice inside him which speaks and says, 'This is the real me' [emphasis added]" (1920, p. 199).

It is also the meaning the late psychoanalyst Heinz Kohut seems to attach to the term "self": ". . . the patterns of ambitions, skills, and goals, the tensions between them, the programs of action they create, and the activities that strive toward the realization of this program are all experienced as continuous in space and time. . . . they are the self, *an independent center of initiative, an independent recipient of impression* [emphasis added]" (1978).

The internally aimed aspect of identity is what Erikson has spoken of most often, though he plainly does not see the self as wholly self contained: ". . . the conscious feeling of having a personal identity is based on two simultaneous observations: the immediate perception of one's self-sameness and continuity in time; and the simultaneous perception that others recognize one's self-sameness and continuity" (1959, p. 23).

Identity as the total sense of self, perhaps best expressed in the psychoanalytic term "ego identity," has been chiefly of interest in empirical studies of mental health and psychological adjustment. Positive self-concept and high self-esteem have been commonly accepted as indices of good mental health. But the meaning of ego identity is not limited to how one feels about oneself nor to the notion that one's self has some absolute existence. The notion of "total self" subsumes all aspects of one's conscious self-awareness and implies, again to borrow from Erikson, preconscious and unconscious components of great importance (some of which we shall later call, in a social-learning framework, conditioned aspects of ego identity).

The second definition of identity is the one most pertinent to Jewish identity and the one that has chiefly interested social scientists because it pertains directly to the study of social groups and their relationships, to ethnicity and ethnocentrism, and to intergroup and cross-cultural conflict. It is also easier to study empirically than is self-concept. It might best be called "social identity" or "group identity."

Group identity, to use Barry Schlenker's words, is "the point of intersection between the individual and other people" (1984, p. 71). It is, in other words, a person's sense of self in relation to others, or, one might say, the sense of oneself as simultaneously an individual and a member of a social group. People have a variety of social selves or group identities because they take a variety of social roles in life. But some are obviously more important and enduring than others.

Erikson believes that one's group background is fundamental to one's ego identity: "True identity," he says, "depends on the support which the young individual receives from the collective sense of identity characterizing the social groups significant to him: class, nation, culture" (1964, p. 93). He means that the psychology of the social groups from which the individual comes is a large determinant of individual ego identity. Even so, group or social identity, both logically and as it is inferred or measured in social science research, is plainly experienced subjectively as a *component* of ego identity, which is the broader concept. "Social," "group," "ethnic," or "role" identities, however labeled, are aspects of total ego identity, not separate or independent processes. When Jean Phinney studies the "self-identification," "self-labeling," and "self-definition" of children from different ethnic groups, or when Geneva Gay correlates psychological well-being with "post-encounter ethnic identity," they are exploring the place of group identity in ego identity.

William Cross systematically differentiates Personal Identity (PI) from what he calls Reference Group Identity (RGO): Personal Identity contains such "universal" components of personality as anxiety level, dispositions toward introversion and extroversion, depression and happiness, concern for others, psychological well-being and self-esteem. Reference Group Identity includes one's values, perspectives, worldviews, religious beliefs, socioeconomic characteristics, occupational identities, and attitudes toward one's different reference groups. In Cross's empirical studies, the two kinds of identities usually turn out to be unconnected.

"Ethnic identity," so called, is the kind of group identity most studied nowadays. Ethnicity comprises the binding qualities of groups whose members think they are alike by virtue of some combination of common ancestry; patterns of values, social customs, perceptions, or behavioral roles; language usage; or rules of social interaction that group members share (Phinney and Rotheram, 1987, based on Shibutani and Kwan; McGoldrick, Pearce, and Giordano; Barth; Ogbu).

Jewish identity is, of course, one (at least) case of social or reference group identity. Simon Herman calls it a special case of ethnic identity which "needs to be studied within the framework of the study of ethnic identity in general," but which is peculiarly different from other ethnic identities in its "blend of religious (traditional) and national (peoplehood) components so inextricably interwoven that to pull them apart not only weakens but distorts the Jewish identity" (1989, p. 107). How Jewish identity actually differs psychologically from other ethnic identities in terms of its components, its formation, and the functions it serves in ego identity, however, is an empirically moot point.

The Psychology of Identity Formation

Personality development theories talk about how total ego identity is formed, and we shall explore them first because much of ego identity is formed and visible before social, or at least ethnic, identity becomes visible. But both personal and social identity formation are continuing parts of the same overall process. Even when they can be seen separately, their paths merge and cross repeatedly throughout life.

Personality development theories are typically "stage," or sequential, theories borrowed from a biological model that treats mental growth as a process which, like physical growth, goes through fairly distinct and inevitable phases. The most celebrated of all such doctrines, of course, is Sigmund Freud's theory of psychosexual stages. Erik Erikson's more elaborate series of personality stages is an emended variant of it. Both are *general* personality theories, concerned with all aspects of ego identity development, albeit chiefly with its emotional and affective aspects.

The cognitive development theory of Jean Piaget is a close second to Freud's in the scholarly popularity contest, perhaps by now even a first in view of the recent intense interest of scientific psychology in cognitive processes. The late Lawrence Kohlberg's moral development theory is a variant of Piagetian theory which applies the cognitive stage model to the ways in which children learn moral reasoning. Less well known are Robert Kegan's thoughtful attempt to integrate cognitive, moral, and emotional development into stages that span the life cycle, and James Fowler's effort to integrate Piaget, Erikson, and Kohlberg in a cognitive and affective "faith development" theory which covers religious belief over the life span.

Calling these theories of *ego identity* development is not to ban *social identity* from ego but only to emphasize the comprehensiveness of "ego identity." The cognitive processes Piaget catalogued are what Freud called "secondary process" or realistic thought, important parts of one's total sense of self. Moral sensibility, religious faith, and social identity, which Kohlberg tried to assess, are yet other important dimensions of ego identity.

Social Identity Formation

Herbert Kelman, James Marcia, Jean Phinney, and William Cross, among others, have each proposed developmental social identity theories directly applicable to empirical research on ethnic identity. Henri Tajfel, with his colleagues John Turner and Michael Billig, and with many other

European social psychologists, has constructed an important *nondevelopmental* social identity theory, well buttressed by experimental support, which ought to be studied along with the developmental theories to better understand group identity formation. But Erikson (building on Freud) was the first psychological theorist to see the role of social referents in ego identity formation in early childhood.

Erikson emphasizes the way such influences as family, society, and reference group interact to shape the individual. He derived this view from Freud's (1914 and 1938) idea of how the influence of critics (at first parents, later educators), "milieu," and "public opinion" assault the elementary narcissism of early childhood.

> Surrounded by such mighty disapproval, the child's original state of naive self-love is said to be compromised. He looks for models by which to measure himself, and seeks happiness in trying to resemble them. Where he succeeds he achieves *self-esteem*. (Freud 1914, as quoted by Erikson 1980, p. 19)

> . . . what is operating . . . is not only the personal qualities of these parents but also . . . the tastes and standards of the social class in which they live and the characteristics and traditions of the race from which they spring. (Freud 1938, pp. 122–123, as quoted in ibid., p. 20)

Though Erikson never defines identity exactly, his view remains consistent that identity is "a sense of being at one with oneself . . . and . . . at the same time, a sense of affinity with a community's sense of being at one with its future as well as its history—or mythology" (1974, pp. 27–28). So personal identity is always influenced by the larger group, and at some point one's self-concept or self-image may consciously include belonging to a larger group, which is, of course, what happens when children recognize their ethnic identity.

> Child training . . . is the method by which a group's basic way of organizing experience (its group identity, as we called it) is transmitted. . . . The growing child must derive a vitalizing sense of reality from the awareness that his individual way of mastering experience . . . is a successful variant of a group identity and is in accord with its space-time and life plan. (Erikson 1980, pp. 20–21)

The psychological centerpiece of the whole business may be the process of identification, in which young children emulate adult and other models and gradually realize that their individuality overlaps with the traits of a whole group.

Herbert Kelman's theory of identity, which, incidentally, he developed with specific interest in Jewish identity, describes three substages in the process. First is *compliance,* where the child acts as, say, the parents wish only in order to please them and avoid their disapproval. Next comes *identification,* a more profound psychological stage, where the child is trying to absorb the qualities of the parents—to become them by acting (and feeling) like them. And this evolves into a third and final *internalization* stage, in which the adopted traits are the child's own property, free and clear, no longer magical efforts to co-opt the parents' powers or personalities. With reference to Jewish identity formation, says Kelman, it is the achievement of this third stage which enables an enduring and authentic identity to prevail.

The burden of the larger group is built into the child's individual identity sense, even though that sense is first transmitted by parents' approving the child's imitation of the roles they model and disapproving the child's failure to comply. The parents' roles are themselves derived from the larger social group they belong to, so the roles seem "natural" to everyone. In its effect on identity development, this says, the family of early childhood is a small version of the larger society. Since there are many other agencies of identity formation outside the family, (e.g., school, community, information media, and street experience also shape identity), the growing child has conflicts over reconciling and integrating them. Adolescence is especially fraught with crises because the child then starts to seriously test adult roles. Crises then recur, just as identity continues to change, throughout adulthood. Identity integration is a lifelong job.

Freud and Erikson's view of identity development is easily rendered into the idiom of modern social learning theory because the main ideas are the same: Children observe and imitate that which is given value for them by cherished adults. The learning is both positive and negative. They learn to admire and approve of that which is admired and approved and to reject and avoid that which they are taught is hateful and contemptible.

Classical Conditioning as the Foundation of Identification

What stimulates children's admiration or rejection in the first place (what motivates it, what fuels it, what empowers it) is nothing intrinsic to the objects of their attention. It is rather the importance that their parents attach to those objects, on the one hand, and the power of the emotional response that the parents simultaneously stimulate in the children toward themselves (the parents) on the other! Neither Freud nor Erikson nor Kelman says much about the importance of these underlying Pavlovian or classical conditioning aspects of early identity formation as the underlying events on which social learning and imitation is ultimately based, presumably because they take them for granted. But the importance of the classical conditioning paradigm is great because it speaks to the *power, intensity,* and, perhaps, *long-range durability* of the feelings children have about the content of what is to be learned. Classical conditioning establishes the physiological connection (in this case emotions) which gives urgency to feelings in relation to previously neutral and meaningless symbols. This connection can motivate both positive and negative responses to whatever aspects of the cultural and social context the stimulators of powerful emotions (prototypically parents) wish to affect. The basis of group identity is the emotional meaning that gets attached to the group, not the intellectual qualities that may later be associated with it.

In small children, the basic feelings are those connected with parents—love, safety, security, power. The symbols they attach may or may not have arousing properties of their own—chicken soup smells good; white tablecloths, lighted candles and gleaming silverware look good. When such symbols are coupled with rare enough occasions and odd enough times (as when small children stay up later than usual), as well as with the strong approval which parents confer on them, a soft spot in the heart for them, i.e., an automatic and unrationalized positive emotional response, is fixed (conditioned) from that time on. The same things, for the same reason, may apply to the smells of snuff and herring, or to old polished benches, old books, strange colors, daddy's attention, and the oddly beautiful sounds of the synagogue on the High Holidays.

You may correctly call this a "chicken soup theory of early Jewish identity formation," I suppose, but do not dismiss it out of hand on those grounds. Lenin was not just "whistling Dixie" (to say the least) when he said that he could guarantee the ideology of children he got hold of before the age of seven. He was probably wrong about the ideology. But he was probably right about the *emotional dispositions* which could be enduringly attached in children's minds to many of the symbols and slogans and people who represented that ideology. In World War II, sophisticates made light of the patriotic slogan, "I'm fighting for Mom and apple pie!" Millions of fighting soldiers, on the other hand, may have been moved quite seriously by it. The personal significance of such slogans depends on the *depth of feeling* they arouse, not on their intellectual value.

Ethnic awareness. The emotional conditioning of identity is best implemented before the emergence of ethnic awareness because it lays the groundwork for that awareness to be strong and positive. Ethnic awareness happens, according to Phinney and Rotheram's summary of empirical studies (1987), by age three or four. Ethnic preferences for one's own group (or rejection of it) become apparent soon after, roughly between five and seven; and ethnic attitudes start to crystalize by age ten (Table 1).

Awareness is not the same thing as salience and thus a far cry from any meaningful identity. Awareness of a superficial group membership does not imply searching for any meaning in it or being committed to preserving or promoting its interests. If anything, such awareness starts as a relatively trivial datum in children's consciousness.

Piaget and Weil (1951), for instance, found that children below the age of eight are confused by the multiplicity of identities they might claim. When asked whether they were Genevese, young children who lived in Geneva answered yes. To the question, are you Swiss, they replied no. Yet children two years older are able to respond yes to both questions and will understand the inclusive nature of their city and country identities (Rose 1989). David Elkind's interviews of five-year-olds turned up similar responses to questions of the same type: "Are you Jewish? 'Yes.' Is your family Jewish? 'Yes, all except the dog. He's a French poodle.' "

The process of identity search and commitment may not really begin until adolescence—and even then may not become a serious concern until the middle adolescent years.

Identity as Social Comparison Process

Meanwhile, the dawning of ethnic awareness puts the label on the emotional disposition toward group membership which helps not only to cognize (and eventually intellectualize and rationalize) good feeling about it, but also to establish boundaries between one's own and other groups. These boundaries help to solidify the sense of membership by a continuing process of *social comparison* between "us" and "them" which, at its most effective, both clarifies the differences and reinforces one's satisfaction at being "one of us." This starts between the ages of four and ten, more or less. It continues forever.

Henri Tajfel and John Turner's theory. The theory developed by

Table 1
Stages in the Development of Ethnic or Racial Concepts and Attitudes

Goodman (1964)	Porter (1971)	Katz (1976)	Aboud (1977)
		Early observation of cues (0–3)	
Ethnic awareness (3–4)	Awareness of color differences (3)	Formation of rudimentary concepts (1–4)	Unawareness of ethnic affiliation
		Conceptual differentiation	
	Incipient racial attitudes (4)		Awareness of groups leading to social comparison
		Recognition of the irrevocability of cues	
Ethnic orientation (4–8)	Strong social preferences with reasons (5)	Consolidation of group concepts (5–7)	Awareness of group affiliation
		Perceptual elaboration	
		Cognitive elaboration	
Attitude crystallization (8–10)		Attitude crystallization (8–10)	Curiosity about other groups

Note: Numbers in parentheses are approximate ages.
From Jean S. Phinney and Mary Jane Rotheram, eds., *Children's Ethnic Socialization, Pluralism and Development,* California: Sage Publications, 1987.

Henri Tajfel of the University of Bristol approaches identity in a wholly *non*developmental way. Sometimes called the Tajfel-Turner theory, it gives a strictly *social* perspective on the *nature* of identity but does not speak to its origins. It ties positive identity to group belonging and to the invidious comparisons between one's own and other groups that result.

The theory says, essentially, that when people are assigned to virtually any group (which does not have negative connotations for them), then merely as a result of belonging, "they immediately, automatically, and almost reflexively think of that group, an in-group for them, as better than the alternative, an out-group for them, and do so basically because they are motivated to achieve and maintain a positive self-image" (Brown 1986, p. 551).

Almost inevitably, the process causes *ethnocentrism*. Roger Brown believes that "ethnocentrism is universal and ineradicable. . . . it has been traced to its source in motives deeply rooted in individual psychology (Tajfel, 1981; Tajfel and Turner, 1979), and the source is the individual effort to achieve and maintain positive self-esteem. That is an urge so deeply human that we can hardly imagine its absence" (Brown 1986, p. 534).

Dozens of experiments support the theory, demonstrating people's need to use in-group membership invidiously. Joining virtually any unstigmatized group lends itself to ethnocentric sentiment, even if "membership" comes from mere random assignment to the "blue" or "red" team in the "color wars" at children's camps. Mere labeling as a member inspires people to invent positive stereotypes about their group and negative stereotypes about other groups. Brown finds it "really a rather mysterious effect: a 'pull' or force to favor the in-group, without usually even knowing you are doing it" (p. 546).

Ethnocentrism does not automatically make people hostile to the out-group, however. The need to be fair "has always also had a significant effect, mitigating favoritism. What has not appeared is generosity to the out-group" (p. 548).

Now, all theories agree that a main psychological function of identity is to give one a positive *self-image*. But the Tajfel-Turner theory says that feeling positive toward one's group *automatically* serves this goal. It also addresses the problems of low self-esteem which result from negative views of one's own group, but those issues are outside the scope of this essay.

The Middle Ages of Identity Development

Children start to make social comparisons of their own and other groups by first grade, and these comparisons help crystallize their sense of in-group membership by age ten or so. By age eight, they unequivocally distinguish their own identity from other groups. Until then, however, they may think that ethnicity is inconstant and changeable. Some black children think they will become white if they use makeup; some Jewish children think they are Eskimos if they dress in Eskimo clothing. The ones who knew they would still be Jewish were children who said that they would not be themselves otherwise or that Jewishness was an internal quality, not a way of dressing (Aboud 1987). The sense of ethnic constancy is established by age ten.

The next few years, however, are the dark ages of ethnic identity literature. Whether Freud's latency period is accepted as such or not, little is happening here among identity's scholars, whether or not there is much development among the kids. Erikson speaks of it as a time for learning to do tasks and develop skills.

Empirical studies of this period focus on self-concept and self-esteem. A considerable sense of self-identity has developed by this time, but the results on self-esteem are conflicting. Wylie's thorough review of the literature concludes that there is no clear evidence of any connection between positive self-esteem and age (1979). There is a connection with ethnicity at this age, however, as "minority children become increasingly aware of the lower status, power and economic resources of their own ethnic group in society" (Spencer 1987).

Maybe during this period children are consolidating awareness of their own group and comparisons to others. Maybe they are internally getting ready for the mental and physical growth spurts to come. Either way, note that this is the period when formal Jewish education in the United States is most active—gearing the kids to bar mitzvah and bat mitzvah—but this may be the *least* salient period for mining their potential commitment to Jewishness!

Since Jewish education during this period is not likely to be abandoned, it is worth speculating that its identity component would be most strengthened if it concentrated on teaching skills, as per Erikson's idea that skill learning is the primary task of the (Freudian) latency period, and of promoting in-group feeling, since the sense of ethnic constancy needed for that purpose is by then already established in children's minds.

Adolescent Identity: Search and Commitment

Adolescence is the harvest time for identity theory (and is becoming so for empirical research) because it is the developmental time for mental struggle about independence and adulthood and the roles that characterize them. Ethnic identity becomes more salient now because it is so pertinent to these issues and because, by adolescence, children have developed the cognitive skills for exploring it.

Most writers think that the college years are the heart of this period, but Jean Phinney has found that a substantial proportion of black and white eighth-graders and most tenth-graders of all groups are already engaged in the *search* for their (adult) ethnic identities (1988; 1989). How long it takes to find them and make *commitments* to them, not successfully achieved by everyone, is another story.

There is a sequence of steps in the process of adult identity formation. It has different substages, it seems, depending on which study or theory one looks at, but as Phinney has accurately seen, most of them can be subsumed under one of three phrases: an *unexamined* stage, in which kids are aware of their ethnicity and of some other identity roles but not much concerned with them; a *search* phase, in which they are aroused by the issues and maybe troubled by them; and an *achieved* phase, also called a *commitment* phase, in which they have come to terms with ethnicity and other major identity roles (Table 2) (Phinney 1989).

I will not elaborate specific theories of ego and ethnic adolescent identity formation in detail. But some details of some theories make clear how many common elements there are in adolescent identity struggle across ethnic groups and social roles, including those involving Jewish identity. They will be familiar to all who remember their own adolescent identity struggle.

James Marcia, for instance, expanded Erikson's work on ego identity in empirical studies of occupational, religious, and political views and values of late adolescent boys. He found four identity "statuses" among them: *diffusion,* meaning lack of concern about adult identity; *foreclosure,* meaning unreflective acceptance of the values of parents and other models without personally exploring them; *moratorium,* meaning a personal search for adult roles and values; and *identity achievement,* meaning a satisfactory matching of adult values and roles to their personal interests (1968). "Foreclosure" kids may end up with the same identities as "achieved" kids, but without struggling to get them (moratorium) or being able to articulate afterwards how they got them. "Diffuse" kids may or may not wake up to the struggle; some will "foreclose" without it; others will stay diffuse forever (continuing the pattern of some of Phinney's white tenth-graders who said they had no ethnic identities).

William Cross, studying black adolescents, has developed an identity model, based on Marcia's, which charts the staged movement of individuals from negative to positive attitudes toward their ethnicity. It will resonate to Jews whose own identity development was concerned with anti-Semitism, oppression, and the Holocaust. The stages are: *pre-encounter,* during which ethnic identity is either subconscious or is dominated by majority group values, perhaps denigrating the values of one's own group; *encounter,* during which a dramatic personal experience

Table 2
Stages of Ethnic Identity Development and Ego Identity Statuses

	1. UNEXAMINED ETHNIC IDENTITY Lack of exploration of ethnicity Possible sub-types:		2. ETHNIC IDENTITY SEARCH (MORATORIUM) Involvement in exploring and seeking to understand meaning of ethnicity for oneself	3. ACHIEVED ETHNIC IDENTITY Clear, confident sense of own ethnicity
Phinney (1989)	A. Diffuse: Lack of interest in or concern with ethnicity.	B. Foreclosed: Views of ethnicity based on opinions of others.		
Cross (1978)	Pre-encounter		Encounter	Internalization
Kim (1981)	White identified		Awakening to social political awareness	Incorporation
Atkinson et al. (1983)	Conformity: Preference for values of dominant culture		Dissonance: Questioning and challenging old attitudes	Synergetic articulation and awareness
Marcia (1966, 1980)	Identity Foreclosure	Identity Difussion	(Identity crisis) Moratorium	Identity achievement

From Jean S. Phinney, "A Three Stage Model of Ethnic Identity Development in Adolescence," Paper presented at the Third Annual Conference on Ethnic Identity, Arizona State University, Tempe, Arizona, March 1989.

(usually negative, such as prejudice or discrimination) breaks one's previous mental set and makes it necessary to seriously confront one's ethnic identity for the first time; *immersion-emersion*, during which people becomes steeped in exploration of their background culture. The "immersion" part is a period of intense ethnic involvement and affiliation, which may be accompanied by ethnocentricism, anger, depression and elation, and high levels of ambivalence about one's own group and the majority group. "Emersion" occurs when the extreme attitudes and behaviors wear off. The final phase is *internalization and commitment*, when people begin to feel secure and confident in their identity and can maintain a deep sense of ethnic communalism without sacrificing universal values (1978).

Adolescent Jewish Identity

The overall process of adolescent identity formation must apply to Jews as to other groups. The fundamental issues of identity formation that need to be studied across all of them, according to Phinney, include ethnic self-identification (I call myself a . . .); identification with the group (sense of belonging to the group); affirmation (pride in one's group); denial (if I had the choice, I would want to be born into another group); ethnic behaviors (participating in cultural practices of own group); attitudes toward other (nonmajority) groups; exploration and resolution of ethnic identity issues (e.g., trying to learn more about one's own group, knowing where one fits in society vis-à-vis one's ethnic group) (1988). Many of these variables are the concerns of instruments used to study Jewish adolescents.

Empirical studies of adolescent Jewish identity. Since 1955, studies have been trying to assess the components of Jewish identity and their connections to American identity and to such ego identity variables as self-esteem. Piazza catalogued the Jewish identities of college students as "traditional," "ambivalent," and "indifferent." Zak (1972), expanding Kurt Lewin's earlier work, assigned categories of "assimilated," "acculturated," "marginal," and "alienated."

More research attention has gone to the *contents* of identity components than to their quality, however. Rinder (1958) and Brenner (1961) clustered Jewish identity into *national, racial, religious,* and *cultural* dimensions (Klein 1977). Zak (1972) found that Jewish and American identities were orthogonal for American students (being high on one was uninformative about the other), but other studies of American and Israeli students have found conflicting results (Phinney 1989).

My students and I used a repertory of more than twenty existing measures to construct our own adolescent Jewish identity content measure.[1] The final 100 or so items in it were assigned to nine subscales suggested by previous research.[2]

1. *Anti-Semitism.* Sensitiveness to past, present, future anti-Semitism in America; Holocaust; Jewish jokes.
2. *Culture.* Interest in Jewish literature, music, food, and customs.
3. *Jewish education.* Level of positive experience in Hebrew school.
4. *Ethnicity.* Feeling of connection to the Jewish people, sharing a common destiny;
5. *Group pride.* Feeling comfort and pride in being seen as Jewish vs. wanting to "pass."
6. *Israel.* Interest in and commitment to the State of Israel.
7. *Observance.* Practices in regard to major religious events and rituals.
8. *Religion.* Attitudes toward religious practice and ideas.
9. *Values.* Salience of Judaism's morals and ethics.

The component dimensions indicated are much the same ones that elaborate the ethnic identity concerns of other groups than Jews. Like them, moreover, responses have been compared to self-esteem scales, with some interesting findings. As with some studies of other ethnic groups, Rutchik (1968) and Klein (1977) both found that self-esteem tended to correlate positively but ambiguously with strong Jewish identity. But Klein found that the religious, racial (our ethnic), and cultural dimensions of Jewish identity were negatively correlated with the self-esteem of *women*. In a test of her work, using my scale, Kenneth Carr found a high negative correlation (-0.65) between the reported self-esteem and religious observance of *Orthodox* women only!

---

1. The instrument is intended for eventual use across age levels and, with modifications, on different Jewish and non-Jewish groups. English, French, and Hebrew versions of the Jewish questionnaire and a Spanish-language non-Jewish version are being tested. Items were revised from: Minkin & Slade: Jewish Identity Interview (1988, unpublished); Herman: Jewish Identity Questionnaires (1974); James Marcia: Identity Status Interview (unpublished); Zak (1972); Woocher (1984); Sandberg: Jewish Identity scale (1986); Horenczyk: Jewish Identity Dilemmas (1987, unpublished); Elkind: Jewish Identity Interview (1961); London Teen Questionnaire: Problem Behavior (1987, unpublished); Offer et al.: Self-Image Questionnaire (1984); SL-Asia: Asian Identity Questionnaire (1987); Asian American Attitudes Survey (unpublished): Asian Attitudes Questionnaire (unpublished); Fowler: Faith Development Interview (1981).

2. Statistical internal consistencies of these subscales are satisfactory. Factor analysis derived nine factors which, correlated with the hypothesized subscales, suggested that the scales were independent.

Standardized scales of this kind may be important for many aspects of Jewish identity study. They are now helping my students to compare Jewish attitudes within nuclear families and to evaluate the impact of spending a summer in Israel on educational or recreational programs. Used on adult populations in large sample surveys of American Jews, as well as on youth populations, such scales should help us understand better the correspondence between the expressed Jewishness of the adult community and its adulthood-seeking progeny.

Questionnaires inevitably lack psychological depth, however. They will be worth more if they are accompanied by sensitive interviews. In-depth study will tell us something about the relative importance people put on different aspects of Jewishness and, in the case of adolescents, will tell us more about the search process by which Jewish youngsters arrive at adult commitments. Such information, in turn, can be valuable for revising and, perhaps, for personalizing Jewish educational curricula for high school and college students. And it may tell us something about what to expect of these kids in the future with respect to their involvement in American Jewish life.

Do Jews Differ in Other Things Than Jewishness?

Scales of Jewish identity, so far, do not address other aspects of behavior that might differentiate Jews from other kids, such as attitudes toward achievement or general political and social views—qualities that *do* distinguish the American Jewish community as a group from other subgroups. So we cannot know from them what bearing Jewish background has on aspects of personal identity that are not consciously Jewish but may have been profoundly influenced by being Jewish, albeit unconnected to the Jewish community. Most American Jews are unaffiliated with the Jewish community—but their social and voting patterns seem to be the same as those of other Jews, and not those of non-Jewish Americans.

That question gets to the heart of Erikson's observation that most of identity is preconscious and unconscious. This is not said, in this case, as advocacy of the existence of a "Jewish group psyche" (Erikson does not talk about a racial unconscious), but it does leave unanswered the question: Do Jewish kids differ from other ethnic groups by *more* than the fact that they can enter American society less encumbered by race than blacks and Asians and freer of socioeconomic obstacles than blacks, Hispanics, or Native Americans? No one has yet asked if they are more comparable to other American white, wealthy *religious* groups than to other ethnic groups or speculated on Simon Herman's suggestion that the multifaceted interaction of tribal, religious, and national identities may have predictably peculiar effects on them. Scholars have only barely compared American Jewish youngsters with Israelis on Jewish identity, and not at all on other aspects of their personal identities or social views which may or may not be related to it. None of these questions has been raised in empirical comparisons of American Jewish kids with Canadian, British, or Mexican Jews.

Identity Education

The quality of a group identity depends largely on the affective attachments children make to the group at different stages of their psychological growth. Different educational processes are most conducive to these attachments at different times. If one were to structure an educational program in this connection, it might say:

1. In early childhood, use classical conditioning and social learning (observation and imitation), as ethnic awareness starts to develop, to lay the emotional groundwork for positive affects (love) about the group.
2. In middle childhood and early adolescence, use social comparison of groups, as ethnic constancy and group boundaries start to crystallize, to instill group pride.
3. In middle and late adolescence, inspire exploration and discussion (choice), as cognitive skills mature and the quest for adulthood takes shape, to facilitate search and commitment to the group.

A final word on the last point. The search for adult identity among privileged American adolescents (as most Jews are) is not only a problem of finding adult social, occupational, and ethnic roles—it is, more generally, a problem of having to swim in a sea of choices in an almost normless and highly anonymous society. The existential issue of adult identity search, for many sensitive young people, is therefore one of *authenticity*, that is, of how to make meaningful and lasting commitments to adult enterprises whose moral sanction, finally, rests on nothing more nor less than the personal feelings of the person making the choice.

In such a milieu, education toward a group identity cannot succeed without guiding the quest of choices in ways which leave searching youth feeling free to choose. American Jewish youth, almost all of them students, do feel free to choose, perhaps imperiling the American Jewish community of the future by choosing to marry "out" or to disaffiliate. Even so, the boundaries of acceptable intervention are firmly set within that framework of freedom, and educational programs must work within them. Such programs can (and should) be affective and experiential, not merely intellectual. Inspiring mentors and role models and moving personal experiences, as in college retreats, religious celebrations, and trips to Israel or to Dachau, may be key components of them. But they must all be *convincing*, not *coercive*, if they are to work.

References

Aboud, Frances E. "The Development of Ethnic Self-Identification and Attitudes." In Phinney, Jean S. and Mary Jane Rotheram, eds., *Children's Ethnic Socialization, Pluralism and Development*. California: Sage Publications, 1987, 32–55.
Brenner, L. O. "Hostility and Jewish Group Identification." Unpublished doctoral dissertation, Boston University, 1961.
Brown, Roger, *Social Psychology, The Second Edition*. New York: The Free Press, 1986.
Carr, Kenneth. "More Is Less: Sex Differences in the Relationship Between Jewish Identity and Self Esteem." Unpublished Paper, Department of Psychology, Harvard College, 1989.
Cross, William E., Jr. *Rethinking Black Identity: Nigrescence*. 1978.
Erikson, Erik H. "The Concept of Identity in Race Relations: Notes and Queries." *Daedalus*, 95, 1966, 145–171.
Erikson, Erik H. *Dimensions of a New Identity: The 1973 Jefferson Lectures in the Humanities*. New York: Norton, 1974.
Erikson, Erik H. *Identity and the Life Cycle: Selected Papers*. New York: International Universities Press, 1959.
Erikson, Erik H. *Identity, Youth, and Crisis*. New York: Norton, 1968.
Erikson, Erik H. *Insight and Responsibility*. New York: Norton, 1964.
Gay, Geneva. "Implications of Selected Models of Ethnic Identity Development for Educators." *Journal of Negro Education*, 54, 1985, 43–55.
Goldberg, Arnold, ed. *Advances in Self Psychology*. New York: International Universities Press, 1960.
Herman, Simon N. "The Study of Contemporary Jewish Identity." *American Jewry*, 1988, 107–115.
Isaacs, Harold R. "Basic Group Identity: The Idols of the Tribe." *Ethnicity*, 1, 1974, 15–41.
James, Henry ed. *The Letters of William James*. Vol. 1. Boston, 1920.
Kelman, Herbert. "The Place of Jewish Identity in the Development of Personal

Identity." *Issues in Jewish Identity.* New York: American Jewish Committee, 1977.

Klein, J. W. "Jewish Identity and Self Esteem." Doctoral Dissertation, Wright Institute, 1977.

Marcia, James E. "Development and Validation of Ego-Identity Status." *Journal of Personality and Social Psychology*, 3, 1966, 551–558.

Phinney, Jean S. and Mary Jane Rotheram, eds. *Children's Ethnic Socialization, Pluralism and Development.* California: Sage Publications, 1987.

Phinney, Jean S. "Ethnic Identity in Adolescence and Adults: A Review of Research." Paper presented at the biennial meeting of the Society for Research in Adolescence, Baltimore, MD, April 1988. (Submitted for publication.)

Phinney, Jean S. and Steve Tarver. "Ethnic Identity Search and Commitment in Black and White Eighth Graders." *Journal of Early Adolescence*, 8, 1988, 265–277.

Phinney, Jean S. "Stages of Ethnic Identity Development in Minority Group Adolescents." *Journal of Early Adolescence,* 1989, in press.

Phinney, Jean S. "A Three Stage Model of Ethnic Identity Development in Adolescence." Paper presented at the Third Annual Conference on Ethnic Identity, Arizona State University, Tempe, Arizona, March 1989.

Piaget, Jean and Anne-Marie Weil. *International Social Science Bulletin,* 3, 1951, 570.

Rinder, I. D. "Polarities in Jewish Identification." In M. Sklare, ed., *The Jews.* Glencoe, Illinois: Free Press, 1958: 493–505.

Rose, Andra. "Identity and Collective Happiness." Unpublished paper, Department of Education, UCLA, 1989.

Rutchick, A. "Self Esteem and Jewish Identification." *Jewish Education,* 38 (2), 1968, 40–46.

Schlenker, Barry R. "Identities, Identifications, and Relationships." In V. Derlega, ed., *Communication, Intimacy, and Close Relationships.* New York: Academic Press, 1984, 71.

Sklare, Marshall, et al. "Forms and Expressions of Jewish Identification." *Jewish Social Studies,* 17, 1955, 205.

Spencer, Margaret Beale. "Black Children's Ethnic Identity Formation: Risk and Resilience of Castelike Minorities." In Phinney, Jean S. and Mary Jane Rotheram, eds., *Children's Ethnic Socialization, Pluralism and Development.* California: Sage Publications, 1987, 103–116.

Wylie, Ruth C. *The Self Concept,* Vol. 2. Nebraska: University of Nebraska Press, rpt. 1979.

Zak, I. "Dimensions of Jewish American Identity." *Psychological Reports.* Tel Aviv University, 1972, 891–900.

Response to Perry London and Allissa Hirschfeld

IRVING WHITE

It was with increasingly complex feelings as an American Jew that I read with interest Perry London's very objective, carefully researched, and well-documented paper on defining the psychological dimensions in such a formidable construct as "identity," let alone "Jewish identity."

First, let me express my sense of appreciation to Perry for the thoroughness of his paper, for his academic conscientiousness in laying out the complex definitions of identity and for reviewing some of the basic psychological research in the larger field of identity. His efforts were careful, cautious, and legitimately comprehensive and operationist. His paper reminds me that the current social scientific community finds it necessary to avoid the "softness" of the so-called armchair thinker and to tread lightly in areas that are essentially nonempirical or at least not easily reducible without losing something in the process. Clearly, identity is just such a construct.

I stand before you as a psychologist, eager to become a catalyst for effective action in troubled times for our people, somewhat less cautious than is academically prudent today, and ready to trust my intuitions as a researcher and as an informed Jew. Here I stand ready to throw myself into the stormy waters of the problem of Jewish identity with somewhat less precision than Dr. London, with lesser regard for operationist definitions and procedures, which I have too often found to be neither predictive nor to add much to understanding. I have come here today with a hope for a revival of the philosophical and humanistic confidence in our ability to feel and observe and for the Wilstein Institute to help recreate the ferment and vision of milieus which produced explorers and thinkers such as Sigmund Freud, Eric Erikson, Bruno Bettelheim, even Mordecai Kaplan, and many others. I still revere all those who began their struggle with the issues of identity out of the trust of their own inner processes, feelings, and observations which led to theory construction and activism.

Obviously, with such an intuitivist bias, as one who is moved and stimulated by the human experience itself, that is, by the inner phenomena—the *neshamah* issues, to borrow from another modality—and much less so by the atomization process which characterized logical positivism, particularly when applied to Jewish identity, I enter into this dialogue with a feeling of both impatience and of foreboding danger.

The very thoroughness and objectivity of Dr. London's paper, and the emotional distance which I sensed he kept, set a tone that perhaps warns one away from one's feeling and senses in an area that demands the fullness of such experience. I believe that such a retreat prevents us from making fruitful use of the consensual and existential common denominators of Jewish identity that most of us would trust in talking about the crisis of American Jews with our colleagues after dinner, with our students or teachers, and with our spouses. Yet when we label ourselves "scientists," we close down on such existential realities.

Dr. London's paper does indeed remind us that there is *no* single definition or psychological construct relating to identity formation that we can *all* accept without reservation as fruitful for research or for heuristic purposes. But it is in this sense that his paper may be too safe and cautious, failing to offer many of his valuable personal experiences, observations, or even feelings which could become the basis for promising and stimulating new hypotheses or at least exploratory hunches into understanding the issues of Jewish identity in our day. Perhaps we need the authority and profundity of a psychological Maimonides to write to our present-day leadership in a transcendent and clarifying epistle. Or we need the creative arrogance of a Sigmund Freud to help us renew our right to challenge and break through the institutionalized restrictions to our power of thinking and feeling. I believe we need to step back and once more concern ourselves with ideographic truth in research, with ideas and observations that *feel* existentially right to us *now* in our cultural milieu. And we must formulate such observations into new constructs which tell us we are *really* talking about the psychological problems and issues of Jewish identity in America today so that we can move forward in our understanding.

Dr. London refers to two observations about Jewish identity which I believe are the most relevant in approaching our conference today.

First, Jewish identity has an organicity which indeed may be unlike any other collective identity, thereby making sociological analogies to other religious or ethnic identifications somewhat less valuable as a model for our own thinking than we care to admit and making measurement even more difficult.

And second, perhaps, more important for our immediate purposes, Dr. London states that there is not much formal psychological research on Jewish identity as separate from identity at large.

If we accept these two observations, we have a wide-open framework in which to observe the Jewishly "perplexed of our times," to quote Nachman Krochmal, and to enter into such turbulent phenomena with a renewed sense of inquiry and exploration.

In the spirit of creative affirmation of the role of observation and feeling in our research task, let me make a few personal statements about the underemphasized dimension of choice in my own process of Jewish identification, a dimension which offers some new directions for specific research into the unique problem of Jewish identity.

I grew up in a neighborhood that, in retrospect, was my model for my conception of the Jewish community in general, and for my sense of Jewish identity in particular. Humboldt Park in the Chicago of the 1930s and 1940s was a square mile of *pluralistic* Jewish styles and behaviors that included the full spectrum of Jewish immigrant types, from the totally observant religious Jew to the unobservant radical left-wing Jew, whether Socialist of the Arbeiter Ring variety or out-and-out Communist. The clear fact—at least in my nostalgically biased memory—was that the dominant foundation-stone of Jewish existence for every Jew in this multi-colored spectrum was that of the specialness of the Jewish people and of the ideal archetypes that it produced. It was a milieu in which there was relatively little censure and relative freedom to choose within the confines of commitment to Jewish peoplehood and to some form of behavioral acknowledgment of holidays and rituals.

Paradoxically, it was only when I entered the Chicago Yeshiva at the age of twelve, a terribly judgmental and *misnagdishe* yeshiva, located far from my neighborhood, that I felt a major *impairment* of my growing organic identity as a young, active, and vital American Jew. The moralistic and behavioral borders then closed in on me both psychosexually and Jewishly. It was in those ambivalent, often oppressive years that I became aware of my need for masculine Jewish "heroes" with whom I could identify, the most potent of whom were the Palestinian Jews (in those days, a "Palestinian" was almost always a Jew who elected to live there and not an Arab) as well as those young Jews who were preparing for aliyah and to fight for their people.

In my comparison of available Jewish models among my teachers at that time, there was no contest as to which prototype was my ego-ideal. On the one hand, there was the black-coated, black-bearded Rabbi Kaganoff, who once chastised me for not wearing a yarmulke by meticulously pointing out the gilgulic link between such an omission and the crime of murder ("one sin begets another"), and on the other, there was the displaced Palestinian Irgunist, Dr. Haim Bar-Dromo, who had gotten stuck in the United States during the war and was given the job of teaching Tanach at the yeshiva—a man who was determined to fight for his people and indeed took the first boat he could get back to Palestine in late 1945. Between these two prototypes, my own choice was clear. Bar-Dromo was the winner, the "hero" who helped convert my Hebrew from Ashkenazic in accent to Sephardic. Soon after, when I changed my davening to Sephardic Hebrew, I also became a potential Zionist hero to myself rather than a scared, compliant ghetto *yeshiva bochur*.

Thus, in my early to mid-adolescent years, I might have defected from Judaism altogether if I had felt that the only Jewish identity was the one available to me at the yeshiva through its collective myth and through its dominant archetypes. My own positive awareness of a viable alternative came from a neighborhood with its contrasting archetypes and from the one heroic model with whom I identified at the yeshiva.

In my later adolescent and young adult years, I experienced the impact of several other personalities who further reinforced and qualified my Jewishness in a way that complemented the underpinnings of Jewish identity that were first constructed in my own family and in my neighborhood.

In my third year at the Jewish Theological Seminary, I decided that I wanted to better understand myself and my vague motivation for wanting to become a "Jewish leader." I entered into a modified Jungian analysis with an old German Jew who was an M.D. in psychiatry, a Ph.D. in philosophy from Heidelberg, and a talmudic scholar to boot. His freedom to explore the nooks and crannies of human experience and to make meaning out of such experience reinforced within me the value of openness and exploration into my own Jewishness as well as my career motivations. It was his paternal concern combined with his intellectual excitement that turned me toward psychology as an integral part of my Jewishness and not as a contradicting one.

At the same time, I had personal experiences with two Seminary faculty members which added still more complexity to my ideal Jewish model as well as a diversity that required a volitional reintegration of my evolving sense of Jewish identity.

Simply speaking, I became aware of the process of choice in the kind of Jew I was becoming.

I must give you one anecdote relating to the first of these archetypical Jewish personalities, for reasons which I shall soon explain. The Seminary had a lecture course in Midrash which the upper classes were required to attend. The class was taught by Mordecai Kaplan, who was at an advanced age.

It was the habit of many of the students to have friends sign them in every other week, a feat that they would reciprocate each following week, so that all the students who were involved in the scheme were enabled to cut at least half of the class meetings throughout the year.

One beautiful spring day, as usual, only a handful of students showed up to the Midrash class. The signing-in process occurred *prior* to the actual class, leaving an attendance sheet that was loaded with ghost names on Professor Kaplan's desk. I don't remember the exact Midrash— it was on some significant portion from Leviticus—but it was one which Professor Kaplan decided needed immediate student feedback. He called on the first name that was signed in—no response. The second name— no response. The third name, and so on, until he looked up toward the class in this long lecture hall. I shall never forget the look of sad dismay on his old face as he realized he had been duped, and probably had been for years. "I cannot believe that you are the future of our Jewish leadership in America—I will not be a part of this," he mumbled to us in his stupefaction, as he gathered up his papers, put them in his briefcase, and slowly rose to leave the room. "I am going upstairs to Dr. Finkelstein's office and am resigning today."

Those of us who were there were shocked to see this great man of American Judaism so traumatized and ready to forsake a relationship of at least forty years to the Seminary because of the moral lapse of our fellow students. Quickly, a group of us were chosen to chase after the old professor, head him off before he got on the elevator, and implore him to return to the classroom, assuring him of the betterment of our ways.

Four of us ran down the hall, all of us in tears, as we caught him getting onto the elevator. We did manage to get him back to the classroom, where he presented us with one of the most impassioned and, I suspect, profound *musar* lectures on absolute ethics in Judaism and the meaning of the Jewish "character."

I had never been quite so morally moved by any comparable experience to that point. Kaplan's character—not his theology—was another critical adult model of Jewish identity that took on great significance for me, providing me with a conscious moral refinement of personal identification in my Jewishness. The second of my two archetypes from the Seminary was, of course, Dr. Abraham Joshua Heschel, who demonstrated that to be a Jew means to enter into the moral drama of real life in America.

I have wandered into some of my own memories of at least a few of the forces which consciously shaped my own Jewish identity. A key question that must be focused on is: what are the critical common dimensions in what I have called *volitional identification* that must be observed in-depth and with the flexibility to cross nomathetic borders and break through the artificial constructs that separate "personal identity" from "group identity," compartments which often alienate the developmental psychologists from the sociologists and anthropologists?

First, from my own experience, it would seem important to study the choices among volitional identification models available, and the collective myths which they symbolize; that is, to explore the various symbolic meanings—the "image," to borrow from communication and marketing theory—of the "collective Jew," the choices among available prototypical Jewish models that currently transcend or separate Jewish reference groups, communities, and subcultures. In the process of Jewish "growing up," what is the array of values and meanings inherent in various images of the collective Jew which provide volitional identifications of choice and which define different types of Jewish segments, both of the affirmative and nonaffirmative types?

Certainly, within this category of exploration, the image of Israel—the changing meaning and value of the particular collective symbolic Jew called the "Israeli," both that of the prototypically perceived leader as well as the Israeli citizen—has had a profound influence on Jewish identification in America.

Another key question: how do the models of an American non-Jewish archetype intersect with those of the Jewish variety in the cause of one's affirmation of self and of collective?

I have emphasized the role of volitional identification, which can be more easily explored and studied, as contrasted with the characterological identification of early formative years, which is already the subject of voluminous theory and research. I believe that the former phenomenological construct must take on a new importance in our research.

The entire issue of such chosen archetypes, both of the individual and the collective, it seems to me, must be better understood in the development of the organic Jewish identity—that is, the conscious and preconscious choices that flow freely between the artificial compartments of so-called personal and collective identity.

Whether one is "sociological" in orientation, that is, organized toward exploring the *collective* of groups and institutions, or whether one is "psychological" in being oriented toward exploring individual phenomena, we can all agree at least on the *starting points* of research. All of us must recognize the interdependence and nonseparability of self and society in the actual development of Jewish identity. The bottom-line of "data" in this minefield of exploration must be both holistic and in-depth.

Constructs which are designed primarily because they are precise in definition and because they bring order and replicability to the so-called measurement function of research may have little existential validity for the Jew involved in a crisis of identity. The Humpty-Dumpty of Jewish identity cannot easily be put back together as a meaningful phenomenon by the operationist simply by his quantitative reconfiguration of so-called empirical data.

My comments have been stimulated by the empirical and definitional concerns of Dr. London's thorough paper. However, my observations might be self-indulgent if I did not make some specific recommendations about research.

I believe that it is mandatory for us to pull back to another model of empiricism in research than that of logical positivism or reductionism, namely, using our holistic power of observation and integration, wherein validity is drawn from the human experience itself, and where we employ replicable judgment techniques in which the validating "judges" are theory-rooted observers who remain in touch with the relevant human phenomena that are the basis of "data."

The methodological question of *who* and *what* shall we study should be based only on the need to explore that which feels existentially valid to us at this embryonic stage.

I would like to recommend a segmentation technique that will enable holistic judges to observe what I would call "magnifying glass" segments of Jews whose experiences may hold the key to the critical volitional identification issues of our day.

The interfacing role of their individual personal models, their collective symbols and myths, and their "heroes" must be explored in an in-depth retrospect to shed light on what has been *missing* in their prior life and what they feel can be *gained* in their newly affirmed Jewish life.

1. Affirmative identifiers
   Hozrei b'teshuvah, Jewish "born-again" and "newborns" who have made the choice to believe and behave in what appear to be highly traditional ways.
   Chauvurot members, both of the synagogue-affiliated and the non-synagogue-affiliated variety.
2. "Steadfasts"
   Those Jews who have always been and still are—by their own definition—strongly and affirmatively identified as Jews, including formal affiliations with the Jewish community, whether Reform, Conservative, or Orthodox.

For cross-cultural contrast, three other affirmatively identified "magnifying glass" segments appear to be critical in this exploration.

3. Non-Jewish converts to Judaism
4. Israeli-based olim from America

and, most recently,

5. Soviet Jewish dissidents
Soviet Jews who have studied Jewish history, learned Hebrew, and who have practiced some form of Jewish ritual in the face of societal censure. (Obviously this group may not be as available for our research as are the former groups.)

And on the negative side, the attrition elements, for we must learn from our *defectors*, actual and imminent. Several such "magnifying glass" groups are relevant to this exploration of the volitional factors in their chosen identifications.

1. Nonaffiliateds
The segment of Jews who currently *choose* to have no formal relationship to *any* structure within the Jewish community, religious, political, or philanthropic.

Not only do we want to know *who* these people are but *how they differ* from the "affiliateds" in terms of their perceptions of personal models and current collective symbols and myths about the Jewish archetype.

2. Jewish intermarrieds who have committed to their spouses' lifestyles and non-Jewish preference.

Finally, perhaps the most negatively identified, to coin a paradoxical term:

3. Active converts out of Judaism, including cult members.

In the panoply of experience inherent in the above segmentation of "magnifying glass" groups, I believe that we can explore the human dynamics and phenomenology that link the "personal" and "social" compartments of Jewish volitional identity, that we can isolate the common positive identification models and symbols that unite the affirmative segments as well as those that exert a negative, retreating influence.

Methodologically speaking, we are absolutely not ready to "measure" even if this were hypothetically possible. I therefore recommend the in-depth participant observation of such segments by psychologists, anthropologists, and/or sociologists in a first-wave series of focus groups and in-depth interviews that maximize openness of expression with only a minimum of focused guidance from such moderators.

I believe that the time is ripe for initiating new explorations into the foundations of positive Jewish identity as well as the shifting sands under negative Jewish identification.

I believe that the inner soul of Jewish identity in America must be examined in its quest for *authenticity* and *spirituality* that goes beyond the structuralism of operationist research, from the academician's perspective, and gets beneath the quantitative "fact" of philanthropic or "temple" institutional affiliation, from the point of view of the Jew as the *object* of our exploration.

Understanding the volitional context of Jewishness, that is, the conscious partnership between the ego and the community as well as the "spiritual" foundation of one's Jewishness, are the deep phenomenological waters into which we must, as Moses did, throw ourselves. This is not a time for academic safety in precision and measurement but rather one of quest and risk. It is an adventure in which we all can share and benefit.

Response to Perry London and Allissa Hirchfeld

CHAIM SEIDLER-FELLER

I will focus on two issues: the identity of today's Jewish college student and the question of Jewish spirituality. To the first I bring a campus perspective.

It's a confusing time for Jews on the campus today—they tend to be classified as part of the white majority and are no longer considered a minority by the university administration. What's more, the Jews have self-identified with the white mainstream, gaining admission to fraternities heretofore regarded as WASP strongholds. And they are part of the power structure, with an unprecedented number of Jews serving as university administrators.

Yet, at the same time that Jews are busy "making it" on campus, they sustain a gnawing sense that they are different even though they can't quite seem to put their finger on what exactly constitutes that difference. To complicate matters, this redefinition of Jews on the part of the university and by Jews themselves coincides with the rise of ethnic consciousness in general and the willing acquiescence of the university to the demand that it become a vehicle for promoting ethnic identity. So, while Jews are being stripped of their particularity, i.e., their ethnicity, *ethnic identity* is becoming the most significant category of self-identification on the campus. Witness the recently approved Berkeley requirement in ethnic studies that incorporates no overtly Jewish component.

The confusion that results from this set of forces may indeed be partially responsible for the inordinate emphasis placed on anti-Semitism by Jewish students, and for the emergence of the struggle against anti-Semitism as the motive force in their collective Jewishness. This is fascinating in view of all the indications that anti-Semitism is not a significant factor in American public life, and certainly not at the university, where Jews have fared so well. Moreover, the current Jewish student cohort grew up in relative comfort and safety, without any direct experience of anti-Semitism. Yet—taking UCLA as an example—if one were to peruse last year's issues of *Ha'am*, the Jewish student newspaper at UCLA, one would have to conclude that Jewish students must be under siege. The March issue, for example, featured a front cover with a burning cross over which was emblazoned in red, "Louisiana Burning." The story of David Duke's election shared the coveted center track with another event of equal relevance to the campus situation: the success of a right-wing party led by a former Waffen-SS officer in West Berlin in elections. And the May issue carried a piece on Holocaust revisionists, another on Neil Sher, who prosecutes Nazi war criminals as director of the Department of Justice's Office of Special Investigations, and a feature on Jews for Jesus that quoted what is by now a notorious statistical distortion: "in the last 19 years more than 100,000 Jews have succumbed to efforts of groups like 'Jews for Jesus.' "

If this is not enough evidence of an obsessive invocation of anti-Semitism, then the following plain-spoken editorial written by this year's Jewish Student Union president in *Ha'am*'s February issue clearly makes the case:

JSU State of the Union

Anti-Semitism. It is a word we have all heard for years, from the first time we stepped into a Hebrew school class. We all know that anti-Semitism exists. We have all heard stories of the Holocaust. Many of us have grandparents, aunts, uncles, or cousins who perished in the concentration camps. But still, many of us choose to deny that anti-Semitism is a contemporary reality.

Many Jewish students today have never been the victims of anti-Semitism. We have grown up among other Jewish families. We have been allowed the luxury of practicing our religion, of reading the Torah. Nobody has tried to bar us from attending particular schools or working in specific places. We are not forced to live in small ghettos, as were many of our ancestors.

But still, it is very important to remember that anti-Semitism and ignorance is [sic] far from gone. This month we heard from West Germany's Speaker of Parliament Philipp Jenninger that Hitler's years in power were "fascinating" and that they "created an atmosphere of optimism and self-confidence" among the German people. But what Mr. Jenninger must remember is that this "optimism and self-confidence" was built at the expense of six million lives.

Still, you might think that this sort of anti-Semitism does not affect you. Unfortunately, this is not the case. Closer to home, we can point to anti-Semitic comments last year from the Black Student Alliance, charging that "the Jew controls the media" and that the dean of UCLA's graduate school of Architecture and Urban Planning, who happens to be Jewish, is prejudiced against minorities. And just last month, the Chicano-Latino newsmagazine *La Gente* made several insensitive remarks in regard to the reallocation of Kerchoff Hall office space, calling UCLA's Jews "white & wealthy."

We all have a choice to make. We can stand up and respond to such anti-

Semitism or we can deny our Judaism. One way to control the increasing anti-Semitism on campus is to become involved in Jewish organizations. Building a strong Jewish community at UCLA is the only way to show others on campus that the Jewish students refuse to tolerate such racial slurs. Show the entire campus that you care about stopping anti-Semitism at UCLA. Become involved!

This is a remarkable document, a contemporary classic, written by a student of privileged background who has surely never confronted even one iota of discrimination in her life. Nevertheless, she beats the drum of anti-Semitism and, in a manner reminiscent of the most perverse fundraising campaign, establishes anti-Semitism as the underlying rationale for Jewish involvement. Why then does the most secure generation of Jews in history feel compelled to fabricate an identity founded on vulnerability? Numerous explanations come to mind.

1. In the absence of positive motivation for being Jewish, occasioned by the fact that this college generation is the most Jewishly illiterate to have reached the campus, students have naturally latched onto that which is most familiar and reliable, victimhood, to fill the void and function as a stimulant for inducing Jewish identification. This is reflected by the fact that enrollment in the Holocaust course at UCLA has consistently outstripped the combined registration of all other Jewish Studies courses offered on campus.

2. The focus on anti-Semitism is a consequence of our possession by the Holocaust dybbuk, the one that Harold Schulweis warned us about so many years ago. That is, this generation of Jewish students is the first to have been raised on a steady diet of Holocaust films, novels, memorials, museums, etc., and the natural conclusion that they have drawn from their experience is that the Holocaust is the guiding metaphor of Jewish life.

3. With reference to the confusion regarding ethnic identity alluded to earlier, Jewish students have recognized that, in the current campus climate, rewards and special status are granted those groups that are defined as disadvantaged. Therefore, by adducing their heritage of suffering, in spite of the new reality, Jews can claim their rightful place beside all the official minorities. In this way do Jewish students participate in what Glenn Loury calls "comparative or competitive victimology."

4. Precisely at a time when Jews in the community as well as on campus are turning away from their traditional concern for society's oppressed, anti-Semitism is being utilized as a shield against an abiding sense of guilt and as imagined protection from charges of indifference and prejudice.

In other words, the Jewish identity of active Jewish college students is largely political and is energized by a particular emphasis on anti-Semitism.

And now for some reflections on spirituality and its relationship to the problem of identity.

First, the reasons that spirituality fails to appear as a measured category in any Jewish identity surveys are: (1) these studies were designed by sociologists who were more interested in external behaviors than in the inner meaning of life; (2) spirituality simply has not been a community priority; and (3) it is impossible to quantify. In fact, from the perspective of Jewish essence, the identity "business" is nonsense, a field created by the theologians of contemporary Jewish life—the sociologists—so as to legitimate a Jewish lay leadership that has reveled in its public, outer-oriented Jewishness while completely ignoring the private, inner dimension. The measurements of Jewish identity, therefore, cannot be trusted, and the professionals who compile the data should not be permitted to determine, on their own, the content of Jewish identity. These sociologists, and the rabbis who were created in their image, give us a Judaism of affiliation, of political "tummling," of civil religion, not a Judaism of inwardness and personal meaning. Yet serious consideration of identity should lead instinctually to a quest for essence, and essence must be translated as soul. Where, then, is the *neshamah* (soul) in the discussion of Jewish identity?

Second, if soulfulness were the goal, it could be pursued by—

1. developing curricular materials for Jewish schools that draw on the vast kabbalistic and hassidic tradition;
2. making God come to life by talking about God intelligently (only Chabad yeshivot have as their explicit goal, the bringing of students closer to God—otherwise, God is conspicuously absent from the Jewish vocabulary and curriculum);
3. teaching the virtue of silence and sacrifice;
4. creating religious experiences;
5. promoting small minyanim;
6. placing a premium on piety, humility, and passion;
7. developing a corps of spiritually sensitive teachers and rabbis;
8. utilizing movement, music, and art to enhance ritual and study;
9. unlocking the rich reservoir of the private and personal;
10. transforming text study into a personal encounter with Judaism, with God, with one's teacher, with one's fellow student, and with oneself.

In short, the road to soulfulness can only be paved by a process of privatization that personalizes the excessive communal-public orientation of organized Jewish life.

Third, one of the most successful Jewish organizations in Los Angeles—Aish HaTorah—has a great deal to teach in this regard. Although Aish does not address spirituality in the mystical sense, its leadership does seem to understand the importance of providing personal meaning with a focus on the individual, knowing full well that an important component of the spiritual tradition is that, as distinct from the normative collective approach, it provides a path for the individual devotee.

The success of the Aish program is due largely to the fact that its rabbis study privately with Jewish professionals and lay people in their clients' offices, and that Aish classes for young adults, i.e., for the yuppie *hozrim be-teshuvah* (new Jews), deal with such topics as happiness, marriage, sexuality, and the forty-eight paths of wisdom. That is, Aish HaTorah seems to be addressing the personal psychological needs of the Jew, what Harold Schulweis has been talking about for over fifteen years. How is it that Aish got it and the community at large still doesn't understand?!

As a result of this approach even Aish's fundraising continues to expand. Contrast this with traditional communal agencies and with their programs, their lectures, their priorities as well as with the national leveling-off of Federation campaigns.

Finally, since spirituality is a reflection of a theology of creation rather than of a theology of revelation and covenant, it offers a framework for expressing the universal impulse with which Perry London is so concerned. Alternatively, one might say, it emanates a potential corrective to the harmful consequences of Jewish ethnocentrism. That is, insofar as Jews concentrate on covenant and community as the primary sources of their Judaism, they tend naturally to develop their particularity, for covenant highlights that which is unique to the Jews. However, a spiritual focus, which draws on a creation theology grounded in the notion that all are created in God's image and that all humans participate in the universal soul of Being, would yield a more inclusive, catholic, and cosmic Jewish worldview.

Thus, a well-developed Jewish spirituality, which could serve to balance the tendency to emphasize covenantal collectivity and Jewish separateness, would provide a functional source for Jewish humanism that would link Jews to all humanity.

PART II

The American Jewish Experience

The American Component of Jewish Identity

HENRY FEINGOLD

Let me begin with a confession. I am interested in probing something more concrete than the American component of Jewish identity. Identity contains so many "spongy" variables that I do not recommend it to the Wilstein Institute as a foundation upon which to make policy recommendations. I want, rather, to think about secular identity formation in America and the kind of perception of reality which stems from it.

Few will debate the fact that American Jewry has undergone an intense secularization process. We rarely think about the nature of the process in this society and its relationship to what is loosely refered to as liberalism. Secularization does not yield a "unified field theory" which might explain everything from the absence of an aliyah component in American Zionism to the push to ordain women for the rabbinate in all but the Orthodox branch of American Judaism. It does, however, give us some insight into the uniqueness of American Jewish political culture, which continues to differentiate Jews from other subcultures, and also into American Jewry's remarkable economic performance. Most important, such an orientation highlights the question of Jewish survival in America, which is what the Wilstein Institute will focus on in the forthcoming decades. The question we really want to know is whether the unaffiliated, the largest and still fastest growing "branch" of American Jewry can be persuaded to use their considerable influence for a sectarian Jewish interest in a future crisis.

This quest has an important history. During the Holocaust rescue, advocates quickly became aware that access to the Oval Office was in the hands of a coterie of nominally Jewish advisors to the President. Anti-Semites refered to them as the "Jew Deal," but in fact they were usually only nominally, and sometimes unhappily, Jewish. They did not reject their faith but did not want to be known solely as Jews. For the most part there was little success in getting the Rosenmans, Cohens, Frankfurters, Lubins to use their influence, but when Henry Morgenthau, perhaps the closest Jew to Roosevelt, was mobilized, the rescue effort shifted into high gear. Students of the Holocaust now wrestle with the question: what if we had reached these secular influential Jews earlier, would it have made a difference? It need not even have been the "Jew Deal." The Manhattan project, which built the atomic bomb, was staffed with a disproportionate number of Jewish physicists. Most of them were refugees who had already felt the lash of Nazi anti-Semitism. The Allies felt themselves in a life-and-death struggle with the Axis in which the development of the bomb played a crucial role, especially after the battle of Stalingrad, when Berlin prattled endlessly about a new secret weapon. What if Einstein, Szilard, Teller, Bethe, Wigner, Oppenheimer, and their like-minded non-Jewish colleagues in physics had insisted that some serious attempt be made to rescue Europe's Jews? These scientists were not considered Jews and therefore no attempt was made to mobilize them for a Jewish purpose that was really a human purpose. They were a secularized Jewish elite who held a new kind of power because of their knowledge of physics or chemistry or mathematics. The group which composes the technocracy and operational elite, without which no complex society can operate, remains disproportionately Jewish and philo-Semitic like Sakharov. There is still no Jewish bridge to these groups, which, in the absence of numbers, represent an important source of power.

Who are these Jews? Simply stated, a secular Jew is one who believes that it is possible to be Jewish without being Judaic. Jewishness refers to the ethnic peoplehood component; Judaism refers to the religious element. In the premodern period, Jewishness and Judaism were inseparable, as were church and state, art and religion, ethics and etiquette. Today, however, it is one of the many bifurcations that modernity has left in its wake.

In America there are some unique aspects to the secularization process which are rooted in its historical experience. There is a much greater emphasis on individuation, sometimes called self-actualization. America is the society where self-fulfillment and its concomitant, autonomy or freeness, is virtually creedal. It is that primacy which subordinates virtually every other ideology, religious or political, which would stake a claim on how life should be lived. The ideology of self has been so strong in American history that it has sometimes overshadowed the authority of the state and of society. This is the reason why a secular Jew in America cannot be compared with a secular Bundist in Poland. In the case of the latter, the fetters of ideology are present. He remains communalized. He is free, but only to be a better Bundist or Zionist. The pattern is the same for the religious sensibility, which is internalized or privatized. In practice the American Jew may station himself someplace between the opposite poles of secularity and religion, so that few are purely one thing or the other. But the commitment is to fulfillment of self, and Torah, aliyah, class struggle, or any of the numerous ideological aspirations which have at various times enthralled Jews are accommodated only to the extent that they do not interfere with that primary commitment.

Many of the problems Jewry contends with today stem directly from America's freeness. A faith which commanded at Sinai is today compelled to rely on persuasion. There is no other way to communicate with the free. The laity shows a tendency to place itself at the center where the deity used to be. Where once there was eternality, today there is concern for the here and now. We relieve pain and pursue convenience. Where once there was corporateness which permitted Jews to address the one God with a single voice, today there is individuation. Each Jew has become a tribe of one, and there are many voices. Where once there were extrinsic controls embodied in sacred law to guide the perplexed, today we have internalized controls which in many cases are only partially imbibed by the free.

Most of these alterations in Judaism are attributable to the process of modernization and have been endlessly documented and grieved about. We know less about what has happened to Jewishness, the ethnic peoplehood component of Jewish identity. It is the American variant of that new secular identity, and the communal structure and political culture it has created, which shapes the context of this discussion.

Almost at once we are beset by the first of several paradoxes concerning American Jewish identity formation. Undoubtedly American Jews are the most avidly secular of all America's subcultures. By all rights they ought to have been melded into the great mass of American culture a long time ago, since secularization entails privatization of religious feeling as well as a new sense of individuality. Traditionally, the former served as the cornerstone of Jewish particularism and the latter led inexorably to a weaker link to the group, detribalization. American Jewry has in fact been fervently involved in the private pursuit of "happiness," which is usually defined as the accumulation of property and estate. They have now moved beyond the founding Episcopalians in level of formal education and its correlative, per capita income. Yet they remain America's most politically engaged and activist group. Survey research consistently informs us that they are the most involved in the political process, the most well informed, the most active culture carriers this nation possesses. One observer has called them the "merchandizers and packagers" of American politics.[1] They are the nearest thing America has to the *citoyen* envisaged by the French Enlightenment. At the same time their persistent communalism is reminiscent of the *polis* of classical antiquity. American Jews are at once the most separatist and activist constituency in the nation. Adherents of an ancient faith, persistently accused of clannishness and separatism, are today ironically, America's fiercest advocates and staunchest citizens. They are exaggerated Americans in acting out the success ethos of American public culture, and yet also retain much of their distinctive communal perspective and style.

A second paradox, encountered in trying to delineate the political component of American Jewish identity, involves its internal inconsistency. Clearly, that identity has developed along recognizable American lines. When meeting with Jews of other nations, American Jews are recognized for their Americanness and share the admiration and sometimes contempt that identity calls forth. In Israel there is a longing for American olim, not only for the fulfillment of the Zionist dream, but also because they are considered to be efficient problem-solvers, democratic-minded, disciplined, and educated. However, in America Jews are not considered to be cut from precisely native cloth. This may account for the oft-heard observation that in Israel American Jews feel like Americans, and in America they feel like Jews. It is the unique political culture of American Jewry which is its most distinctive fingerprint. Their sense of engagement and activism and their confidence are anchored in the liberal founding principles of the nation. More significantly than anything else, it is the election returns which inform America that Jews remain different.

There is nothing quite like the world of American Jewry. Though a pocketbook interest would indicate otherwise, in their politics, American Jews are the least bound of all political constituencies to the free-market economy which has yielded such remarkable private well-being for them. In their political culture they advocate a deep government intrusion to solve specific social problems, whether it includes AIDS or drugs, cults or gays. Yet their socioeconomic status clearly indicates that they are less affected by such problems, and when they are, their relative affluence affords them a measure of protection. This, however, barely seems to affect their basic assumption that government can and should try to solve these problems. It is deeply embedded in their political culture. Even the most repeated question posed by their historians, which deals with the indifferent role of the Roosevelt administration toward the rescue of their European brethren during the Holocaust, is based on the assumption that government should have done more to rescue them. American Jewry, to be sure, is quintessentially American, but clearly it is an Americanism of a peculiar sort. It is that facet of their political identity which serves as a focus for the next portion of this discussion.

Jewish identity is an amalgam produced by the American-Jewish transaction. Historically the bridge connecting them is a coexisting Hebraic cultural stream which sends signals to both the American host culture and its Jews. That has created a confluence which accounts in some measure for the extraordinary access American Jewry has had to the promise of American life and its willingness to biologically absorb its Jews. To this day Jerusalems, Jerichoes, Bethlehems, and other biblical place-names are commonplace on the American geographic map. Not only were Jews "present at the creation" of America, but the creation itself had a Hebraic cast. As late as 1925 Calvin Coolidge reminded the nation that it was a "Jewish mortar which cemented the foundations of American Democracy."[2] The Bible was important in eighteenth- and nineteenth-century America, and the Jews were the people of the book. No better legitimation could be asked for.

If the earliest linkage of Jews to the American enterprise was biblical and Hebraic, the second linkage was through a mutual attachment to the principles of the Enlightenment. If America was the Enlightenment's favorite child, then the "Jews of modernity" are its stepchild. Much of the historical development of this nation occurred after the Enlightenment, whose principles were enshrined in its founding documents in their most pristine form. Similarly, modern Jewry traces its emancipation and much of its recent development to the same movement. The ideologies which have had the greatest play in the Jewish arena, from the *Wissenschaft* of the Reform and Conservative branches on the religious front, to Zionism and socialism on the political and cultural, find their roots in it.[3] The channels of the American-Jewish transaction are especially broad. The American influence on Jewish identity formation demonstrates that this nation acted as a carrier of the Enlightenment principles which served as the most crucial shaping influence in its modernization. American Jewry became modern and secular through its Americanization.

Once that is understood, the political identity of American Jewry comes into better focus. Stemming from the Enlightenment, American political culture is liberal, and so too is the political culture of American Jewry. I do not mean here to conjure up images of the dread "L-word" of the recent national election. From a historical perspective George Bush was biting his own leg when he associated liberalism with failure. The libertarian principles of the Republican platform, which depend so heavily on the private sector of the economy, are as much the heir of eighteenth-century American liberalism as is the welfare statism of the

Democrats. Both are rooted in the Enlightenment. "America is conservative," noted Gunnar Myrdal, the well-known student of the American scene, "but the principles it seeks to conserve are liberal, even radical."[4] But, as played out in American history, an internal inconsistency in those principles, which has been fully imbibed by American Jewish political culture, becomes apparent. It serves as the axis on which American politics revolves. On the one end of that axis is liberty, on the other end, equality. The inconsistency can be noted in the famous slogan of the French Revolution, "Liberty, Equality, Fraternity." If there is liberty to develop our unequal talents, then how can there be equality? Yet if liberty is allowed full rein, can the ties of community, which is the meaning of fraternity, be enduring?

There are in fact two distinct historical streams which served as the ideological foundations of this great nation. The first stems from the English Enlightenment, as represented by such thinkers as John Locke, and is concerned largely with the protection of the sphere of freedom of the individual citizen. We limited the power of government by dividing and separating its power so that the sphere of individual liberty would be enhanced and secure. The second has Hebraic roots and was developed by thinkers of the European Enlightenment. It is embodied in the concept of *Rechtstaat*, which can be translated as "just state" or the state that pursues justice. The first was libertarian, the second egalitarian. American liberals adore and embrace both despite their incompatibility. Liberalism is not a systemic ideology advocated by a particular party or interest group but a potpourri of principles, which acts as the motor to push American politics forward. It does so by seeking out the latest regnant tyranny which is imagined to infringe on either liberty or equality and attaches the need for reform to the political agenda. The ensuing political dialogue may in one period concern the freeing of the slaves and in another the power of the trusts or the rights of the working man. Most recently it has aimed to expand the equality of women, whose rights are imagined to be curtailed by sexism.

The connection between liberalism and American Jewry should by now be clear. I do not mean to suggest that Jews are the originators of the liberal principles on which this nation is founded. But Jews are historically associated with the grouping of ideas associated with the *Rechtstaat* aspect of liberalism. It was not only that their prophet Amos counseled them to pursue justice but that the breakdown of the medieval ghetto walls, which Jewish historians have called emancipation, stems from liberal ideas.

Predictably Jews have demonstrated a longer and more intense commitment to liberalism than any other subculture. The only example of a formal introduction of the term "liberal" into American political history occurred in New York State in 1938 when the Liberal party was chartered. It was organized and sponsored by a Jewish labor union, the ILGWU. Its predecesor, the American Labor party, called itself "the party of the permanent New Deal." The modern welfare state traces its roots to many sources, including Mussolini's corporate state, but on the domestic scene the actual programs, such as old-age pensions, unemployment insurance, medical care, public housing, and paid vacations, were pioneered in the Jewish labor movement and pushed forward by Jewish social workers. The process of using the instrument of the state to assure greater equality can be traced to Louis Brandeis, who at the turn of the century alerted the nation that the swashbuckling individualism America had inherited from its nineteenth-century pioneering frontier ethos was tipping American society into such inequities that the democratic system itself was at risk. For Brandeis, private power was as likely to be abused as the government power which so concerned the forefathers. The answer was clearly limitation or regulation, just as the forefathers had limited the power of government. Brandeis was only marginally Jewish, but his view was reinforced by the habit of looking to government to monitor the system and keep liberty and equality in balance in the political culture of the Eastern immigrants who brought with them their social-democratic political proclivities. These ideas differed considerably from those of American Progressive reformers like Brandeis but shared with them the notion that government needed to play a greater role in maintaining the fairness of the economic system. One could cite other illustrations of the Jewish commitment to the egalitarian/statist aspect of liberalism.

It is important to understand that for various historical reasons, Jews associated themselves with the egalitarian *Rechstaat* dimension of liberalism even while they took full advantage of its libertarianism to advance themselves. Their astounding mobility, which began in earnest during the twenties, was living evidence that the system was not closed. Fully a generation earlier than other immigrants who came after 1881, Jews achieved a firm foothold in the middle class. They did so despite the growing corporateness of the system and despite efforts to restrict them. This was the purpose not only of the immigration laws of 1921 and 1924, but also of the attempt by the nation's elite institutions to limit the enrollment of Jewish students and on the private level to deny them access to managerial positions in the nation's leading corporations.[5] However, Jews were highly successful in working their way around such roadblocks. The development of a commercial elite after World War II, the so-called egg-head millionaires, who made their fortunes by combining a professional skill with traditional business acumen was actually the third example of Jewish success in business in American history.[6] Whatever else the Jewish grievance in America might be today, it cannot be based on the complaint that the economy was closed to Jews. Jewish political behavior stands apart and is in fact in conflict with the economic position Jews hold in society.

The easiest way to explain the startling inconsistencies of American Jewish political culture is to note that, more than any other American subculture, the Jews have inherited the ambivalence regarding the use of power which is inherent in the duality of American liberalism. It has also been reinforced by their own historical experience in the Diaspora, which required that they maintain a delicate balance between loyalty to the nation and the use of power to further their group interest. It was their great wealth unprotected by power which made Jews so vulnerable in Western society, according to Hannah Arendt. On the one hand, liberal political culture seeks to limit the power of government so that the sphere of individual liberty may be broadened. On the other, the injunction to pursue justice which is part of the *Rechstaat* approach to liberalism requires a government armed with sufficient power to do so. Liberty and equality are at loggerheads, not only in American politics, but in the Jewish political persona.

The freeness of the libertarian element of American liberalism is linked to American Jewish identity formation, and so it is interesting to note how it impinges on the communal development of American Jewry. We have already learned that the basic currency of American modernization is liberalism. It has been described as a mood or cast or even a context rather than a logically consistent ideology. There are many aspects to the potpourri of ideas which compose liberalism. Here we concentrate on only one, individuation, the priority given to creating the legal and economic context for the actualization of the individual citizen. That is what the libertarian aspect, inherited from the English Enlightenment has come to mean.

America furnishes a free atmosphere in which the individual citizen can best fulfill himself more intensely than in most other societies in the West. To be sure it has not been extended equally to all groups, as any native Indian or person of African descent can testify. But even here there is a corrective process, furnished by liberalism itself, to extend "liberty" to include previously excluded groups.

Individuation, however, is no simple matter, since it has inherent in it the possibility of community dissolution. To furnish freeness (not freedom) without limits can lead to chaos. The forefathers were not unaware of such a danger and relied on something called "republican virtue" to maintain an orderly community. Liberals are optimistic about the potential of humankind to voluntarily achieve such order. Their model that it could be done was the classical Greek *polis*. That assumption was made before the rapaciousness of the "robber barons" in looting the public weal had occurred. Then what holds the assumption of freeness in place today when merely a look at the graffiti in the New York subway or the fantastic rate of criminality suggests a society out of control because it is too free? For moderns the answer is found in the new social sciences associated with modernity, especially sociology and psychology. These view the maintenance of social order in terms of social controls. The most effective social controls ideally are those instilled in the maturation process of modern man which are internalized. Ostensibly, modern man stops for red lights and pays his taxes, not because of government coercion, but because he is self-governing. He has internalized little policemen who keep him law-abiding. It is part of the process of modern secular identity formation.

In America, it becomes more clear daily that not all people are capable of such internalization of controls. As the extrinsic controls of government, family, church, school and the various socialization agencies are removed in the name of freedom and individualism, the index of social chaos rises. Free societies are not expected to be orderly in the totalitarian sense. The trains are sometimes late. But to be functional it is understood that they must also possess a modicum of orderliness and civility. The priority given to freeness has meant freeing the citizenry from the ties that bind and control. The tendency is to weaken extrinsic controls in the name of freedom only to discover that there are many who have not been able to replace them with internalized controls. The result is that the more widely freedom is expanded in the name of the founding liberal principles, the more palpable disorder becomes in American society. The socializing agencies of modern societies are made weaker in the name of freedom and individualism. Having lost church, tribe, and family, modern man becomes his own lonely tribal chieftain and does for himself what used to be done in the context of community. One reason social scientists call our time in history postsecularism is because it is clear that for many, life based on purely secular principles cannot be lived fully.

What has this to do with American Jewry? Clearly American Jews are America's most successful internalizers. That is what their rapid embourgeoisement and their civic virtue are about. But increasingly they are compelled to live in an America which does not seem to be able, because of the very notion of freeness, to furnish the environment in which individual self-fulfillment is assured. The evidence is in dozens of manifestations that we are in a cycle of dissolution. It is not only the loss of a technological edge or evidence that the American education system does not deliver a level of skills sufficient to cope with modern life. The drug wars in our cities are out of control and the casualties are enormous. That is only the most obvious symptom of chaos. Life, especially in America's cities, has become cheaper, and its quality has diminished. For Jews, then, the promise of American life, which acts as fuel for their remarkable energy, may at some future point be threatened, not by anti-Semitism, but by the failure of the American experiment with which they have cast their lot. Clearly all indications point to the fact that Jews are not immune from the malaise which seems inherent in freeness. It is still true that when the Gentile world sneezes, the Jewish world catches cold. Their children are disproportionately attracted to cults, their alcoholism and addiction rate is rising, their strong family ties are weakening. How could it be otherwise? They are America.

The dilemma posed by individuation and freeness is no less troubling when viewed from a communal perspective. Individualism does not bode well for the traditional corporate character of Jewish life. From the need for a quorum for prayer to the rituals of birth, marriage, and death, Judaism is groupy. The covenant is between the Jewish people and the one God, not merely each individual Jew. In America that corporate communal character is diminished. In its place there are 5.5 million tribes of one. The number of Jews who voluntarily choose to affiliate themselves with congregations or secular organizations is comparatively small. The fastest-growing branch of American Judaism has been the nonaffiliated. There is no longer a power to order a free Jew to his Jewishness. He cannot be commanded. He is free and must be persuaded. The free secular Jew chooses those aspects of the religious culture which please him. His criteria for belonging are comfort and convenience, which are important in the American secular life-style. Like all modern men his loyalties, after commitment to self, are multiple. The American Jew is no longer only Jewish. He is also a lawyer and professional, a golfer anxious to better his game, and an American, committed to all that entails. Many of the trappings of traditional Judaism have been abandoned. Survey researchers ask the definition of Jewishness, and American Jews are hard-pressed to answer. Unfailingly they speak of certain feelings in their hearts; however, they are often plagued by cardiac arrest.

This brings us full circle to our original observation regarding American liberalism and its Jewish twist. We have noted that American Jewish political culture has played its primary role in advocating a stronger government role in maintaining equality even while fully using the freeness of America to toll a remarkable economic achievement. The Judaic concept of freeness, embodied in the word *herut*, is related to but not identical with the one America has inherited from the English Enlightenment. Jews cherish freedom, of course, but in their history it has always been associated with necessity and responsibility. Jews are never merely free to do what they desire. This concept is embodied in Halakhah and borne out by their historical experience in the Diaspora, where their freedom was usually limited. They are free to meet their responsibilities as Jews, to be better Jews. To be free does not mean to be an antisocial accumulator of wealth. It is not a freeness that can be expressed outside or against the community. Rather it is bound by community fiat and is expressed through community.

We are told that a Jewish slave has a slave for a master, and we go as far as to thank providence for giving us the poor so that we can fulfill our obligation for tzedakah. It is that different approach to the notion of freedom which continues to shape the political profile of American Jewry. It is that which differentiates American Jewry from other subcultures.

Jews who no longer adhere to the tradition are rarely hostile to what their parents once were. They are merely once removed from it. They have not made a Faustian pact with the devil. Can such Jews be mobilized for a Jewish need even when they are no longer directly involved in the community? It would not be the first time in Jewish history that Jews with special skills or influence were enlisted for a Jewish cause. We sponsor endless survey research which traces the inexorable process of secularization. Do they still love Israel? At what rate are they intermarrying? Do they light Sabbath candles? We learn that they do less of these Jewish things. How could it be otherwise when they are less Jewish. But they are also superbly educated and produce men of enormous moral stature like Natan Sharansky. They possess the skills crucial to the efficient working of society. That is in fact an integral part of the secular-religious transaction. If the Wilstein Institute seeks a mission, it does not need to repeat what we already know beyond a doubt, that modern American Jews have a different perception of what they are as well as how life should be lived. We need to know more about secular identity formation, secular perception, and the secular elites to which so many

Jews belong. The security of American and world Jewry may well depend on it.

Notes

1. Stephen D. Isaacs, *Jews and American Politics* (Garden City, 1974), preface.
2. *American Hebrew*, May 8, 1925, p. 831.
3. On the impact of the Enlightenment on the Jews, see Jacob Katz, *Tradition and Crisis* (New York, 1961).
4. Gunnar Myrdal, *An American Dilemma: The Negro Problem and Modern Democracy* (New York, 1962), foreword; see also Allen Gutman, *The Conservative Tradition* (New York, 1967), pp. 3–4.
5. Henry L. Feingold, "Investing in Themselves: The Harvard Case and the Origins of the Third American-Jewish Commercial Elite," *American Jewish History* 67, no. 4 (June 1988): 530–553.
6. The term "egg-head millionaires" was used first in "The Egghead Millionaires," *Fortune*, September 1960, p. 172. It found its way into Nathan Glazer and Daniel Moynihan's *Beyond the Melting Pot* (Cambridge, 1963), p. 155. It was actually the third commercial elite generated by American Jewry. The first was developed during the colonial and national period by the Sephardic Jews. Called popularly "the Grandees," it was based largely on ocean commerce. The second was the German-Jewish banking elite popularly known as "Our Crowd."

Response to Henry Feingold

HOWARD I. FRIEDMAN

Thank you very much. I hope you will permit an initial digression on my part that has nothing to do with the subject assigned to me but is something that I would just like to get off my chest. In listening to the discussions, particularly about the relations between American Jewry and Israel, I think I heard a general theme that one's reactions these days largely turn on whether one sees oneself as a hawk or a dove and that disenchantment with Israel tends to reflect dovishness in the reactor far more than it does hawkishness—at least in the formulation that Steve Cohen made. I think, from an American-Jewish point of view, that misses much of the reality. The reality is that hawkishness and dovishness in the existential reality of Israel are equally authentic, and indeed it would be hard to imagine a modern state in the conditions that affect Israel that did not have its share of hawks and doves. Our responsibility there, as in so many other areas, is not just to translate our own policy preferences into our support syndrome but is rather to recognize the authenticity of each expression, and to embrace enthusiastically the reality that there is a process in Israel—an open *process*—that permits and indeed assures, in my optimistic frame of mind, the ultimate resolution of that internal conflict. For American Jews it is not just a matter of deciding who you agree with or whether or not you are disenchanted because a free and open process has support but, more importantly, of American support itself.

I approach this task with a good deal of trepidation. I must say to you that I am a lay person in every sense of the word. I am a lay person if one thinks in terms of rabbinic and lay, and I am certainly a lay person if one thinks in terms of academic and lay. I have no data or surveys that I have conducted. I have only a smattering of general reading. Therefore, I would like to share with you the perspective of a person who is referred to at times as a spokesman, but only for very narrow interests. I have spent a good deal of time being active in the Jewish community, and today I will tell you how the symbiotic dynamic of being both an American citizen as well as a Jew governs my activity in the Jewish and general community.

David Gordis, at the outset of the conference, indicated that one of the objectives of the Institute is to bring together both a lay and an academic perspective. Today I will share with you how I am affected by these dual traditions. I'm going to talk largely in terms of the impact of these traditions or these sources or values in the public policy arena. This is the area of most concern to me, and I think that is the place where the uniqueness of the symbiosis between American and Jewish value system is most important.

Generally, when I knew that Henry was going to present a paper, and David asked me to respond to it, I told him I would really have very little to say because I am one who has learned from Henry over the years. And I've learned that I generally say amen to Henry. But let me not so much respond to Henry as share with you the reactions I have to the general subject matter and some of his insights into it. To do that I need to begin with the starting point of analysis in dealing with the subject.

The starting point begins with a fascinating book by Chaim Raphael called *The Springs of Jewish Life*, where the author identifies, over the four-thousand-year history of the Jewish people, what generates creativity and the pursuit of well-being on the part of Jews wherever they are located. Let me just take a moment to give some of the guidelines that I derive from Chaim Raphael. He says,

> There is a dynamic in Jewish consciousness that in every age has infused Jewish existence with a new transforming existence. Jewish life has not been merely resilient but creative. The form of this creativity has never been predictable. One knows only that it will be tuned in a decisive and original way to the varieties of backgrounds in which Jews find themselves. The hallmark is a sense of urgency which is inspiriting, intellectually and emotionally, and exploration of life that seeks and generates fulfillment. The identifiable heritage into which Jews are born offers a base of endless interest but if we are assessing their creativity, this is only part of the story. In some ways, certainly, the Jews have established their character through the exploration of their own heritage. In other ways, the sense of fulfillment is a mark of Jewish absorption in the world outside, giving and receiving, and in this dual process, enlightening man's vision. If Jewish identity reinforced itself through the centuries in its oppositional stance to Christianity, it flowered in a different way through taking root in the rich civilization which Christianity gave birth to in Europe, and the same process was evident in the Muslim world in its periods of high culture. So much is usually written about the Jewish contribution to the Christian and Muslim worlds that the other, equally important point tends to get overlooked. What about the contribution of these worlds to the Jews? It is not a question of

weighing one against the other but rather of recognizing what being a part of a wider society has meant for the substantiation of Jewish identity. The Jew living in a free society draws on a cultural heritage far wider than a Judaic past and is enriched by this broader heritage, and yet expresses it with a tone or mood that takes in unfailingly his dream of Jerusalem.

The insights that I find in Raphael are terribly important to our subject. One may only be a cursory student of Jewish history and know that as the Jewish people encountered Hellenism the Jewish people were historically affected. It is also true that as the Jewish people encountered Islam, the same thing occurred. Jewish experience in the Enlightenment and the Emancipation had a historic effect upon the nature of Jewish identity and the nature of Jewish thought. One cannot deal meaningfully with Maimonides, as Harold pointed out last night, without steeping oneself in Aristotle. Moses Mendelssohn, to a considerable extent, is a reflection of Leibniz. Krochmal without Kant and Hegel is not really explicable.

What is the transforming experience, then, of this incredible, unique phenomenon in Jewish history—the encounter between the Jewish people and American society? Henry has a very felicitous phrase for that—he calls it the "American-Jewish transaction." Can it be that this historic encounter has no more consequence than to describe demographically or sociologically what has happened to Jews living in America? Or is there some impact upon the raw materials and sources for the evolution and development of Jewish thinking that has emanated from this historic encounter? Henry tends in his paper to treat the Jews in America largely sociologically as a subculture in American society, and he points out, quite rightly, in the political profile of American Jews, for example, a major deviation from what would normally be expected in political behavior patterns. He talks about the wrestling Jews have to do with the internal tension of liberty and equality, and this wrestling which modern people—not just Jews—have to deal with. But I do not believe that he addresses the key question—at least the key question for me—and that is the impact on the development of the Jewish ethos, particularly in the field of public policy making, which results from that encounter. What is the internalized reality of Jewish consciousness born of the American experience?

I will suggest to you what has been important to me. I think the American experience is absolutely unique in the four-thousand years of Jewish experience, primarily because of two factors which go to the very essence and heart of America as a society. One is the celebration of the idea of freedom itself—America is a society that is predicated on freedom.

This is not necessarily totally unique in Jewish history, but in terms of the depth of the commitment to freedom, I believe that it is. Secondly, the complete devotion of the ethos of this country to the very idea of pluralism. Pluralism is not just a notion that is the flip side of freedom that says you can do what you want and you can do it in varying ways. Pluralism, in the American experience, sort of taking off from Madison's tenth paper, is the notion that it is a good thing for the society if people articulate their interests and their concerns for the total society out of their group roots. I believe that *is* unique in Jewish history. I don't know where else Jews have lived in a society that affirmatively dictates that the society expects from them the expression of those things which go to their group identification, and further tells them that it is incumbent upon them to participate fully in the society as Jews, or as whatever else they may be, in order that the society may derive the benefits from those diverse inputs. Those are very unique facts and circumstances of the American experience which surely should at least be looked at from the point of view of what does that mean in terms of the Jewish experience in the world. I don't believe it is captured simply by looking at the demography and the sociology of American Jews, nor do I believe that it is anywhere near captured by pointing either with pride or with dismay to the deviant, if I can use that word, political behavior of American Jews. Nor is it augmented by a sense that even Jews in this country are exposed to and vulnerable to whatever elements of social pathology the society generates, including the social pathology emanating from the things that Henry talked about—namely, the individualization of values, the tendency to create chaos in society because of the excessive individualism of the society.

Let me say a word or two about the political profile. The political profile points with pride to the fact that Jews tend to be, at least to the extent of some 65 percent in the last election, political liberals—and that's a very difficult phrase, but it denotes political liberals in terms of whatever is the conventional standard. The fact that this is so is sometimes cited as the expression of Jewish values in the American setting. Those who are expressing a preference for political liberalism are seen as being more authentically Jewish than the other 35 percent of Jews who seem to vote in a fashion that is inconsistent with Jewish values. I would suggest that if the political profile of American Jews were more evenly divided between the two parties, or if, shudder the thought, a majority of American Jews voted Republican rather than Democratic, it would not materially change the impact that we can derive from the fact that there has been an encounter between Jews and the United States. We need far more understanding than we have of this rather startling and interesting phenomenon of the political profile of American Jews. I don't believe that we know a great deal about it except the tendency—either of those like Irving Kristol who deplore it or others like Leonard Fein who embrace it. I think its one of those things that an Institute like this might profitably do—really try to explore what it is in the makeup of the American Jewish value system that has created this divergence.

But let me go beyond this because I don't think the political profile goes to the heart of the effect of American life upon Jews. One limited element that clearly can be seen in terms of the impact of America upon Jewish life is that the existence of freedom in this country has, I believe, had an effect upon the expression of religious conviction in this country. While the Conservative and the Reform movements both started not in this country but in Germany, under somewhat different circumstances to be sure, they flowered in this country, and if one looks around the world, while there are places where Reform and Conservative Judaism have taken some root, I think it is fair to say that it has been the American experience that has really provided the opportunity for major development of the Conservative and Reform movements as authentic expressions of Jewish life, and they carry with them a uniqueness born of the American experience. It's very important that this has happened, because I believe that part of the freedom syndrome, if you will, of America is, as Peter Berger has explained so poignantly, reflective of the prime importance in this society of the concept of freedom of religion—not because freedom of religion is important to the inner soul or inner well-being but because a society that emphasizes freedom of religion is, by that very act, indicating the possibility of there being a transcendent dimension to life itself. And once a society recognizes that transcendence is possible, it then recognizes that all values do not necessarily stem from the society, that human beings may discover something more durable. Freedom of religion, as Peter Berger has told us, is really the prime freedom, ultimately more important for the reasons that he stated than freedom of expression and freedom of association, as important as those freedoms are. But the possibility of the transcendent and the right to inquire into it lies at the very heart of that part of the American freedom ethos.

If you look at the general field of public policy formation in this country and the role of Jews in it, I think one has to proceed from the importance of pluralism as a value that has affected Jews in this country. The notion of pluralism, as I said a moment ago, places an affirmative obligation upon people as groups to participate in the policy formation process. This is a new factor in Jewish life generally, but it is a factor that speaks volumes in terms of the importance of the American experience.

What, then, are the values from the Jewish experience in the world, honed in the American transaction, which have informed and should inform the affirmative participation by Jews in the public policy formation field? I do not accept the notion that they are essentially survivalist and defensive notions, that we participate in the process only to protect Jewish interests or to fight anti-Semitism or to accomplish other narrow Jewish concerns. I believe that the significance of our participation rests on the very fact that we are required to draw on what is available to us in our tradition as a way of contributing to this society. We are the paradigmatic group in America that has responded to that imperative of the American experience—the notion of pluralism accompanied by the affirmative responsibility of participation. As we have learned as a community, we are effective in doing this not just as an interest group wielding either financial or electoral clout—we have some financial clout, to be sure, but in the total American experience I'm not sure it is that significant, and we have a little bit of electoral clout but basically insignificant—I think Steve Bayme had his finger on it the other day. We are effective as a group participating in the policy formation process to the extent that we supply *ideas*, hopefully honed from the Jewish experience, which are then persuasive to the general community. And the secret of success for us as a paradigmatic example of American group life has been our ability not just to confront and challenge the system by insisting upon what we are entitled to as we see it, but by providing linkage between the ideas we advance, to be sure from a Jewish source, and broader American concerns.

The support of this country for Israel, for example, is not, in my opinion, just a function of AIPAC and Jewish electoral and financial clout. I don't suggest that there is not some marginal significance to those things. Ultimately, however, it rests upon the notion that we've been very successful in inculcating that there is an American interest that happens to coincide with what it is that Jews are pressing for. And that is a terribly important thing for America generally, because to the extent that we can act as a paradigmatic example of group life, we have a message for other groups in this country. Your activity affirmatively in the political process in America is dependent upon your providing the same kinds of linkage, the kinds of things that make pluralism not just a divisive Balkanization of a country but a source of new energy that helps provide linkages from diversity and thereby provides unifying purpose to society.

A monolithic Jewish view in the public policy area, in my judgment, is not helpful to that kind of objective of Jewish participation. And the very existence of diversity among Jews augments rather than dilutes the power of the Jewish community to provide linkage ideas. The notion that Jews speak with only one voice, and if they don't that they somehow weaken themselves, is a faulty premise, and in any event it is no longer a premise that anyone can expect to continue. We need to be able to make a virtue of the fact that there are divisions among Jews on a whole host of subjects.

What are these values that should activate the Jewish participation in the political process? I do not believe that they are values which simply constitute a series of planks in either a liberal or a conservative platform. To me being Jewish, using these diverse sources of identity, comprises a number of things, but surely includes these. It denotes a certain kind of world view, a scheme of values, a philosophy of life in this world, a sophisticated memory of the past, a profound and abiding commitment to the future, an insight into the character of societies and social organizations, a staying power in the face of adversity, and above all, a commitment to community as a source of values.

Let me be more specific as to what should be the informing values from the Jewish experience as one deals in the public policy formation process. These are certainly some of them:

- The idea that people acquire their values and their identity through the community rather than through a process of individual selection.
- The idea that human beings are charged with responsibilities rather than given the opportunity for self-fulfillment as the guiding purpose of life. Privatism is *not* the touchstone.
- The idea that human beings are in partnership with God in the ongoing but never-ending task of perfecting the world, and that the primary responsibility of life is to contribute to that process, knowing full well, and indeed insisting upon it, that the process will not and cannot ever be concluded.
- The idea that the world is redeemable and is not condemned to a bleak fate.
- The idea that work is communally purposeful, and that through work individuals contribute to the process of perfecting the world.
- The idea of full freedom of inquiry, including the full right and obligation of dissent, even as to the most sacred propositions. The Jewish ethos is premised upon law, but it is equally premised upon quarreling with the law.
- The idea that human beings, both individually and collectively, are responsible for history.

- The idea of social harmony as an objective of the social process—that peace is an unalloyed good, and that civility is the primary instrument for its attainment.
- The idea of social justice—not just in its superficial aspect in terms of helping the poor and the needy, but in its broader and more profound aspect, dealing with the health of society itself, and the obligation of creating conditions in which all acquire a constructive stake in society. I would even go beyond this to say that social justice based upon these kinds of factors means a deep and profound commitment to the development and maintenance of society generally rather than an exclusive preoccupation with the poor and the needy.
- The idea that procreation is an obligation of life, not for the mere survival of the Jewish people but for assuring that there will be people following us who will engage in the ongoing perfecting of the world.
- The idea that human life itself is the primary value, and that its condition is to be improved in this world and not serve as preparation for another world.

Now this, obviously, does not exhaust the list of Jewish values. But I submit to you that these elements tell one something about a mindset and an attitude of mind rather than a prescribed series of political positions that do indeed constitute what the Jewish input can be in society. I cannot find in Amos or Hosea, for example, anything that tells me that it is more Jewish or less Jewish to either support or oppose a nuclear freeze. I can find there the requirement that I be concerned about peace, but it doesn't tell me anything about whether nuclear freeze and its support or its opposition is more or less Jewish. It seems to me that these are the kinds of issues which should activate American Jews, and to a considerable extent have, as they participate in the public policy formation field.

Jewish life in the last half of the twentieth century, and as we now go into the twenty-first century, is really centered in two places—Israel and America. For America, we as Jews are party to a unique phenomenon in Jewish history, and the Jewish ethos is being developed in this country in a fashion that should command our attention in terms of its impact upon what changes the Jewish ethos really reflects as a result of this encounter. I would hope that this process would be viewed, if not by ordinary Jews expressly, as least by the "haunted air," in Lionel Trilling's phrase, that they breathe—and that the process would be characterized by an incapacity on their part to distinguish between Rosenzweig and Niebuhr as providing lodestars for their spiritual identification; that both Buber and Dewey provide philosophical underpinnings to them, and that they respond to the song of both Bialik and Whitman. We dilute the historical significance of what this country has provided to us as a group when we make it almost trivial by saying that we should be political liberals in order to be Jews. And I think Irving Kristol does them some wrong when he says that one must be a political conservative. But above all, we dilute that significance when we then say that those who might disagree with us are somehow less Jewish than ourselves. In addition, I must say to you in all candor that I think one of the things that has characterized the political profile of American Jews is the tendency for those who acclaim the political liberalism of American Jews to suggest that those who are of a different mind are less Jewish. I rarely hear the 35 percent suggest that the 65 percent are less Jewish. The genius of the American-Jewish encounter is that it has provided American Jews with an opportunity that is truly singular when viewed from the perspective of Jewish history. It has been hospitable to them, and wants their input. We do not deliver that input well when we arrogate to whatever political position we may have some kind of moral, authentically Jewish dimension, and suggest that a different position does not have that moral dimension. I think that in general the experience of American Jews in the public policy formation field is consistent with what I have been saying—even though individual Jews may not articulate it.

The American encounter with Jews is one of the great civilizing experiences in the world and is certainly *the* most civilizing experience for Jews. Whether we will survive as a Jewish people in this country because of the things that Henry has talked about—the openness to freedom and individual rights—is, of course, part of the conundrum of life itself. There is every reason to draw upon the sources I have talked about in making the Jewish experience in this country the kind of experience which people of your training in fifty years will characterize as comparable to the historic encounters between Jews and Hellenism, between Jews and Islam, and between Jews and the European Enlightenment. That characterization will mark the flowering of Jewish life in a free society—ultimately the fulfillment of the most ancient of the Jewish imperatives for life in the larger world.

Jewish Identity in the Changing World of American Religion

JONATHAN D. SARNA

Efforts to foretell the future of the American Jewish community date far back to the nineteenth century, and for the most part the prophecies have been exceedingly gloomy. Former President John Adams predicted in a letter to Mordecai Noah in 1819 that Jews might "possibly in time become liberal Unitarian Christians." A young American Jewish student named William Rosenblatt, writing in 1872, declared that the grandchildren of Jewish immigrants to America would almost surely intermarry and abandon the rite of circumcision. Within fifty years "at the latest," he predicted, Jews would be "undistinguishable from the mass of humanity which surrounds them." Just under a century later, in 1964, *Look* magazine devoted a whole issue to the "Vanishing American Jew," at the time a much-discussed subject. More recently, in 1984, Rabbi Reuven Bulka, in a book entitled *The Orthodox-Reform Rift and the Future of the Jewish People*, warned that "we are heading towards a disaster of massive proportions which the North American Jewish community simply cannot afford."[1]

So far, thank God, all of these predictions have proven wrong. The Jewish people lives on. Some might consider this a timely reminder that (as someone once said) "prediction is very difficult, especially about the future." Others may view our continuing survival as nothing less than providential: evidence that God, in a display of divine mercy, is watching over us. A third view, my own, is that precisely because Jews are so worried about survival, we listen attentively to prophets of doom and respond to them. Gloom-and-doom prophets function historically as a kind of Jewish early-warning system: their Jeremiads hit home and produce necessary changes. For this reason, contemporary prophets, much like the biblical Jonah, are often fated to spend their lives as "self-negating prophets." Their widely publicized prophecies, instead of being fulfilled, usually result in the kinds of changes needed to "avert the evil decrees."

With this in mind, I should like to focus here on a basic change in the character of contemporary American religion that seems to me fraught with serious implications for American Jewish identity in the coming decades, and which is all too little discussed in professional Jewish circles. Specifically, my subject concerns the decline of the Judeo-Christian, Protestant-Catholic-Jew model of American religion, and the growth of non-Judeo-Christian religions, particularly Islam. While, broadly speaking, I see this development as part of a larger process that Robert Wuthnow understands as nothing less than "the restructuring of American religion,"[2] I am going to focus here on the subject at hand, and postpone discussion of other aspects of this "restructuring" for another occasion.

To understand the decline of the Judeo-Christian, Protestant-Catholic-Jew model of American religion requires first a brief excursion into history. For well over a century after the Constitution was promulgated, a great many Americans still believed that they lived in a Christian, often more narrowly defined as a Protestant country. The First Amendment did not bother those who held this view, for they believed, following Justice Joseph Story, that

> The real object of the amendment was not to countenance, much less to advance Mahometanism, or Judaism, or infidelity, by prostrating Christianity; but to exclude all rivalry among Christian sects, and to prevent any national ecclesiastical establishment, which should give to an hierarchy the exclusive patronage of the national government.[3]

"Christian America" advocates were also not bothered by challenges from non-Christians. Given late-nineteenth-century figures showing that Protestant churches outnumbered all the others by a factor of more than ten to one, dissenters could be safely dismissed, if not altogether ignored.[4]

Even the Supreme Court agreed in 1892 that "this is a Christian nation." The justice who wrote that decision, David Brewer, the son of a missionary, subsequently defended his views in a widely published lecture unabashedly titled *The United States: A Christian Nation* (1905).[5] Jews certainly objected to this formulation, and consistently battled against the whole "Christian America" idea. But they did not make a great deal of headway.[6]

The more inclusive conception of America as a "Judeo-Christian" nation, referring to values or beliefs shared by Jews and Christians alike, developed only in the twentieth century, though adumbrations of it may be found a century or more earlier. Mark Silk, whose account I follow here, traces the contemporary use of this term to the 1930s. "What brought this usage into regular discourse," he writes, "was opposition to fascism. Fascist fellow travelers and anti-Semites had appropriated 'Christian' as a trademark . . . 'Judeo-Christian' thus became a catchword for the other side." Using a wide range of examples from this period, Silk shows how "Judeo-Christian" gradually became the standard liberal term for the idea that Western values rested upon a shared religious consensus. "We speak now, with still inadequate but steadily expanding understanding, of the Judeo-Christian heritage," Hebrew Union College president Julian Morgenstern thus wrote in 1942. "We comprehend, as we have not comprehended in all of nineteen hundred years, that Judaism and Christianity are partners in the great work of world-redemption and the progressive unfolding of the world-spirit." Ten years later, President-elect Dwight D. Eisenhower spoke of the "Judeo-Christian concept" that formed the basis of "our form of government." "As of 1952," Silk concludes, "good Americans were supposed to be good Judeo-Christians. It was the new national creed."[7]

Side by side with this creed, there developed in America a new and more pluralistic model of how the nation's religious character should be conceptualized and described. Earlier, the standard textbooks, from Robert Baird's *Religion in America* (1843) to William Warren Sweet's *Story of Religion in America* (1930), adhered to what might be called the "Protestant synthesis"; they were overwhelmingly concerned, as Sydney Ahlstrom points out, with "the rise and development of the Protestant tradition."[8] With the twentieth-century decline of mainline Protestantism, the remarkable growth of Catholicism, the interreligious assault on wartime and postwar hatred, the rise of the interfaith movement, and the coming of age of non-Protestant intellectuals, this synthesis broke down. In place of the "Protestant tradition" paradigm, there arose a new tripartite model of American religion, the familiar trinity of Protestant, Catholic, and Jew.

As early as 1920, before this ideology had fully crystallized, "leaders of the Protestant, Catholic and Jewish groups united in an appeal to the people of America to help safeguard religious liberty from the menace of bigotry, prejudice and fanaticism." Seven years later, the National Conference of Jews and Christians was established (the name was changed in 1938–39), and by design it had three co-chairmen: Newton D. Baker, Protestant; Carlton J. H. Hayes, Catholic; and Roger W. Straus, Jew. The NCCJ's education program featured hundreds of local "round tables," each one "a body of Protestant, Catholic and Jewish leaders" who joined together "to further the aims of the National Conference in its community." Everett R. Clinchy, the NCCJ's longtime executive director, soon developed this idea into a full-scale ideology, arguing that America consisted of three coequal "culture groups," each of which made valuable contributions to American life and should be encouraged to flourish. Within two decades, this tripartite approach to American religion was enshrined in countless symbols, from "equal-time" radio allotments on NBC to the famous Chapel of Four Chaplains, "an interfaith shrine" commemorating the 1943 sinking death—"standing on deck, arms linked, praying"—of four army chaplains, one Catholic, one Jewish, and two Protestant, on the S.S. *Dorchester*.[9]

What did more than anything else to make "Protestant-Catholic-Jew" a household concept was a book that appeared in 1955. Written by Will Herberg, recently characterized by David G. Dalin as "one of the most interesting Jewish intellectuals of the last half-century," it made the case for "the pervasiveness of religious self-identification along the tripartite scheme of Protestant, Catholic, Jew." According to Herberg, America had become a " 'triple melting pot,' restructured in three great communities with religious labels, defining three great 'communions' or 'faiths.' " "Not to be . . . either a Protestant, a Catholic, or a Jew," he warned, "is somehow not to be an American."[10]

By the mid-1950s, then, both the Judeo-Christian tradition and the "triple melting pot" had become firmly entrenched components of American identity. Both models—and they were clearly linked—pointed to a more pluralistic understanding of America, an America that embraced Jews as equals. For Jews, all too used to being cast in the role of persecuted minority, this was a pleasant change. Indeed, it was so congenial that in a paper entitled "The Basic Task of the Synagogue in America," the Conservative Jewish lay leader Maxwell Abbell matter-of-factly read these assumptions back into history. "Americans," he explained, "have always spoken of the Judeo-Christian traditions as the basis of the religious life of the modern world, thus giving us Jews credit for the basic elements of this tradition. Americans have always spoken of the three great religions of this country as Protestantism, Catholicism and Judaism, despite the fact that we Jews number only about five million out of about 160 million population."[11]

Abbell, and I think many other Jews as well, understood that Jews did not quite deserve the coequal status that America accorded them. They apparently hoped that Jews might compensate for their manifest numerical inequality by making a substantial contribution to American life. But there was a great danger here that I think we are only now beginning to appreciate: namely, that there was a large and indeed growing disjunction between myth and reality. Neither the Judeo-Christian tradition nor the "triple melting pot" adequately or accurately conveyed the full extent of American religious pluralism in all of its complex manifestations. For a long time, Americans lived with this disjunction, cognitive dissonance notwithstanding. Jews found their exaggerated status particularly convenient; an overwhelming number of Americans believed that Jews formed a far larger proportion of the nation's population than they actually did, and treated Jews accordingly.[12] But today these myths are dying. It behooves us to know why they are dying, and what the implications are for Jewish identity in the coming decades.

Mark Silk demonstrates that the Judeo-Christian idea first met with resistance as far back as the 1940s. Criticisms included the charge that the concept was fuzzy (Harvard's Douglas Bush, for one, asked for "fuller hints of what the Hebraic-Christian tradition, to which all pay at least vague lip service, actually does or can mean in modern terms for modern men of good will"), and that it obscured age-old Jewish-Christian differences. The concept was further attacked in the wake of the 1967 Six-Day War, an event that exposed deep theological fissures between Jews and Christians, especially with regard to Israel, and hastened a trend toward greater Jewish self-pride. More recently, "Judeo-Christian" has been attacked as a rhetorical ploy used by right-wing elements in order to promote an exclusively Christian political program.[13]

The so-called triple melting pot proved no more adequate as an explanatory concept. It seriously underestimated the importance of ethnic differences, totally misunderstood the significance of Evangelical Protestantism, and wrote off other American faiths completely, as if they did not exist at all. David Dalin points out that "even as Herberg was writing, new evangelical sects were arising and older ones were undergoing revitalization. Less than five years after the publication of *Protestant-Catholic-Jew*, the sociologist Seymour Martin Lipset could note that such fundamentalist sects were 'far stronger today than at any time in the 20th century,' and that the much-heralded growth in church membership was taking place precisely among these 'fringe sects,' rather than within the traditional Protestant 'mainline' denominations in which Herberg placed so much stock."[14] Admittedly, Herberg's model did help pave the way for subsequent discussions of American "civil religion." But the triple melting pot by itself was scarcely an adequate depiction of American religion in the 1950s, and was even less adequate thereafter.

Today, assumptions about America's Judeo-Christian character and its Protestant-Catholic-Jew makeup confront an even more critical problem: the rapid growth of American religions that are not Protestant, Catholic, or Jewish, and are totally outside the Judeo-Christian spectrum. I refer principally to Islam, among the fastest-growing religions in the United States, but we should also bear in mind the presence in America of so-called hidden religions (the term is J. Gordon Melton's), including metaphysical faiths, Eastern religions, Psychic or New Age religions, and the like. Sociologists Wade Clark Roof and William McKinney found in 1985 that non-Judeo-Christian faiths commanded the loyalty of twice as many Americans as Judaism and that nearly one American in ten reported no religious affiliation. In other words, at least 13 percent of all Americans do not fit our standard assumptions about America's religious character. This represents more than a fourfold increase in just thirty years, and there is every reason to believe that the number of these "exceptions" will continue to expand at a rapid rate.[15]

From the point of view of American Jews, the growth of American Islam merits special attention, especially given the organized Muslim community's hostility to Israel. Islam's emergence as a major American faith has failed until now to elicit much discussion in Jewish circles, probably from a fear of appearing religiously prejudiced. I am not familiar with a single scholarly study of what this development means to Jews, certainly none that investigates how Islam's rise may affect Jewish identity and life in the decades ahead. No detailed study can be attempted here either, but given my topic, "Jewish Identity in the Changing World of American Religion," some preliminary remarks are in order.

Historically, individual Muslims came to America as early as the colonial period. Small numbers of Muslims are known to have lived in various communities in the nineteenth century, but always as individuals; there was no organized Islamic presence. During the era of mass immigration (1880s–World War I), migration from what was then called Greater Syria increased owing to a wide variety of factors: political and economic insecurity, agricultural problems, overpopulation, the decline of the Ottoman Empire, and the lure of economic advancement in the New World. Most of the immigrants were actually Christian Arabs, but a number of Muslims came too—"they hoped to earn as much as possible and then return home."[16] The oft-told story of the small Muslim community established near Ross, North Dakota around 1900 demonstrates the difficulties that Muslims faced in a non-Muslim environment. To Jewish ears, the story sounds remarkably familiar.

> Before a mosque was built in ths 1920s, prayer and ritual were conducted in private houses and led by the best informed among the group. Without a mosque for almost 30 years and without any cultural reinforcement from newcomers, the Muslims rapidly lost the use of Arabic, assumed Christian

names, and married non-Muslims. The community dwindled as children moved away, and the mosque was abandoned by 1948.[17]

The most visible early centers of Islam in America were in Michigan, especially in the Detroit and Dearborn areas, for many Arab immigrants took jobs at the Ford plant. Other Muslim communities were established in East Coast and Midwest industrial centers. But given immigration restrictions and assimilation, the number of Muslims in America remained small—"a little over 100,000"—into the early 1960s. Since then, the nation's Islamic population has mushroomed, owing both to large-scale immigration (14 percent of all immigrants into the United States are now Muslims) and to thousands of converts, especially blacks. Significant Islamic communities may be found in New York, Los Angeles, Chicago, Detroit, and Toledo, Ohio. One recent study lists 598 mosques and Islamic centers operating in the United States, and estimates the number of American Muslims as "somewhere in the range of two to three million"—a conservative estimate.[18] "The high rate of birth, the growing number of converts, and the continuing flow of immigration," the study's authors conclude, "make it possible to predict that by the first decade of the twenty-first century Islam will be the second largest religious community in the United States."[19]

The Muslim community stands in the forefront of those who seek to break down the Judeo-Christian, Protestant-Catholic-Jew models of American religious life. Quite understandably, Muslim leaders feel that these models are exclusivistic; they imply that Muslims cannot participate as equals in American society. "We'd like people to start thinking of the U.S. as a Judeo-Christian-Muslim society," said Salam Al-Marayati, spokesman for the Muslim Political Action Committee. Another Muslim told researchers that he looked forward to the day "when all will say 'Catholics, Protestants, Jews and Muslims.'"[20] While such a change would not go far enough for those Muslims whose ultimate goal is to bring about an Islamic state in America, and would certainly not meet the needs of those whose faith is neither Judeo-Christian nor Muslim, it does bear out our earlier analysis. America's religious identity is changing; the way Jews understand American religion must change as well.

What are the implications of these changes for American Jews and American Jewish identity? Given what we have seen to be the rather poor results of earlier efforts to foretell American Jewry's future, I might be forgiven if, echoing Amos, I declared myself to be neither a prophet nor a prophet's disciple, and left it at that. But since the organizers of this conference have instructed me to pay special attention, at the very least, to the policy implications of my analysis, let me suggest ten possible changes that we may see in the years ahead, bearing in mind my earlier caution concerning self-negating prophecies. Some of these changes relate broadly to the new world of American religion that Jews must confront; the rest deal more narrowly with the growth of Islam, and its possible ramifications.

1. The one-time familiar trinity of Protestants, Catholics, and Jews will, in the future, almost surely give way to a much wider religious circle. At the very least, we shall have to include Muslims in the company of religious insiders; more likely, we shall have to expand the circle to include the full range of American religious denominations, Eastern religions as well as Western ones.

2. Our image of American religion will have to change to comport more closely than it now does with statistical realities. As such, Jews may find themselves placed on an equal footing not with Protestants and Catholics, but, ironically, with Muslims, for both represent major world religions comprising less than 3 percent of the total U.S. population. A hint of what lies in store may already be found in J. Gordon Melton's *Encyclopedia of American Religions* (1978). The encyclopedia claims to explore "the broad sweep of American religions and describes 1200 churches." It divides American religion into seventeen "religious families," only ten of which basically follow Christian beliefs and practices. Jews do not even rate a religious family of their own in this classification; instead they are grouped together with Muslims, Hindus, and Buddhists under "the Eastern and Middle Eastern Family." "The inclusion here of the Jews, Hindus, Buddhists and Muslims in one family," J. Gordon Melton explains, "is based on shared characteristics, peculiar to their American sojourn, without negating their fundamental differences."[21]

3. Given the move away from the triple melting pot view of American religion, and the almost inevitable devaluation of Judaism's place in the panoply of American religion, Jews in the next few decades will have to endure what mainstream Protestants went through earlier in this century: the experience of status-loss, of feeling almost dispossessed. The rise in status that Jews experienced when the triple melting pot image gained ascendancy will, I believe, be partially if not wholly reversed. As a result, the Jewish community will have to learn how to live with a radically different image of itself—a much less flattering one.

4. As a consequence of all of the above, American Jews will receive far less textbook and media attention than they do now. Where for some years Jews benefited from a disproportionate share of religious attention, almost on a par with Protestants and Catholics, now they will have to

adjust their expectations down to a more realistic level in keeping with the Jewish community's actual size and significance.

5. Jewish political power in the years ahead may also fall into decline. As politicians become aware of America's changing religious situation, many may feel less inclined to listen when Jewish lobbyists come calling. Political power in America is, of course, more than just a function of numbers; organization, intelligence, experience, participation, and money also count for a great deal. But given countervailing pressure from constituents actively hostile to Jewish interests, the knowledge that America's Jews are a less significant group than they used to be cannot but have some impact. In the coming years, Jews will have to work much harder to achieve their goals and will not be able to take their power nearly so much for granted.

6. Israel may well suffer the most from these changes. The declining status of American Jews, coupled with the rise of American Islam and the growing political maturity of the American Muslim community, will make it much more difficult in the years ahead for massive aid to Israel to win congressional approval. Already, the Muslim Political Action Committee is promoting pro-Palestinian policies. Having learned much from watching how Jewish political lobbyists work, American Muslims intend to increase their political activities in coming elections, and hope to elect a Muslim to Congress by 1992.[22]

7. For a few decades, at least, we are likely to see a return in this country to the rhetoric of religious triumphalism. Faiths new on the American scene and flush with fresh converts often delude themselves into thinking that theirs is the faith of the future, the religion that will bring The Truth to all Americans and unite them into a single all-embracing church (or mosque). Almost inevitably, this pious hope stirs up religious fervor, spurs the faithful to participate in religious crusades, and successfully thwarts liberal efforts aimed at promoting interreligious harmony. Catholics, Jews, and mainstream Protestants know from experience that sooner or later all such hopes are doomed to disappointment; religious monism is not the American way. But this may well be the kind of lesson that every faith community must learn anew for itself.

8. Until this and other lessons *are* learned, interfaith conversations will become much more difficult. In the past, leading Jews, Protestants, and Catholics have, if nothing else, established certain properties that permitted them to interact; they all learned to practice what John Murray Cuddihy calls "the religion of civility."[23] Faiths previously excluded from the mainstream do not necessarily share these proprieties, and may in some cases openly scorn them—witness the intemperate rhetoric of some

fundamentalist preachers or of Black Muslim leaders like Louis Farrakhan. Unless (or until) a new generation of religious leaders from a much broader spectrum of faiths can be initiated into the niceties of religious conversation, progress can scarcely be expected. Discussions will either prove too limited to be meaningful or too acrimonious to be helpful.

9. On the brighter side, the rise of Islam and the widening parameters of American religion may in the long run promote closer Muslim-Jewish relations. Confronted with surprisingly similar kinds of religious problems in a society that is still overwhelmingly Christian, Jews and Muslims have every reason to learn to work together in support of common interests. Moreover, the neutral American environment should make possible a level of religious interaction between Jews and Muslims that would be unthinkable either in Arab countries or in Israel. For reasons that I have already outlined, I do not expect serious interreligious conversations to take place in the near future. But the history of Catholic-Jewish relations over the past century in America demonstrates that change is possible. Given what Robert Wuthnow writes about the "decline of denominationalism"[24] in recent decades, improvements may come about even sooner than we think.

10. Finally, the changing world of American religion may prompt Jews fundamentally to reevaluate their agenda and goals for the years ahead. If Jews are to be known once more as a religious minority, a so-called dissenting faith, they may want to act the part, just as they did decades ago. This means that Jews would focus first and foremost on their own interests, next on those issues of special concern to religious minorities, and only third on the great social and political agenda that majority faiths worry about. Historically, the Jewish community played a tremendously important role as leader and spokesman for America's religious minorities. It did more than any other faith community to promote inclusive theories of American life (the melting pot and cultural pluralism) and religious liberty for all. Jews, in my opinion, have had far less impact as yea-saying members of the religious majority, and have squandered precious resources on issues about which they have little new to say. By refocusing priorities back toward minority-group issues—particularly the age-old American question of minority rights versus majority rule—Jews may actually make more of a mark than they did as members of the religious "establishment." Such a refocusing would not only strengthen Jewish minority-group identity, but would also have the additional advantage of promoting group survival as a weapon against intermarriage and assimilation.

Let me close with this final thought. Jews have done exceedingly well in this country, both in the old days when they were viewed as members of a religious minority roughly akin to Turks and infidels, and more recently when they became part of the religious majority, grouped together with Protestants and Catholics in a "triple melting pot." The fact that yet another change is now taking place should thus occasion concerned vigilance, but not necessarily alarm. Indeed, we have seen that some of the implications of this change may actually turn out to be positive. Moreover, it is a mistake to assume that Jews are merely the objects of history, tossed about by forces totally beyond their control. While Jews may not be able to do anything about the realignment of American religion and the growth of American Islam, the way they respond to these challenges may in fact make a great deal of difference. American Jews survived earlier challenges, prophecies of doom notwithstanding, because Jewish leaders responded to them creatively—with wisdom, discernment, and flexibility. Let us hope that our present leaders can do as well.

Notes

1. John Adams to M. M. Noah (March 15, 1819), reprinted in Moshe Davis, *With Eyes Toward Zion* (New York: Arno, 1977), p. 19; W. M. Rosenblatt, "The Jews: What Are They Coming To," *Galaxy* 13 (January 1872): 60; Thomas B. Morgan, "The Vanishing American Jew," *Look* 28 (May 5, 1964): 42–46; Reuven P. Bulka, *The Coming Cataclysm* (Oakville, Ont.: Mosaic Press, 1984), p. 14; see also Stephen J. Whitfield, *American Space, Jewish Time* (Hamden, Conn.: Archon Books, 1988), pp. 171–191.

2. Robert Wuthnow, *The Restructuring of American Religion: Society and Faith Since World War II* (Princeton: Princeton University Press, 1988).

3. Joseph Story, *Commentaries on the Constitution of the United States* (Boston, 1833), as reprinted in John F. Wilson and Donald L. Drakeman, *Church and State in American History* (Boston, 1987), pp. 92–93.

4. Robert T. Handy, *A Christian America: Protestant Hopes and Historical Realities* (New York: Oxford, 1971), p. 118.

5. Morton Borden, *Jews, Turks and Infidels* (Chapel Hill: University of North Carolina Press, 1984), pp. 62–74; Naomi W. Cohen, *Encounter with Emancipation: The German Jews in the United States, 1830–1914* (Philadelphia: Jewish Publication Society, 1984), pp. 98–100, 254–256.

6. Jonathan D. Sarna, *American Jews and Church-State Relations: The Search for "Equal Footing"* (New York: American Jewish Committee, 1989), esp. pp. 4–10.

7. Mark Silk, *Spiritual Politics: Religion and America Since World War I*

(New York: Simon & Schuster, 1988), pp. 40–53. Silk provides numerous other quotations from this period in addition to the ones I have used here. See also Silk's "Notes on the Judeo-Christian Tradition in America," *American Quarterly* 36 (Spring 1984): 65–85. In a forthcoming article, Benny Kraut will argue that the Judeo-Christian concept actually arose in the 1920s as part of that decade's interreligious "goodwill" movement. I am grateful to Prof. Kraut for sharing his material with me prior to publication.

8. Sydney E. Ahlstrom, *A Religious History of the American people* (New Haven: Yale University Press, 1972), pp. 8–12; see also R. Laurence Moore, *Religious Outsiders and the Making of Americans* (New York: Oxford, 1986); and more broadly Henry W. Bowden, "The Historiography of American Religion," in *Encyclopedia of the American Religious Experience*, ed. Charles H. Lippy and Peter W. Williams (New York: Charles Scribner's Sons, 1987), vol. 1, pp. 3–16.

9. Everett R. Clinchy, "Better Understanding," *Universal Jewish Encyclopedia* (1942) vol. 2, p. 257; Louis Minsky, "National Conference of Christians and Jews," ibid., vol. 8, p. 114; Benny Kraut, "Towards the Establishment of the National Conference of Christians and Jews: The Tenuous Road to Religious Goodwill in the 1920s," *American Jewish History* 77, no. 3 (March 1988): 388–412; idem, "A Wary Collaboration: Jews, Catholics and the Protestant Goodwill Movement" (forthcoming); Alex J. Goldman, "Alexander D. Goode," in *Giants of the Faith: Great American Rabbis* (New York, 1964), pp. 311–329; see also Lance J. Sussman " 'Toward Better Understanding': The Rise of the Interfaith Movement in America and the Role of Rabbi Isaac Landman," *American Jewish Archives* 34 (April 1982): 35–51.

10. Will Herberg, *Protestant-Catholic-Jew: An Essay in American Religious Sociology*, (rev. ed. (New York: Anchor Books, 1960), esp pp. 256–257; David G. Dalin, "Will Herberg in Retrospect," *Commentary* 86 (July 1988): 38–43.

11. Maxwell Abbell, "The Basic Task of the Synagogue in America," *Torch*, Winter 1955, reprinted in Milton Berger et al., *Roads to Jewish Survival* (New York: Bloch, 1967), p. 153.

12. Charles H. Stember et al., *Jews in the Mind of America* (New York: Basic Books, 1966), p. 77.

13. Silk, *Spiritual Politics*, pp. 42–44, 142–146, 180.

14. Dalin, "Will Herberg in Retrospect," p. 42.

15. Wade Clark Roof and William McKinney, *American Mainline Religion: Its Changing Shape and Future* (New Brunswick, N.J., 1987), esp. p. 17; Silk, *Spiritual Politics*, p. 181; for an exhaustive survey of non-Judeo-Christian religions, see G. Gordon Melton, *The Encyclopedia of American Religions* (Wilmington, N.C.: McGrath Publishing Co., 1978, 1985). These "exceptions," it should be stressed, are not for the most part avowed secularists. Americans are simply defining religion in ways that they rarely if ever did before. For a valuable compilation of survey data regarding "unsecular America," see Richard J. Neuhaus, ed., *Unsecular America* (Grand Rapids, Mich.: Erdmans, 1986), esp. pp. 115–158.

16. Anthony B. Toth, "The Syrian Community in New Castle and Its Unique Alawi Component, 1900–1940," *Western Pennsylvania Historical Magazine* 69 (July 1986): 221–239; Newell S. Booth, Jr., "Islam in North America," *Encyclopedia of the American Religious Experience*, ed. Charles H. Lippy and Peter W. Williams (New York: Charles Scribner's Sons, 1987), vol. 2, p. 725. For earlier sources, see George Dimitri Selim, comp., *The Arabs in the United States: A Selected List of References*, Mideast Directions bibliographies of the Library of Congress (Washington, 1983).

17. Alixa Naff, "Arabs," in *Harvard Encyclopedia of American Ethnic Groups*, ed. Stephan Thernstrom et al. (Cambridge, Mass.: Harvard University Press, 1980), p. 132.

18. Yvonne Yazbeck Haddad and Adair T. Lummis, *Islamic Values in the United States* (New York: Oxford, 1987), p. 3. *Time*, May 23, 1988, p. 49, quotes Carol Stone's estimate of 4,644,000 Muslims, and *New York Times*, February 21, 1989, p. 1, speaks of "6 million Muslims in the United States."

19. Haddad and Lumis, *Islamic Values in the United States*, p. 3; *Time*, May 23, 1988, p. 49, makes the same point: "U.S. Muslims are expected to surpass Jews in number and, in less than 30 years, become the country's second largest religious community, after Christians."

20. *Time*, May 23, 1988, p. 50; Haddad and Lumis, *Islamic Values in the United States*, p. 161.

21. Melton, *Encyclopedia of American Religions*, vol. 1, pp. vii–xii; vol. 2, pp. 307–354. Melton's idiosyncratic classification scheme is, of course, easy to criticize. His depiction of American Judaism is filled with gross errors, and his inclusion of Jews for Jesus under "Mainstream Judaism" is offensive.

22. *Time*, August 23, 1988, p. 50. Writing in the wake of the Six-Day War, the Arab sociologist Abdo A. Elkholy dreamed of a far more radical agenda for Arab Americans. "Many of the great national movements which have changed the course of our modern history started abroad," he pointed out. "Could it be that future historians will focus on the Arab elites in America and their role in a sweeping Arab revolution which would unify the Middle East and liberate it from both international Zionism and military domination and corruption?" See Abdo A. Elkholy, "The Arab-Americans: Nationalism and Traditionalism and Traditional Preservations," in *The Arab Americans: Studies in Assimilation*, ed. Elaine C. Hagopian and Ann Paden (Wilmette, Ill.: Medina University Press, 1969), p. 17.

23. John Murray Cuddihy, *No Offense: Civil Religion and Protestant Taste* (New York: Seabury, 1978).

24. Wuthnow, *Restructuring of American Religion*, pp. 71–99.

Response to Jonathan Sarna

DAVID ELLENSON

Jonathan Sarna has pointed to recent developments and trends within the world of American religion that are fraught with implications for the manner in which American Jewish identity and political power will be manifested in the decades ahead. It is particularly significant that he identifies the rise of Islam in the United States as a matter of special note to American Jews. Few, if any, other commentators have brought this item to the attention of forums such as the one in which we participate tonight. Thus, it is with a sense of gratitude for his thoughtful and erudite presentation that I offer several comments occasioned by Dr. Sarna's work.

As with every respondent, there are items which I might have chosen to emphasize that Dr. Sarna did not. For example, the growth of women's presence within the contemporary world of American Judaism has already had a significant impact upon American Judaism and American Jewish identity in several ways. Women's visibility in the public and institutional spheres of American life and their appearance in the pulpit in many mainline Protestant denominations, and even some Evangelical Protestant sects, have had their parallels in the Jewish world. The ordination of women as rabbis in the non-Orthodox movements of American Judaism has caused many Jews to ponder the way God is imaged and discussed in our tradition. The sexist nature of much of our liturgical language and the role that humans play in the construction of religious ritual have also come to the forefront of the consciousness of many American Jews in the shaping of their Jewish identity. This discussion of the impact of feminism upon American Jewish identity could certainly continue. I cite it here merely to illustrate the point that the factors that impinge upon the issue of identity are multifaceted, and no single paper could possibly consider all the variables potentially relevant to such discussion. It is important, however, to acknowledge this and keep such matters in mind before feeling satisfied that we have completed our consideration of the issue before us tonight.

This said, it is now appropriate to turn to Professor Sarna's paper and its important and well-argued thesis. Essentially, Dr. Sarna has argued that the decades ahead will witness the decline of the notion that there is a Judeo-Christian ethos that informs the core value of American people. Along with that, the Protestant-Catholic-Jewish model of American religion will wither as there will be a concomitant growth in non-Judeo-Christian religions, particularly Islam, in the near future. The implications of these developments, as Dr. Sarna sees them, are several. Paramount among them, however, are the predictions that Jews will no longer receive the media attention and prominence they have formerly possessed as a group—they will experience "status loss." Secondly, with the rise of American Islam and the decline of Jewish religious significance on the American scene, Jewish political power in the United States will become attenuated. Israel "may well suffer the most from these changes," as American support for Israel's government may well erode as a result. There are other interesting and provocative positions Dr. Sarna garners from his analysis. However, I would like to focus on these.

First, I am not certain that the predicted decline in Jewish political influence in the United States will occur. Secondly, even if it does, I am not certain that this will lead to an attenuation of American support for the State of Israel. That is, I am not certain that U.S. government support for Israel stems principally from the political influence of American Jews. Rather, the source for our government's support for Israel may arise from the role that Israel plays in the mythology of a Christian America as well as from the fact that Israel, for all its problems, may well be the best strategic ally the United States possesses in the all too often volatile Middle East. I am, of course, not a political scientist. I offer these thoughts to indicate that even if Dr. Sarna's forecasts about the decline of American Jewish influence and the rise of Islamic presence in the United States are correct (and I believe they are), they might not lead to a diminution in U.S. support for the State of Israel.

However, let us assume that it is the power and influence of the Jewish community that assures American governmental aid to Israel. I am not sure even then that it would be the factors cited by Dr. Sarna alone that would account for the erosion of the political power of the American Jewish community. Rather, and this would be especially true in the short run, it may be that internal Jewish communal controversy over current Israeli governmental actions and policies may do more to splinter Jewish political unity and influence in this country than the external factors Dr. Sarna correctly identifies. The majority of America's Jews are fundamentally liberal and moralistic. Prophetic interpretations of Judaism tend to inform their sense of authentic Jewish religion and identity. Given such an internal American Jewish ambience, it is inevitable that communal debate and disagreement over the wisdom of Israeli governmental positions will grow. Indeed, the 1980s have already borne ever-increasing witness to this phenomenon as communal debate over the war in Lebanon, negotiations with the PLO, and the ongoing intifada have indicated. The diversity of opinion on Israeli political policies expressed by many American Jews mirrors what one might more readily expect from an Israeli public. This was not true a decade ago. Such divisions of opinion surely cannot escape members of Congress, or anyone else who either is exposed to the national media or reads the Jewish press.

Furthermore, the rise of intermarriage, the non-Orthodox affiliation patterns of most American Jews, and the symbolic import of the "Who is a Jew?" debate in the light of these facts is another reflection of the community's divisions, both internally and with Israel. Over 90 percent of the intermarrieds, when they do affiliate or convert, do so with non-Orthodox institutions or rabbis. The "Who is a Jew" debate has thus had the effect of forcing most American Jews to recognize that their form of Judaism is disenfranchised in Israel and that many of their friends and, more significantly, their families, as well as their rabbis, possess a status that would be questioned there. This is why the debate elicited the furious reaction it did from American Jewish leaders. More important for our concerns is that it indicates a rift between and among Israeli and American Jews that may grow more intense over the next decade, with untoward consequences for the unity of the American and worldwide Jewish communities. Finally, given the political sophistication various right-wing Orthodox groups in this country are displaying, as well as their dissent from the traditional posture of church-state separation with which America's Jews have long been associated, it is unclear whether there is the significant "center" of American Jewish political consensus there formerly was. In sum, there may simply be too many spheres of influence, too many competing factions within an admittedly small community, for the Jewish community to unify and exert the same degree of influence it might have formerly possessed. The pluralism our community now displays—for all the reasons cited above—may be as, if not more, significant than any other factor in accounting for a decline in Jewish political influence in the immediate future.

Finally, I would offer another view of the meaning that the rise of Islam and other religious traditions—and the concomitant decline of the Judeo-Christian ethos in America—might possess for future American Jewish religious and ethnic identity. To begin, I am not sure that the "triple melting pot" model of American identity was ever one that truly embraced "Jews as equals." Let me explain. The major characteristic of

Jews living in the Western world during the last two centuries has been to acculturate, to take on the cultural characteristics of the dominant host societies in which we Jews have lived. In the United States, this has been as true of Jews of Eastern European origins as it was of the German Jews who preceded them. Yet such acculturation exacts a cost. As John Cuddihy has noted, the passage from particularism to a broader particularism—what is often called universalism—is often an "ordeal" for the members of the group who are making the journey. For the "journey" toward cultural integration often causes the Jews, or any other minority similarly situated, to internalize negative stereotypes.

American Jews have felt, in significant ways, the conflict inherent in trying to have maintain an *authentic* Jewish identity while living in a non-Jewish world. On the one hand, Jews have had an intense desire to acculturate, to take part in the American celebration of the melting pot. We have successfully done this as individuals by eagerly accepting the benefits the American nation has had to offer us and by participating as fully as possible in every sector of American life. Communally, we have also accepted the labels American society has conferred, precisely because such labels have bestowed and ascribed status upon us that we so desperately have desired. We have accepted, with little protest (Arthur Cohen's famous book, *The Myth of the Judeo-Christian Tradition*, remains a notable exception), the ideal of a Judeo-Christian ethic and have applauded our role as one of the three prominent American faiths.

Yet, in doing so, we have betrayed a sense of unease and insecurity in this land of unparalleled freedom and opportunity. For we have known that America, protestations to the contrary notwithstanding, has largely been a white, Protestant, male affair. We have primarily accepted the notion of a Judeo-Christian ethos because it has allowed us to mask an "otherness" we might otherwise have had to confront, and it has given us a means to respond to an indictment we might otherwise have had to admit is essentially correct. That is, when an Arnold Toynbee caricatured Judaism as a "fossil," as a relic from an ancient Near Eastern tribal civilization otherwise dead, he did not necessarily mean that Judaism as a religion was moribund. Rather, he was saying that Judaism was culturally insignificant, and that after the creation of the Hebrew Bible, the Jews as a people left the central stage of history. This view, however difficult it is for us to acknowledge consciously, has been the normative view of Western civilization until our own day. Look at virtually any course on Western civilization given in any university in the United States today to confirm it. Past generations of American Jews have tacitly accepted this view. Scores of apologetic works "proving" Judaism's decisive impact upon this or that element of Western history were written precisely because our ancestors felt that the value and legitimacy of Judaism could not be affirmed in its own right. These works betrayed our sense of unease and inferiority when confronted with a Gentile society we considered superior. We have welcomed the notion of the Judeo-Christian ethos and have applauded our place as one of America's three great religions because it has allowed us to deny the power of the Toynbee view. However, this should not obscure our internalization of the negative stereotypes inherent in that view. It is in light of this that I would offer an additional assessment of the significance and meaning that the demise of the Judeo-Christian myth may hold for American Jewish religious and cultural identity.

The decline of this ethos, I would submit, may well help to create a healthier American Jewish identity. Many more American Jews, in the present decade as well as in the years ahead, may now be freer to approach their past and search out their roots because they sincerely believe that the Jewish heritage may address human needs and answer the quest for personal and communal identity and belonging in ways more compelling than the previously dominant Protestant model. I am not speaking here of a narrow ethnicity or religious identity. Rather, I am applauding the fact that in recent years America has evidenced a genuinely more pluralistic model of cultural and religious life.

The burgeoning of Jewish studies on college campuses, for example, and the demands made in the past two decades to include such studies within university curricula, bespeaks the growing sense of self-confidence contemporary Jews feel about their Jewishness in American society. It also reflects the greater ability of the United States to tolerate a multicultural, pluralistic societal model. No longer ashamed of their past, American Jews, as well as women and other ethnics, claim that their cultures are valid ones that the American nation must include in its canon. It is not parochial, this new form of identity. However, it does assert that one need not reverberate *only* to the literature of New England to find a valid American identity. One can supplement and discover it through one's own cultural heritage as well. This, I would submit, explains in part the rapid growth of day schools in contemporary America. Increasing numbers of Jews are asserting the legitimacy of their cultural heritage and see it as a viable option for their children in a multicultural America.

For these reasons, I would acknowledge the legitimacy and correctness of much of Dr. Sarna's analysis. However, the demise of the religious models of post–World War II America may simply serve as the harbinger of a more genuinely pluralistic and mature model of American Jewish identity and community in the century ahead. Rather than lament the decline of the older model, we ought, in many senses, to applaud it. It offers new challenges and new hope as American Jewish identity takes shape in the years to come.

Response to Jonathan Sarna

STEVEN BAYME

Jonathan Sarna has offered a provocative and thoughtful analysis of the realignment of American religion: the decline of the triple melting pot, the explosion of the myth of the Judeo-Christian tradition, and the rise of American Islam. In that context Sarna has entered the debate concerning the future of American Jewry and, to some extent, has come out on the pessimistic side. At the least, he qualifies many of the Pollyannish predictions that proclaim American Jewry to be in an age of revival, renaissance, and resurgence. Reflecting upon his paper, I also come out somewhat on the pessimistic side, but perhaps for different reasons. I'd like to take issue with some of his hypotheses as well as build on some of his constructive suggestions.

The first theme is that of Sarna's explosion of the myth of Judaism as being coequal with Christianity. In his view, Judaism is about to experience a decline, or as he puts it, "an inevitable devaluation of Judaism's place in the panoply of American religion." The basis for this prediction is almost entirely a numerical and statistical analysis. Yet it is no secret that Jews have never been a large nation either in America or elsewhere. The promise given to Abraham that "your children will be as the sands of the sea and the stars of the universe" pales by comparison with Moses' pronouncement in Deuteronomy that "you are the smallest of all the nations." What has been at the root of American Jewry's and American Judaism's status in America has had very little to do with demography. This is not to say that we should not be concerned with demographic factors. But, in my opinion, the status of American Judaism has much more to do with the power of Judaic ideals and values, the high position accorded Judaism in the panoply of theological truths and in the range of ideas that color the American value system. Jewish intellectuals' influence in American society has not rested upon the power of Jewish votes but rather upon the verve and persuasiveness of the ideas that Jews are willing to defend.

Let me offer two brief examples. Thirty percent of the professors at elite American universities are Jews. That is an incredible manifestation of the prominence and power of American Jews in American society, in elite sectors of American society, despite the fact that they constitute a comparatively small percentage of this society. On a more personal level, one need go no further back than several years ago to the famous Bitburg event of 1985, where an American Jewish spokesman, Elie Wiesel, felt confident and sure-footed enough to publicly rebuke the President of the United States, saying "That place is not your place." That's a statement of Jewish influence in this country that rests not upon the number of votes supporting Reagan, which was quite minimal, but rather upon the verve and persuasiveness of the ideas and values that Jews are willing to defend. In that sense, I think one question I would raise to Sarna regards his hypothesizing an inevitable decline in the stature of Jews and Judaism in America. Is there evidence of the decline in the persuasiveness and power of Jewish ideas?

My second disagreement relates to his elevating Islam into the wave of the future, or as he puts it, "that the myth of America as inhospitable to non-Judeo-Christian faiths is about to be exploded." Again he offers numerical evidence for the rise of Islam. I'd like to qualify that in several respects. Sarna offers a number of figures as to how many Muslims there are in this country. But the Muslim community in this country is by no means united. A large percentage, for instance, are Turkish Muslims who want little to do with the broader Muslim context. They are Turks of the Muslim faith, but that is as far as it goes in terms of their integration into any broader American Muslim entity. Going beyond numbers, the question becomes, what is the influence of Islam in American society? The best-known Muslims remain Kareem Abdul-Jabbar and Muhammad Ali, figures who have a minimal impact upon the intellectual values and ideals that dominate American society. Edward Said, in a recent book, *Covering Islam*, complains bitterly of how the image of Islam has been distorted by American media. One can argue, of course, that Said is expressing nothing more than the "blame the messenger" syndrome (which afflicts Jews as well). Yet if one looks at how the media have covered Islam, there is a sense of the Arab as being anti-Western, of Islam as being alien to American society. The implicit premise of the famous Abscam scandal, namely, that it takes an Arab to engage in such an act of deception, is indicative of such mistrust. Sarna is quite correct in suggesting that Israel is currently suffering a decline in its standing in the eyes of public opinion. But, I submit, that has far more to do with the actual developments in the Middle East than it does with the rise of Islam in America. In this sense, I again submit that there is no "necessary, inevitable devaluation of Judaism's place in the panoply of American religion." Our high place in American society was never based on statistics.

To dwell on American textbooks, Jonathan suggests fervently that we are about to see fewer Jews portrayed in American textbooks and in far less positive terms. I find this questionable as well. It has been only recently that Jews have entered into the textbook industry. When, a mere ten or fifteen years ago, Columbia University issued its much heralded *History of the World,* for the first time Jewish history was integrated into the overall panoply of general history. In other words, in terms of recent developments in textbook treatments of Jews and Judaism, we have only begun to enter into that world. What is of greater interest is the number of Jews who have entered into the textbook industry. The question is not that of Jewish influence—the question is, how Jewish are these Jews? Are they going to be willing to portray Jews in substantive and rich forms?

There are other areas where I think Sarna is on target. First, in terms of the political dimension, he forecasts a political shrinkage of American Jewish influence. This is probably well taken, since in this area mere demographics do count. Declining numbers of Jews, declining electoral importance of the areas in which Jews live, will obviously take a toll in terms of how much influence the Jews wield in American society. Yet I'm not sure whether this is related so much to the questions that Jonathan raises as it is to two other factors that have been staples of Jewish political life in this country—namely, the virtually one-sided identification of Jews with the Democratic party, which in turn raises the question of, why take Jews all that seriously if their votes are so eminently predictable? Secondly, Jewish political clout and Jewish political influence is also a function of the roles Jews play in the intellectual debate concerning political issues. When Jewish political culture is defined in narrowly liberal terms, the question of the future of Jewish political influence becomes somewhat more questionable. But again, these are not new trends in American Jewish political life—they've been with us for forty or fifty years, since the day of the New Deal. We have not seen any shrinkage of political influence until now, and I'm not sure that they forecast political shrinkage for the future either.

Sarna correctly points out that the rise of Islam, by definition, will cause greater attention to be focused upon the Middle East, in terms that are less favorable to Israel. But again the question here is cause and effect. Undoubtedly, Israel will be subject to considerable criticism in the foreseeable future, not only from American society at large but also within the American Jewish community. Is that a function of the rise of

Islam, or is it a function of greater questioning, distancing, and alienation on the part of many American Jews and American Jewish intellectuals from the realities and the facts in the Middle East?

Irving Greenberg has argued succinctly in a recent article, "The Growth of an American Jewish Political Culture," that AIPAC's political influence rests upon the fact that "minorities will get their way only when it coincides with widely held values and perceptions." Whether Israel will make its case in the American media or in American public opinion is not so much a function of how many Jewish votes there are or how much political clout Jews wield. Rather, it is a function of the extent to which American public opinion identifies and is consonant with the realities of Israel's position in the Middle Eastern conflict, and continues to see Israel as the fulfillment of the basic Zionist dream of building a liberal democracy.

A third area which I think Sarna has raised correctly is his forecast of the growth of religious triumphalism in American society at large. In this respect, the rise of Islam parallels the rise of American Orthodoxy, and Jewish leaders who want to direct their energies toward safeguarding the Jewish future should seek to maximize the resources of the Orthodox, and at the same time to promote the kind of religious pluralism that Jews have stood for. The rise of American Orthodoxy has in many ways defied all the prognostications, and the implications for the future of American Judaism are critical.

Most importantly, we are for the first time witnessing Orthodox affluence: Orthodox Jews have the resources, the money, the power, to express themselves in education, in politics, even in such day-to-day things as running kosher restaurants. Related to this is the growing political clout of Orthodoxy. On Capitol Hill today, for the first time, there are Orthodox lobbyists monitoring legislation that will affect the Orthodox Jewish community. As Sarna correctly indicated, this may raise certain questions in terms of the traditional American Jewish position regarding the separation of church and state. The Orthodox prefer, in many ways, to go back to a nineteenth-century definition of Judaism and other faiths being treated equally, over the alternative of strict separation between the political state and the synagogues and churches within it.

In terms of Jewish identity, the resurgence of Orthodoxy will set forth certain paradigms which will have implications for the broader Jewish community; for example, in terms of the intensity of Jewish family life, where Orthodox rituals often serve as a vehicle of communication between generations that cements families together. It's no secret that Orthodox divorce rates are much lower than those of the Jewish community at large. In terms of Jewish education, the Orthodox have brought much intensity of commitment and verve to support their own educational institutions. At a time when so many are worried about the future of Jewish education, the commitment of the Orthodox to maintain their own institutions sets forth a model or paradigm for the non-Orthodox community. All of this, of course, exists alongside the tremendous furor within the Jewish community over relations with the Orthodox—furor over the "Who is a Jew?" question, religious pluralism here and in Israel. In all these issues, the Jewish community is heading toward increased conflict. The triumphalism in American religion generally feeds upon the resurgence of Orthodoxy and in turn nurtures and enriches that resurgence. I would submit that perhaps the best example is not so much Islam but rather religious fundamentalism in a broader sense—Christian, Muslim, and Jewish. Its implications for the broader Jewish community and for the Jewish future are considerable.

Finally, Sarna concludes on a fairly optimistic note regarding Muslim-Jewish relations. In truth, there may be a precedent here that suggests that while we cannot look forward immediately to a close interfaith relationship with our Muslim friends, the background exists for a religious interchange and dialogue between Judaism and Islam—in many ways a far stronger dialogue than between Judaism and Christianity. One need go no further than the classic example of Maimonides, who, in his famous essay on martyrdom, argued that if a Jew was forced either to convert to Islam or to die, he should convert to Islam, at least superficially, observe Judaism privately, and then escape at the next possible opportunity.

I'd like to conclude with some overall comments on where I think this paper is taking us and its implications for future work. In criticizing Sarna for emphasizing demographics and numbers, I've argued that the strength of Judaism is based on its ideas and not its numbers. In that respect, I think he emphasizes the forms of Jewish life rather than its content. Our real weakness is in the content. Jews have joined the corporate elite. It is not as if we lack influence in America. The question is, how Jewish are those Jews who have attained power? Larry Tisch, the president of CBS, has put this quite explicitly: "The big trick is how you keep the Jews Jewish once they get affluent." In other words, our problem in America is not that we have been denied access to power. The question for us in America is whether we can exercise our Jewishness once we get power. David Biale, in his recent book *Power and Powerlessness in Jewish History*, persuasively argues that Jews have never been as powerful as their enemies proclaim them to be, but also never as powerless as we have claimed ourselves to be. I think that's an accurate portrayal of the situation of American Jewry today and the way we look toward the future. A recent conference on "Jewish-Christian Relations in an Age of Modernity" co-sponsored by the Harvard Divinity School and the American Jewish Committee, assembled a fair number of influential theologians, philosophers, and historians in the chapel of Harvard's Divinity School. Despite the presence of all of their colleagues who were not of the Jewish faith, virtually every Jew in the audience felt no compulsion, no compunction, no guilt, no ambivalence, about criticizing either the Jewish faith and Jewish behavior or the Jewish encounter with modernity. That's a remarkable statement of the self-confidence of American Jewish intellectuals—of our willingness to engage in such dialogue, to be able to criticize ourselves openly, even in the citadels of power that were once closed to us. How Jewish we wish to be within those citadels of power—that's the question that we have to answer.

PART III
American Jews and Israel

Israel in the Jewish Identity of American Jews: A Study in Dualities and Contrasts

STEVEN M. COHEN

Any serious attempt to generalize accurately about the place of Israel in the Jewish identity of American Jews confronts a huge obstacle. Collectively and individually, American Jews' relationship with Israel is riddled with dualities and contrasts. Often, what is true for one group of American Jews is not true for another; moreover, many individuals hold images and emotions that are in tension with one another; and finally, American Jews' attitudes toward and conceptions of Israel-related matters often contrast sharply with those of Israelis, the very people many American Jews are deeply committed to supporting. Thus, when speaking about American Jews' beliefs about and feelings toward Israel, one is often compelled to use such phrases as "While most American Jews . . . still a good number . . . ," or "On the one hand . . . but on the other hand . . . ," or "In contrast with Israelis, American Jews. . . ."

Thus, two-sided generalizations about American Jews' relationship with Israel are unavoidable. Here are some of the more salient and significant:

1. While most American Jews may claim an extraordinarily deep and powerful commitment to Israel, the attachment of many is superficial and fragile.
2. While most American Jews are pro-Israel, very few are Zionists in the way contemporary Israelis use the term.
3. On the one hand, Israel dominates the public sphere of American Jewish identity; on the other, it is virtually absent from the private sphere. For American Jews, pro-Israelism is all political, it is neither cultural nor spiritual.
4. While Israelis experience and express a combination of aspiration and trepidation in thinking about their society and their future, American Jewish involvement with Israel is far more bound up with fear and danger than with hope and opportunity.
5. Most American Jews agree on the need to support Israel, but they divide on which Israeli policies they prefer.

6. One can make a convincing case that American Jewish attachment in the next five years will erode; alternatively, an equally convincing argument contends that it will hold steady.

In seeking to accurately and precisely portray the place of Israel in the Jewish identity of American Jews, much of this paper is organized around these six dualities and contrasts, all of which have important policy and research implications. (Note: Much of the material in the next three sections draws upon Liebman and Cohen [1990].)

American Jewish Support for Israel: Deep but Superficial, Powerful but Possibly Fragile

Ever since May 1967, when menacing Arab military forces appeared to threaten the very existence of Israel, commitment to Israel has functioned as a pillar of American Jewish identity. Community-wide philanthropic campaigns have made support for Israel the centerpiece of UJA-Federation fundraising. Jewish defense and community relations agencies have placed securing American political support for Israel and projecting a positive public image of Israel at the top of their organizational priorities. Jewish political groups in America—lobbyists, campaign contributors, and activists—decide which congressional and presidential candidates to assist and how much help they should offer primarily, and sometimes exclusively, on the basis of the candidates' attitudes toward Israel. News about Israel dominates almost every Anglo-Jewish newspaper and periodical, thereby reflecting and promoting the notion that Israel is probably the single most important item in the public consciousness of American Jews. No other American ethnic, racial, or religious group expresses as powerful an attachment to a foreign "homeland" as do American Jews to Israel. And none seem as completely absorbed by events thousands of miles away.

The surveys of American Jews that I have conducted for the American Jewish Committee almost annually since 1981 repeatedly document the breadth of concern for Israel in the Jewish public (Cohen 1983a and 1983b, 1984, 1987, 1989). Roughly two-thirds claim to care deeply about Israel, and the same number also regard it as a very important part of what being Jewish means to them. The concern for Israel has been so pervasive and passionate that it has led many to observe that Israel is the core component of the religion of American Jews.

But there may be good reasons to qualify this commonplace observation. The pro-Israeli sentiments of American Jews are limited in a number of ways that observers of American Jewish life often overlook. In quantitative terms, the commitment to Israel varies considerably. Not all American Jews are passionately concerned with Israel. On the basis of several surveys, I feel comfortable dividing American Jews into three broad categories covering a wide spectrum of caring, commitment, and involvement. It is fair to say that about one-third are relatively indifferent (and some even hostile) to Israel; another one-third (the middle group) are pro-Israel in a reflexive but not particularly thoughtful, committed, or active fashion; and the final third are passionately pro-Israel, occasionally or even frequently expressing their passion through visible, concrete behavior.

In the indifferent camp are those who, as their responses to the surveys suggest, do not claim to "often talk about Israel with friends and relatives." Neither does about a third of the Jewish population indicate any intentions of ever visiting Israel, or any interest in having their children do so. Approximately this number reject the view that "caring about Israel is a very important part of my being a Jew"; they see themselves as "not very close" to Israel; and they fail to agree with the statement "If Israel were destroyed, I would feel as if I had suffered one of the greatest tragedies in my life." It is true that about two-thirds of American Jews do answer such questions in a pro-Israel fashion. But one-third—the indifferent or even hostile respondents—do not. (Only about 5 percent of the Jewish population feel downright antagonistic, rather than simply indifferent, to Israel.)

Among the pro-Israel two-thirds, almost half (or one-third of the entire population) respond affirmatively to a set of more stringent questions. Roughly a quarter to a third have visited Israel, have family in Israel, have friends there, claim to have had personal contact with an Israeli during the previous twelve months, would want their children to spend a year in Israel, plan to visit Israel in the next three years, and call themselves Zionists. Just a fifth say they feel "very close" to Israel, and more than twice as many claim to feel "fairly close."

Taking these findings together, how does one characterize the central tendency of American Jewry with respect to Israel? Is this a portrait of generally "strong" or only "mixed" attachment to Israel? The answer, of course, depends upon one's definition of these terms, but any answer needs to build in a recognition of considerable heterogeneity in sentiment and behavior.

In short, while support for Israel dominates public life, is part and parcel of the American Jewish consensus of what it means to be a Jew, and is voiced by the vast majority of American Jews, no more than a third (perhaps less) express what could be called a very passionate involvement with Israel, and (as is detailed below) an even smaller minority (no more than a sixth) express what might be called a truly Zionist commitment, in the classical or contemporary Israeli sense of the term.

Thus, part of the argument that American Jewish attachment to Israel is not strong or as broad as it appears to some is based on a perspective which sees the pro-Israel glass as "only" half-full (or perhaps a third-full of even a sixth-full). But the other part of this argument is more qualitative than quantitative in nature. Even granting some ambiguity as to the size of the strongly pro-Israel fraction of the population, there is no such ambiguity about (1) the very limited impact that involvement with Israel exerts on the private, inner Judaic lives of the vast majority of American Jews; and (2) the ignorance of most American Jews concerning some very elementary aspects of Israeli society.

Far more pro–Israelism than (Classical) Zionism

To most American Jews, a Zionist is someone who "believes in the centrality of Israel to the Jewish People" (Cohen 1987). In contrast, to most Israelis, a Zionist is someone who "intends to live in Israel," or, by extension, someone deeply committed to the enterprise of encouraging Jews to settle there.

But classical/Israeli Zionism, in all its ramifications, extends beyond a commitment to aliyah. In the minds of the movement's thinkers and early activists, as well as most Israelis today, Zionism has something to say not only about the value of Jewish life in Israel, but also about the condition of Jewish life outside of Israel. And for the most part, its analysis of Diaspora Jewry and Judaism is not very flattering. Jewish life in the Diaspora (including the United States) is seen as unstable and tenuous, limited and distorted. In the long run, according to this view, the twin forces of anti-Semitism and assimilation threaten the very continuity of the Jewish community outside of Israel. Israelis' dismal characterization of Diaspora Jewry extends beyond the quality of Jewish life to embrace the individual Jew as well. In their minds, American and other Diaspora Jews are plagued by a "galut" (exilic) mentality that precludes them from freely expressing themselves as proud, self-confident, and self-respecting Jews.

Clearly, American Jews reject these aspects of Zionism. They certainly reject the allegation of cravenness, as well as the notion that American Jewish life is inherently limited. On the AJC surveys, hardly any agree with the idea that they could "live a fuller Jewish life in Israel than in the

United States." Even among the more passionately involved segment of the American Jewish population, only a fraction would qualify as Zionists by the typical Israeli's criterion, one which emphasizes commitment to aliyah. Only 15 percent of American Jews claim to have given some thought to settling in Israel, and an even smaller number (just 6 percent) say they would want their children to live in Israel.

While the claim that American Jews are overwhelmingly pro-Israel has some merit, only a very small number accept some of the very basic premises of classical or contemporary Israeli Zionism. This point may seem obvious to American readers, but it is frequently lost upon Israeli *shlichim*, diplomats, educators, and tour guides. All too often, the only language they have to "market" Israel is a modified Zionist language, and their conceptual foundation is a vulgarized form of classical Zionism. Needless to say, this language and conceptualization may not be the most effective way for Israelis to communicate with American Jews.

Israel Commitment: In the Public but not the Private Sphere

Notwithstanding the powerful commitment of a good fraction of American Jews to defending Israel's image and security, American Jewish involvement with Israel has relatively few consequences for the expression of Jewish identity in the private sphere. This statement presupposes a distinction between public and private Judaism, each with its own orientation. Private Judaism assumes a "cultural-religious-spiritual model which takes the individual as its starting point" and for whom "Judaism is a meaning system [providing] the adherent with an orientation to . . . questions of ultimate concern." Public Judaism assumes a "political-secular model [which] takes the Jewish people as its starting-point and concerns itself with its collective existence" (Liebman, 1981). Public Judaism is that which is conducted by communal organizations, primarily in the philanthropic or political spheres.

But the massive Israel-oriented philanthropic and political lobbying apparatus has had relatively little impact on the private lives of most American Jews. Israel (as a society, culture, state, language, or sacred concept) certainly has little meaning for American Jews at the times in their private lives when they feel most keenly Jewish: at life-cycle events (marriage, divorce, birth, mourning) and family celebrations (the Passover seder, Hanukah candle lighting, the High Holidays).

Paradoxically, the observation that contemporary Israel exerts little impact on American Jews' private Jewish identity remains true even though echoes of Israel, from the Jewish past and future, are incorporated into traditional Jewish ritual. Whatever anthropological explanations may be offered for the breaking of a glass by a Jewish groom under the wedding canopy, the Jewish tradition ascribes the custom to the need for one to remember the destruction of the Temple even on the most happy of occasions, a meaning that is probably lost on most members of the wedding party. Few worshipers pay serious attention to some very prominent passages in the liturgy that express the yearning of Jews for their physical ingathering in the Holy Land; and few Passover celebrants regard the concluding chant of the seder, "Next Year in Jerusalem," as a literal obligation.

In addition, few American Jews have any real familiarity with the currents of Israeli cultural and political life. Israeli culture, in other words, is not integrated into the cultural life of most American Jews, even in an English-language version. Very few American Jews have any fluency in Hebrew. Most American Jews are ignorant of even the most rudimentary features of Israeli life. For example, less than a third of the 1986 sample knew (or guessed) that former Prime Minister Menachem Begin (veteran leader of the right-wing Likud bloc) and then–Prime Minister Shimon Peres (head of the Labor Alignment) were members of different parties. Despite the publicity surrounding the "Who is a Jew" affair in 1988, just 38 percent of the 1989 sample could claim that they knew (or guessed) that non-Orthodox rabbis cannot legally marry couples in Israel. Despite the publicity surrounding the intifada, less than a quarter knew (or said they knew) that Israeli Arab and Israeli Jewish schoolchildren do not generally attend the same schools. Less than two-thirds of American Jews know the year of Israel's independence, and less than two-fifths know the year Israel took control of the West Bank. An informal scan of adult education programs sponsored by synagogues and Jewish community centers reveals few lectures and classes devoted to Israel, and most of these focus on the external threat rather than the internal features of Israeli society. At best, Israel—as a rallying point or as a locus for travel and study—serves as an instrument to further American-style Jewish identification. Yet little of the substance of Israeli life enters into the thinking and activities of most American Jews, even the one-third who have been to Israel.

Writing in the *Jerusalem Post*, a Conservative American Jewish educator, now living and working in Israel, observes:

> Today, while support for Israel is conceived of as an integral part of being Jewish, it stands somewhat apart from American Judaism. It is as if the

influences of American life have exorcised the spiritual meaning of Zion from the political reality of Jerusalem.

What remains is an urgent sense of obligation to support Israel, with only faint echoes from the tradition as to the reasons why. Israel in American Jewish education has become an entity to be learned about, to be supportive of and devoted to, and to identify with. But it is not a reality with implications for Jewish self-understanding. (Breakstone 1988, p. 11).

There is yet another way to view the limited extent to which Israel is integrated into conceptions of American Judaism. Social scientist Phillip E. Hammond advances the idea that personal identity, and more specifically religious identity, operates on two levels: one more intimate, essential, and constant; the other more peripheral, voluntary, and changeable. He writes:

We use the concept of identity in two quite different ways in the social sciences. The first way of looking at identity suggests the immutable, or at least the slowly changing core of personality that shows up in all of a person's encounters, irrespective of differing role-partners. The second way suggests the transient and changeable self as persons move from one social encounter to another, offering a somewhat different identity, as it were in each place. The first notion of identity suggests that it is involuntarily held; the second, that it can be put on and off. The first is nourished in primary groups, probably early in life; the second exists precisely because much of life is lived outside of primary groups. (1988, p. 2)

This division of identity into two spheres raises the question of whether American Jewish identification with Israel is in fact part of the core Jewish identity of most American Jews. Alternatively, it may be fair to say that pro-Israelism is primarily situational; it bubbles up or simmers down in connection with the rises or falls in perceived threats to Israel's security and in Jewish efforts to defend that security through philanthropy, political activity, and public relations work. Undoubtedly the extent to which Israel attachment occupies the core portion of Jewish identification varies for individuals and communities, and unfortunately we lack hard evidence on the matter. Nevertheless, it seems fair to say that, for the most part, identification with Israel remains located in the situational compartment of most Jews' identities. It emerges in times of conflict and crisis, such as in response to the Palestinian uprising or to Orthodox parties' attempt to change the legal definition of "Who is a Jew."

In fact, the contrasting Israeli and American Jewish reactions to the

"Who is a Jew" affair and to the Palestinian uprising serve to illustrate the extent to which Israel plays a powerful symbolic role and a very limited substantive role in the Jewish identity of American Jews.

The intifada, which began in December 1987, has been a momentous event in the lives of Israelis. It caused adherents of all political persuasions to reevaluate and sometimes to dramatically modify their previous positions; it disrupted the economy of the country, its military operations and deployment, Arab-Jewish relations, and the family lives of the thousands of reserve soldiers who serve for extended periods in the territories; and it has provoked passionate, often bitter debates about competing visions of the future of Israel, the meaning of Judaism and Jewish morality, and the wisdom of alternative political grand strategies. The impact of the intifada on Israeli society, politics, and economy has been profound, far-reaching, and massive. In contrast, the Israeli reaction to the arguments over "Who is a Jew" in the weeks following the November Knesset elections was far more limited and less consequential. Were it not for the intervention of American Jews, the "Who is a Jew" question would have been seen (no matter how it was resolved) as one more mildly disturbing skirmish between repeatedly conflicting religious and secular forces in Israeli society.

While American Jews certainly were moved by the intifada and Israeli responses to it, they were far more deeply and broadly affected by the fight over "Who is a Jew." True, between a third and a slim majority felt at least somewhat outraged, embarrassed, and critical of Israelis beating Palestinian protesters. But a much larger majority felt that the American press was treating Israel unfairly. The intifada occasioned no major immediate shift in the American Jewish public's thinking about Israel (they have remained, at least on paper, just as close to Israel as before) or about Israeli foreign policies, save for a slight shift in a dovish direction in a few areas. It may be fair to say that most American Jews were as or more concerned by how the intifada looked to the Gentiles than by what it meant to the Jews, Israeli or American.

In contrast, the "Who is a Jew" affair struck deeply and widely. On the 1989 survey, substantially more American Jews admitted to speaking critically or hearing criticism on the "Who is a Jew" matter than on the intifada. A near-consensus was critical of those Orthodox Israelis who pressed for changes in the definition of "Who is a Jew." In fact, roughly a third said that, had the law passed, they would have cut back on their contributions to Israel-related charities, their political support for Israel, and their readiness to travel there.

The reasons for their deeply felt anguish over the controversy are instructive, pointing to the critical symbolic role Israel plays in the lives of American Jews. Almost two-thirds said that the proposed legislative changes would have meant that Israel was declaring some of their family or friends non-Jewish, and that it would have meant that Israel was declaring Conservative and Reform Judaism illegitimate. These numbers demonstrate that in their eyes, official Israel has the potential symbolic authority to invalidate the Jewish authenticity of Jewish individuals or movements. An even larger majority (over three-quarters of the 1989 sample) were upset by the "Who is a Jew" affair because for them it meant that if the legislative changes passed, "Israel would be taking a big step toward becoming a country ruled by narrow-minded Orthodox rabbis." The implication is that Israel is seen by most as belonging to the entire Jewish people, that it affirms and validates the claim of all Jews (Orthodox or not, religious or secular) to Jewish authenticity. In the eyes of many non-Orthodox American Jews, the "Who is a Jew" affair represented an attempt by Orthodox parties to steal Israel away from them and to withdraw Israel's implied sanction of their legitimacy as Jews and of the legitimacy of the type of Judaism with which they choose to identify.

The contrast in leadership reactions to the "Who is a Jew" affair and the Palestinian uprising paralleled reactions in the public at large. For a variety of reasons, Jewish leaders have often expressed mixed, ambivalent, and muted opinions about the intifada. In contrast, the reactions in November and December 1988 to the "Who is a Jew" affair was loud, sustained, unified, and unmistakable. Leadership ambivalence on the intifada and strong consensus on "Who is a Jew?" both reflected and derived from similar reactions among the Jewish rank-and-file.

The "Who is a Jew" issue is a symbolic issue; how to respond to Palestinian nationalism is one of tremendous substantive import. That American Jews (both leaders and the public) reacted so strongly to the first (the symbolic issue) and in a more limited and ambivalent fashion to the second (the substantive crisis), while Israeli Jews reacted so much more strongly to the intifada, is surely understandable. But the contrast also points up Israel's potency as a symbol to American Jews, and its relative weakness as a substantive force exerting impact on the private Judaic sphere of the Jewish identity of most American Jews.

More Fear than Hope at the Root of American Jews' Passion for Israel

It may be significant that the Zionist anthem is entitled Hatikvah, "The Hope." The song speaks of the two-thousand-year-old hope "to be a free people in our land, the land of Zion, Jerusalem." Similarly, with the exception of a prayer for the Israel Defense Forces said in many Israeli congregations (and in few, if any, in the United States), the liturgy's references to Israel are all cast in terms of hope rather than fear. The hope for the restoration of the Temple (accompanied by the coming of the Messiah), the hope for return to Jerusalem, and the hope for the beginning of the "flowering of our redemption," symbolized by the State of Israel, all crop up at various points in the liturgy. Similarly, Zionist thought envisioned (and hoped for) a Jewish state that would serve as the center of the Jewish people and a model for the entire world. Indeed, it is fair to say that most Israelis still abide such hopes even though they differ sharply on how to create that society. While average Israelis are certainly concerned with threats from the Arabs and other sorts of dangers to the well-being of the Jewish state of Israel, it is also fair to say that they are far from overwhelmed by them. Rather, they abide and can articulate a wide variety of hopes and dreams for themselves, for their families, and for the state and society of Israel.

This point may be subtle (it is surely speculative), but it may also be significant. In contrast with the liturgy, Zionist thought, and the orientations of most Israelis, American Jewish feelings about Israel are dominated by fear far more than hope, by nightmares more than dreams. American Jews are more worried by the bad things that can happen to Israel than invested in the good things Israel can create or achieve. It is a truism to note that American Jewish interest in Israel centers around security concerns, by working to prevent the destruction of Israel.

The potency and centrality of fear and vulnerability in the attitudes of American Jews toward Israel emerge in other contexts as well. For example, attachment to Israel is correlated with perceptions of Arab hostility and with perceptions of American Gentile hostility (to Jews and to Israel). In other words, for American Jews, caring about Israel is tied to worrying about the "goyim." To make a modest abstraction from this finding, viewing the world as generally antagonistic to Jews and to Israel comports with a high level of caring about Israel. In contrast, Israelis' commitment to their country is unrelated to their assessment of its vulnerability or of international anti-Semitism; only when a relationship to Israel is built upon fear—as is the case for most American Jews—will Israel attachment be linked with perception of antagonism to Israel and other things Jewish.

Moreover, with the lone exception of fundamentalist Protestants, groups whom American Jews see as friendly or hostile to Jews are also seen, in roughly equal measure, to be friendly or hostile to Israel. Thus, almost half of all American Jews see blacks as both anti-Semitic and anti-Israel. They see political conservatives and Republicans as far less friendly to both American Jews and Israel than are liberals and Democrats. In short, American Jews identify anti-Zionism with anti-Semitism, and, correlatively, they presume that Gentile support for Israel is a sign of friendliness to Jews generally. The fact is that in the general population support for Israel and favorable images of American Jews are statistically unrelated. Anti-Semites tend not to translate their feelings about Jews to opposition to American government support for Israel, and many opponents of U.S. aid to Israel exhibit no overt signs of anti-Semitism. (Jesse Jackson and Daniel Patrick Moynihan, who are seen as consistent—where one is anti-Semitic and anti-Zionist, the other philo-Semitic and pro-Zionist—are not exceptions, but neither are they the rule.) Yet the centrality of fear and perception of vulnerability lead many American Jews to conflate anti-Zionism, anti-Israel positions, and anti-Semitism.

Now, there is nothing wrong with fear and danger playing a role, even an important role, in American Jews' orientation to Israel. But, upon some reflection, many Israelis, Jewish educators, and even some Jewish communal leaders would probably regret that fear virtually dominates American Jewish thinking about Israel. Few of Israel's most passionate enthusiasts in the United States have the fundamental tools to articulate one or another alternative vision of Israel's future. Few think of, let alone imagine, how Israeli society can positively influence the education, spiritual life, communities, and family lives of American Jews. Few know of, let alone utilize, the vast cultural resources found in contemporary Israeli fiction, drama, art, and music. The nearly prophetic visions of those who first sang Hatikvah, of a Jewish state central to the entire Jewish people, have been only partially realized. For most American Jews, even the most pro-Israel among them, Israel is linked more with feelings of fear and thoughts of danger than with sentiments of hope and dreams of opportunity. This is another limit on the quality and perhaps the stability of American Jewish attachment to Israel.

Agreement on Supporting Israel, But Division on Policies

While American Jews, or at least the majority that are pro-Israel among them, are united on the need to lend support to Israel's struggle for security, they are sharply divided on how to do so. The full story of American Jewish divisions over such matters as criticizing Israeli government policies and of American Jews' differing views on the wisdom of particular Israeli policies need not be reviewed here. Suffice it to say that

American Jews are more dovish than Israelis, though not as dovish as the typical highly educated, middle-aged Ashkenazi who, in these sociodemographic terms, is the counterpart of the typical American Jew. What is interesting, and of major policy relevance, is that the divisions over foreign policy do not simply divide the more pro-Israel American Jews from the less pro-Israel population segments. Rather, they occur within the ranks of those most attached to Israel.

It is true that hawkishness and Israel attachment are modestly correlated. Those who express greater concern for Israel, those who are more involved in Jewish organizational life, those who are more religiously observant, and those who find more of their close friends among other Jews are also more likely to oppose both talks with the PLO and offering the Arabs territorial compromise. Nevertheless, the correlation is modest and is even more modest when the Orthodox are removed from consideration. (The Orthodox are both extraordinarily involved with Israel—on several measures—and extraordinarily hawkish.) Among non-Orthodox Jews, the more pro-Israel individuals are only slightly more likely than the less pro-Israel individuals to hold hard-line views on foreign policy issues.

The presence of large numbers of passionately pro-Israel doves represents both a danger and an opportunity. The danger, of course, is that opposition to official Israel government policies will become a source of alienation from Israel or from conventional organized Jewry, which tends to support current Israeli policies. The opportunity lies in several functions pro-Israel doves perform for Jewish life. First, their identification as active pro-Israel Jews makes it more difficult for journalists and political leaders to misinterpret American Jewish discomfort with certain Israeli policies as a sign of weakening American Jewish support or concern for Israel. Second, their visibility lends moral credibility to American Jewish lobbying efforts on matters where there is indeed a consensus. When lobbyists can say, "Even Jewish doves believe . . . ," they can present American Jewry as a reflecting, morally motivated community rather than one given to knee-jerk support for every Israeli position, no matter how unwise. Third, their visibility also makes it possible to prevent the alienation of Jews who are critical of Israeli policies from the pro-Israel and organized Jewish community. It stands to reason that the appearance of a seemingly monolithic Jewry would be less attractive to young Jews who are dovishly inclined than one which appears to include and embrace all pro-Israel Jews, be they hawks, doves, or moderates.

Notwithstanding these functions, pro-Israel doves constitute a problem and a source of friction within organized Jewry. There is little agreement as to how doves should express their views, what they should say, and to whom. The norms of dissent and debate remain uncrystallized and are themselves subject to debate and controversy.

Are American Jews Drifting Away from Israel? Signs of Change in Both Directions

Several recent developments have caused many observers to anticipate declines in American Jewish support for Israel. The two most recent events that come to mind are, of course, the intifada and the "Who is a Jew" controversy. But other disturbing news stories in the last few years have also cast Israel in a poor light and provoked some signs of alienation among American Jews. These include (to mention only the most prominent) the Pollard affair, the violent clashes between religious and secular forces in Israel, the election to the Knesset in 1984 of Meir Kahane, a man perceived by Israelis and American Jews as a symbol of racist and anti-democratic tendencies in Israel, and the invasion of Lebanon, a war whose wisdom was severely questioned by Israelis and Americans alike.

Notwithstanding these potentially alienating events, the survey data collected almost every year since 1981 display surprising continuity and stability in pro-Israel sentiment among American Jews. Their views on Israeli foreign policies may have taken a somewhat dovish shift in 1988 and 1989, but their claims to caring for Israel and involvement in Israel-related activities remain as high (or as low) as ever. (The surveys document some slight decline between 1985 and 1986 in many pro-Israel measures, but this may be attributable to a coterminous change in sampling procedures more than to a real change in attitudes.) The data seem to indicate that attachment to Israel may well be the same as earlier in the decade, or it may have declined, but, if so, only slightly.

Despite the "good news" in the data, there is some reason to question its validity, and there is a large measure of "bad news" as well.

One reason to question the validity of the survey data is that respondents may be committed to reporting what researchers call "socially acceptable" answers so as to conceal some disquieting sentiments bubbling beneath the surface. Major pollsters report that their surveys uncover far more Americans who claim to be dieting and exercising than would seem to be the objective case. In like manner, in the 1986 AJC survey, as many as 89 percent of the respondents agreed with the statement, "I get just as upset by terrorist attacks upon non-Jews as I do when terrorists attack Jews." These responses can be taken only as testimony to the commitment to overt universalism on the part of American Jews rather than as a reflection of their true reactions to terrorist incidents. The more pained reaction to the murder of one Jew—Leon Klinghoffer—in the *Achille Lauro* hijacking, as compared with the murder of 246 U.S. marines by a car bomb in Beiruit, should be enough to convince anyone that the survey data cannot always be taken at face value.

Much of the anecdotal and impressionistic evidence seems to point to some decline in American Jewish support for Israel, even if the quantitative data fail to substantiate such a conclusion at this point. The UJA reported that 1988 collections fell beneath the levels of 1987. Officials interpreted the decline as a response to the change in tax laws, which may have accelerated 1987 donations and depressed those in 1988. This may be the full explanation, or it may be only part of it. In any event, adjusting for inflation, aggregate support for the federation campaigns (which are relevant here because they have been built around Israel) has declined fairly steadily since the mid-1970s.

Another disquieting sign is found in the declining share of federation funds allocated to overseas needs. Every year (or almost), a small committee of major donors in each of scores of communities decides how much of the federation dollar is to be kept in the local community and how much is to be sent overseas to the United Israel Appeal and other recipients. Although Israel receives only about half the overseas allocation, symbolically, it looms largest in the minds of the committee members deciding on how to divide the campaign funds. The aggregate effect of scores of individual decisions across the continent has been to effect a decline in the overseas proportion over the years. From 1976 to 1986, the proportion for overseas needs fell from 55 percent to 46 percent, amounting to a slide of almost 1 percent a year on average. Is a decline in Israel's popularity at work here? Would a more popular Israel have halted this slide? There is no way to answer this question. But these two trends may be significant: sluggishness in total campaign contributions, coupled with a decreasing share dedicated to Israel-related needs.

The "bad news" contained in the admittedly flawed survey data concerns the differences between older and younger Jews. Put simply, younger Jews are less pro-Israel than older Jews. There is no way around this conclusion. Every ten-years decline in age is associated with about a five-percentage-point decrease in pro-Israel answers to each of several questions, and this slide is greater for those who have never been to Israel. Moreover, where very strong support for Israel is the criterion, the age-related slide is even more severe. According to one comprehensive index of several survey questions, the fraction of those over sixty-five who very strongly support Israel is over twice that among those under thirty-five.

One reason for these differences is that younger people have had less of a chance to travel to Israel than their elders. Another is that younger people affiliate less frequently with Jewish institutions (parenthood seems to change that, though). However, even when travel and communal affiliation are factored out of the equation, most of the young-old differences in Israel attachment remain. In other words, were younger people to have traveled to Israel as much as their elders, and were they as involved in Jewish communal life as much as their elders, they still would report lower levels of concern for Israel.

Significantly, younger Jews differ little from their elders in many other measures of Jewish involvement. On the same surveys, controlling for parental status, younger Jews are about as likely as older Jews to report ritual observance, communal affiliation, and feelings of attachment to Jews and Judaism. The decline in Israel attachment is, therefore, not a function of any hypothetical decline in overall Jewish attachment.

The implication of these findings is that, barring unforeseen events or communal intervention, as Jews inevitably age (and die), today's less pro-Israel youngsters will take the place of the more pro-Israel elders, making for an overall decline in American Jews' attachment to Israel. Clearly such an eventuality ought to alarm any supporter of Israel who cares either for Israeli security or who believes that American Jewish involvement with Israel is important in and of itself as a constituent element in what it means to be a Jew.

Implications for Policy and Research

Underlying the foregoing discussion is an idealized model of the American Jewish relationship with Israel, one which needs to be made explicit at this point. The model calls for more substantive involvement of American Jews with Israel. It places a value upon more and broader knowledge of Israeli society, current affairs, political culture, religious trends, and Hebrew language. It also values American Jewish involvement in all these areas. This model (i.e., my model) of the "good Jew" or "good Zionist" also incorporates a basic uneasiness with the quality of Jewish life in the United States (or Israel, for that matter).

The analysis clearly finds American Jewry wanting in these respects. It even raises the possibility that American Jews are growing more remote from Israel, possibly threatening their historic commitment to political and philanthropic support for Israel.

The policy implications here are numerous. To detail them would lie beyond the scope of this paper. Nevertheless, a bare outline of some of the more striking policy consequences might prove useful.

1. Jewish and Zionist educators need to present the ways in which Israel and Israeli Judaism differ from American Jews and American Judaism. Any sophisticated appreciation of Israel starts with the assumption that Israeli Jewish life is fundamentally different from Jewish life anywhere else.
2. The community needs to develop norms of dissent so as to make the best use of pro-Israel doves for the purposes of lobbying and public Jewish education.
3. For the most part, Israel has been marketed to American Jews as a homogeneous whole; in so doing, we have perpetuated the symbolic rather than the substantive side of involvement with Israel. Instead, we need to promote the identification of American Jews with the cultural, religious, or political aspects of Israel that they find most attractive. A sign of success of this strategy would be found in the emergence or expansion of Reform missions to Israel or Friends of Gush Emunim (or Peace Now, or Labor, or Likud).
4. Fundamental to all these efforts is increased travel to Israel. Numerous communal decisions affect the support for and marketing of Israel travel.

A research agenda in this area would investigate the veracity of some of the more controversial points in the analysis, and focus on the practical steps needed to achieve the policy goals mentioned above as well as others that would flow from the analysis.

References

Breakstone, David. 1988. "Woeful Neglect of the Vital Centre." *Jerusalem Post*, July 29.

Cohen, Steven M. 1983a. "The 1981–2 National Survey of American Jews." *American Jewish Year Book*, 89–110.

———. 1983b. *Attitudes of American Jews Toward Israel & Israelis*. New York: American Jewish Committee. Offset, 36 pp.

———. 1984. *The Political Attitudes of American Jews*. New York: American Jewish Committee. Offset.

———. 1987. *Ties and Tensions: The 1986 Survey of American Jewish Attitudes*

Toward Israel and Israelis. 118 pp. New York: American Jewish Committee. Offset.

———. 1989. *Ties and Tensions: An Update.* New York: American Jewish Committee.

Liebman, Charles S. 1981. "American Jews and the 'Modern Mind'." *Midstream* 27: 8–12.

——— and Cohen, Steven M. 1990. *Two Worlds of Judaism: The Israeli and American Experiences.* New Haven: Yale University Press.

Response to Steven M. Cohen

HOWARD MILLER

After discussing this subject almost to the point of stupefaction, I have come to the following twofold conclusion: with the exception of the Orthodox, an extraordinary number of Jewish Americans define their self-image, at any given moment, to a significant extent by the way Israel is behaving; and the advice individual American Jews give Israel and the attitudes they adopt toward Israeli policy reflect how they would like to be seen as individuals.

This is most clearly evident not just in the "Who is a Jew" issue, which, of course, struck to the core of a great many people's sense of identity and power, but also in the reaction to the intifada. I could observe it in discussions with endless numbers of people. When Israel was acting with what individuals considered to be brutality, Rabin's "force, might and beatings" pronouncement, the people that I spoke to, I sensed, felt diminished if they didn't agree with that policy. They saw themselves as brutal because they personally, as individuals, identified with whatever Israel was doing at the moment. Therefore, the advice that is given to visiting Israelis is advice that is less political and military and statecraft-oriented than reflective of something like the following thought: "You ought to behave in this way because if you do, I will feel better about myself. And, therefore, I want Israel to take positions that will permit me to feel good when I look in the mirror, permit me to feel good when I talk to my children, and permit me not to feel embarrassed when I talk to my non-Jewish fellow Americans."

I regard this identification among American Jews of personal self-image with Israeli statecraft and policy as one of some significant danger. I'm not a psychologist, so I don't want to comment on the issues of individuals who invest so much of their identity in others over whom they have no control. But I do think it's something we need to be aware of, because individual morality and the requirements of statecraft are often different. Any nation that attempts to act on the basis of notions of individual morality alone is not long for this world.

We ourselves know that from what we know in our bones about American history and whom we revere. Few leaders have been more ruthless in the use of military force than Abraham Lincoln. And yet we revere him not only because he won, but because we understand that the values he was supporting justified the ruthlessness he employed. Lincoln was simply carrying out ideals also personified by Jefferson, who when he was criticized for violating the law after buying Louisiana, said that it was the duty of the chief magistrate to obey the law, no doubt, but not his highest duty. The highest duty of the chief magistrate, he said, is to defend his people, and if that comes in conflict with any particular law, he must choose the highest duty and then "throw himself upon the judgment of history."

But in relating to the intifada and Israeli policy, we as individual Jews generally do not give advice based on statecraft but rather advice based on the kind of people we want ourselves to be. And that, I think, is a confusion that raises enormously important issues. We know that politics often is a reflection of personality, and nowhere is the extent to which the individual views of people are reflections of their personalities and the world in which they live more clear than in this case. Most of us who live in this well-protected, genteel West Los Angeles world find it difficult to admit what goes on 10 miles away at 3:00 a.m., let alone the reality that exists in other parts of the world. I think it is extremely important, regardless of one's views on what Israeli policy ought to be, for us to come to grips with and understand this extraordinary sense of personal identification.

American Jews and Israel in the Bush Era

STUART E. EIZENSTAT

Jewish identity in the United States is played out in a major way in the American political arena around issues involving the State of Israel (and to a lesser but important exent, Soviet Jewry). But our relationship with Israel is so vicarious and one-dimensional that we may become too easily disenchanted with the difficult political situation in which Israel finds itself. The next several years will be particularly challenging and difficult for American Jews because at one and the same time we must reinvigorate our stagnant relations with Israel, while we help assure that during a turbulent period of change relations between the United States and Israel remain on a firm footing. Just as the Bush administration is seeking to define a new relationship with the State of Israel in light of the intifada, so too the American Jewish community must define a more satisfying, deeper relationship with Israel.

But, in the end, Israel cannot be expected to bear the full burden of Jewish identity in America. We must add our own religious observances if we are to sustain Jewish identification against the chill winds of assimilation.

We live, in the words of the Chinese proverb, in interesting times. Never in recent history has there been such tremendous change occurring so rapidly—most of it positive. The post–World War II world of two superpowers facing each other with their subservient allies through the barrel of a gun is fast disappearing. In its place is arising a multipolar world of many power centers based significantly on economic power. Measured in these terms, the Soviet Union is not a first-rate power at all and the United States is like a runner having difficulty finishing the mile run in first place, looking over its shoulder as faster runners threaten to overtake its lead. From Latin America to the Pacific Rim to Europe, countries are emerging seeking their own place in the sun.

In western Europe we see a growing assertiveness on the part of our allies, particularly West Germany, seeking to put the Holocaust behind it and to assert its own national interests. In 1992, the European community of Western Europen nations will form the greatest single barrier-free trade area in the world. The changes in Eastern Europe are even more profound. Hungary is moving toward a multiparty political system; Poland has recognized Solidarity, which only a few years ago it deemed a threat to its very security, and held elections where contests were permitted and in which Solidarity smashed the Polish Communist party; free-market experiments are emerging throughout the Communist world; pressures for greater independence by Estonia and Latvia, forcibly integrated into the Soviet Union at the beginning of World War II, are a reflection of the increasing yearning of peoples throughout the world for greater freedom and independence.

There is a dramatic march toward democracy as half a dozen dictatorships in Latin America have become democracies over the last decade. China and the Soviet Union have found themselves facing a demand for more self-expression and individual freedom. Gorbachev has recognized this and has tried to steer it in a positive direction. China's leaders have discredited themselves by brutally trying to stem the tide. With more accurate news reporting, the election of a more representative legislature, with calls by the KGB itself for greater legislative oversight, Perestroika is real.

The fundamental changes occurring in the Soviet Union are in significant part due to the collapse of its Marxist economy. Its inability to satisfy the most basic human needs of its people has led the Soviet Union to the most significant retrenchment of Soviet power throughout the world since the Russian Revolution. Mikhail Gorbachev has made a decision of historic proportions that the Soviet Union will play a cooperative role in resolving regional disputes, which have acted as a drain on the weak Soviet economy, so that he can shift greater resources into consumer-oriented industries and agriculture. One regional dispute after another has been the beneficiary. Whether it is Afghanistan, Namibia, Cambodia, or Nicaragua, Gorbachev has rejected the old Brezhnev Doctrine of supporting national liberation movements in order to project Soviet influence throughout the world.

The Bush administration is groping for a way of dealing with these changes, and it appears that at the recently concluded NATO summit the President has begun to find his sea legs and to chart a course which he describes as "Beyond Containment," designed to integrate the Soviet Union into the community of nations.

If current trends continue, it seems clear there will be a major treaty between the United States and the Soviet Union on strategic nuclear arms, reducing the strategic nuclear forces of both countries by up to 50 percent, and the first major conventional arms treaty between the two countries in post–World War II history. If the Soviet Union, as it has promised, passes a new law this year on immigration which institutionalizes the right of Soviet Jews to emigrate, and if this is implemented by continued high levels of Jewish emigration, the way will be paved for a presidential waiver of the Jackson-Vanik amendment, most favored nation treatment for the Soviet Union, and increased trade. Already, President Bush has lifted the blanket prohibition, which our administration instituted in 1979 after the invasion of Afghanistan, on the export of high-technology products from the United States to the Soviet Union.

As one regional dispute after another is resolved, the Middle East stands out in sharp relief as the major trouble spot in the world. Here, too, Gorbachev has recognized that change must be the order of the day. He seems to have come to fundamental conclusions here. First, like other regional disputes, this one also must be eliminated as a source of pressure on Soviet resources; and second, that in order for the Soviet Union to have a greater role in Middle East policy, the road lies through Jerusalem and not simply through Washington. He is clearly moving step-by-step toward a restoration of diplomatic relations with Israel, severed after the Six-Day War in 1967.

A Soviet consular mission has gone to Israel and an Israeli delegation has worked in Moscow since July of 1988. Soviet Jewish immigration levels may soon approach the record high of 50,000 in 1979. An Israeli basketball team was allowed to play the Soviet Union's team in Moscow. Positive statements were made by top Soviet leaders following Israel's role in returning the hijackers of a Soviet plane to Soviet authorities; an Israeli delegation was permitted into the Soviet Union to assist with the Armenian earthquake relief effort.

Even more dramatic, Gorbachev has publicly stated to President Assad of Syria that it is "abnormal" for the Soviet Union not to have diplomatic relations with Israel. More recently, he told Yasser Arafat of the PLO that Israel's security must be considered as an important factor in any Middle East settlement. The Soviet Union did not extend full diplomatic relations to the PLO when it declared Palestine an independent state, has pressured the PLO to accept the Reagan administration's conditions for the opening of a dialogue, and, just within the past few days, has opposed the PLO's bid to enter the World Health Organization. During the recent Baker visit to Moscow, the Soviets publicly had positive words for Prime Minister Shamir's election proposal.

There are other positive signs of change in the Middle East as well.

Iran and its brand of militant Muslim fundamentalism has been in retreat as a result of its loss to Iraq in its eight-year war. Iraq, in turn, rather than rejoin the rejectionist camp with Syria and Libya, is throwing in its cards with a pro-Western group of Arab nations—Jordan, Egypt, and Saudi Arabia.

Egypt's reentry into the Arab League is another positive sign. While Egypt's peace with Israel is not nearly what we had hoped it might be at the time of Camp David, it has nevertheless withstood the pressures of Israel's bombing of the Iraqi nuclear plant, the invasion of Lebanon, the intifada, and Arab pressures on Egypt to reject and renege on the peace treaty. Egypt persevered. Its leadership position at the recently concluded Arab summit in Morocco isolated Syria and Libya and led to a general endorsement of a peace initiative toward Israel.

I am extremely cautious about the PLO and its true motives, in light of its history, the continued conflicting statements of its leaders, and the uncertainty as to whether its peace initiatives are simply a tactical device to destroy Israel by other means. It nevertheless is incorrect to believe that there has been no change. Arafat's statements subject him to physical danger from more radical Palestinians and over time create a dynamic toward negotiation and acceptance of Israel. Indeed, it is the great sacrifices Israel has made and the valor it has shown which have led the Palestinians to realize there can be no military victory and that they will have to accept much less than they want.

Ironically, relations between the Jewish community and Israel have not kept pace with the positive change in relationships between the United States and Israel. Over the past four decades, the two governments have moved from an arm's-length relationship to the warm embrace of two allies.

In 1948, President Truman recognized Israel but imposed an arms embargo at the time of Israel's maximum peril during the War of Independence. A generally hostile Eisenhower administration denied a request for a modest loan in 1953 and forced a unilateral Israeli withdrawal from Suez in 1956 without equivalent Egyptian peace concessions. From 1948 through 1971, total U.S. aid to Israel averaged only about $60 million per year. There was no official state visit to the United States by an Israeli Prime Minister until the mid-1960s.

But the change in the relationship has been truly remarkable over the last twenty years. Israel has become one of America's closest allies. Israel receives $3 billion annually in economic and military assistance, one out of five American foreign aid dollars, and on terms far more favorable than any other country in the world.

During the Reagan era, particularly after the Lebanese fiasco in 1983 convinced Secretary of State Shultz of the unreliability of the Arab world, the relationship became even more intimate, blossoming into a strategic alliance. Today there are permanently established working groups under a 1988 Memorandum of Agreement on foreign aid levels, the Israeli economy, and a third on military and intelligence cooperation. There are joint military exercises, and American ships regularly dock in Haifa. The moral and ethical ties between the two countries remain strong. Israel is appreciated as a stable democracy in a sea of dictatorships, a predictable friend, a country which shares a Judeo-Christian legacy.

There is change. The opening of a dialogue with the PLO is a marked departure of U.S. policy and is leading America to become a broker for peace, as it was in the 1970s.

The unusual warmth and sensitivity of President Reagan and Secretary of State Shultz blinded us to the more basic reality which is now asserting itself in the Bush administration—namely, that it has been and will remain American policy to have close relations with both Israel and Israel's Arab enemies. This is the role of a superpower. The American Jewish community has long argued against an "even-handed" American foreign policy in the Middle East. But, we are returning to just that policy in the Bush administration. That is the deeper meaning of the Baker speech, which in the words of *New York Times* correspondent Tom Friedman was "clinically even-handed." But the relationship is so firmly grounded that it will never revert to the distant one of Israel's first two decades.

There are enormously contradictory trends in Jewish identity in the United States as we are poised to enter the last decade of the twentieth century. The Jewish community is like a corporation, with one healthy core division which is vibrant, healthy, and exciting, while another division is weak, sick, and threatening to imperil the entire enterprise. On the one hand, the pressures of assimilation are enormous and are having corrosive effects on Jewish identity for a substantial percentage of American Jews, while at one and the same time, another group of American Jews, in reaction to the forces of assimilation, has been more authentically Jewish, across denominational lines, than the preceding generation.

Steve Cohen has conducted a recent poll which I find sobering. It shows that one-third of American Jews are relatively indifferent to Israel, another third claim a strong attachment but show no signs of active involvement, and only the last third is both passionately attached to and actively involved with Israel.

Despite the existence of the first Jewish state in two millennia, Jewish identification for a substantial number of American Jews actually dropped.

- Jewish birthrates in America are among the lowest for any segment of American society. Where we were 3.7 percent of the population in 1960, today we are only 2.7 percent. Jewish birthrates are now well below the average of 2.1 births per mother necessary to simply maintain population stability. We are at zero or negative population growth. If current trends continue, there could be fewer than three million Jews by the time our nation celebrates its third centennial in 2076, a tiny percentage of the total American population.
- As we have made it in America, as we have moved out of our ghettos and into mixed neighborhoods, open schools, and accepting institutions, intermarriage has become more acceptable. Interaction with non-Jews has produced a dramatic rise in mixed marriages. Between 1900 and 1920, only 2 percent of marriages involving Jewish were outside the faith; between 1940 and 1960 it was 6 percent. But between 1960 and 1965, it rose to 17 percent, and between 1968 and 1973 to 32 percent. The latest figures in the 1980s show intermarriage rates at 40 percent in San Francisco, 36 percent in Denver, 34 percent in Phoenix, and 33 percent in Dallas. The rallying point of Israel has not stemmed the tide nor offset the pull toward intermarriage. As Rabbi Arthur Hertzberg put it, "the rate of intermarriage in American Jewry in the year 1948, when the State of Israel was proclaimed, was one in twenty; it is today, at the very least, three out of ten."

In only about 25 percent of the cases does the non-Jewish spouse of a mixed marriage convert. Children of mixed marriages without conversion generally have little Jewish identification and are often lost to the religion. Less than one-third of mixed couples report that their children have had or will have a bar or bat mitzvah, and 75 to 80 percent of the children of mixed marriages receive no formal Jewish education.

Jewish divorce rates are also up dramatically over the course of the last four decades, now rapidly closing the gap with the divorce rates in the general population. Studies have shown that households of singles, childless couples, or divorcees show dramatic drops in Jewish identification compared to intact conventional Jewish families. Moreover, the

Cohen Center for Modern Jewish Studies at Brandeis has found that second marriages are twice as likely to be intermarriages as first marriages.

- The total number of Jewish youngsters receiving any form of education has dropped dramatically from 600,000 in 1962 to only 350,000 today. Between 1961 and 1978 there was a 36 percent decline in enrollment in all Jewish schools. Put another way, today only one-third of the approximate 1 million Jewish children between the ages of seven and seventeen in this country are engaged in any form of Jewish schooling compared to two-thirds twenty years ago. And only about 14 percent of Jewish children continue their Jewish schooling into their high school years.
- Only about 75,000 American Jews have made aliyah to Israel and stayed permanently since 1948.
- In inflation-adjusted terms, American Jewish donations to the United Jewish Appeal Federation, the premier institution in the American Jewish community with the closest identification to Israel, have not increased at all since 1974.
- Only about one-half of American Jews are affiliated with a synagogue or temple or give anything to UJA, and less than 40 percent practice any consistent pattern of Jewish ritual observance. American Jews are much less likely than non-Jews to belong to a house of worship.
And yet, remarkably, another segment of American Jewry, I believe smaller than the first, has begun to build a true Jewish culture in the United States. It is not coincidental that this group is also the most closely identified with Israel and Israeli causes, has been inspired by the accomplishments of the Jewish state, and has been invigorated by Israel's existence to live more authentically Jewish lives.
- A higher percentage of Jewish youngsters receiving any form of Jewish education are getting more intensive in-depth Jewish education than was the case a generation before. There are now over five hundred day schools with over 100,000 Jewish students, while less than eighty existed shortly after World War II, almost all Orthodox.
- A rising number of American Jewish families keep kosher at home.
- As recently as 1950 there were only two full-time chairs held by Jewish scholars in American universities whose field of instruction was exclusively in Judaica. Today, Judaic studies are offered at more than 250 American universities.
- For the first time in our nation's history, a Jewish chapel was constructed at the United States Military Academy at West Point.

- Go to any major college campus, such as Harvard, and you will see an incredible number of students wearing kipot, a conscious, visible demonstration of Jewish identity.

Politically, American Jews have come into their own and out of the closet. While already in the early past of the twentieth century Jews were involved in political activities, including pioneers like Louis Brandeis, organized Jewish political activity for specific Jewish causes is a very recent phenomenon.

The American Israel Public Affairs Committee, the registered pro-Israeli lobby in the United States, was organized by Sy Kenen in 1957, but came into its own only after the 1973 Yom Kippur War, when large amounts of U.S. foreign aid started flowing. It is a vocal and remarkably effective public advocate for Israel's interests.

Twenty-five years ago there were virtually no Jewish political action committees. Today, there are seventy pro-Israel political action committees, which in the last election cycle, 1987–1988, raised $4.5 million of the $150 million raised by all political action committees.

The intense Jewish involvement in politics is demonstrated by the increasing number of Jews offering themselves for public office, with all the risk that public exposure entails. The trend is dramatic and healthy and can only occur in an atmosphere in which Jews feel secure. In the 92nd Congress a decade and a half ago, there were only two Jewish senators and twelve Jewish House members. Today, in the 101st Congress, there are eight Jewish senators and thirty-one Jewish members of the House, many from states and districts with small Jewish populations.

In the House of Representatives, many of the Jewish members of Congress, such as Mel Levine and Howard Berman from the state of California, have taken prominent positions on the House Foreign Affairs Committee and have become active champions of Israel's causes.

In addition, there are now some 250 Jewish state legislators across the country with their own national Jewish organization, the National Association of Jewish State Legislators.

This extraordinary explosion in Jewish political activity has occurred for a combination of three reasons.

First, it is a form of repentance for the Holocaust. A recognition first pierced the consciousness of the American Jewish community at large in the mid- to late 1960s of the complicity of the Roosevelt administration and the failure of the American Jewish community to more actively press it to intervene to stop the atrocities against Jews of which that administration was aware. Bayard Rustin had threatened to take to the streets if

President Roosevelt did not provide greater civil rights protection to blacks during World War II. The American Jewish community simply did not feel secure enough to openly challenge and threaten the White House over the plight of European Jewry. Today, American Jews are driven by a determination not to let Jews threatened anywhere be forgotten—Israel, Ethiopia, Iran, or the Soviet Union.

The second factor in the remarkable political involvement of American Jews is the reduction in barriers to all minority groups as a result of the civil rights movement for blacks in the 1960s. American Jews, much more than they realize, were major beneficiaries of the civil rights movement. Institutions once closed were opened. Jews felt more comfortable and secure—a necessary ingredient for a minority's active and open participation in the political process.

The American Jewish community has been willing to take on the President of the United States on issues like the Arab boycott (which was negotiated at the White House between American Jewish organizations and the American business community), the sale of fighter planes to Saudi Arabia during the Carter administration, or AWACs planes to the Saudis during the Reagan administration. This is healthy and has helped sensitize the American political system to issues important to Jews.

The third factor was the dramatic impact of the 1967 war. This galvanized American Jewish opinion and created an identification point with Israel beyond anything that has happened before or since with the exception of the creation of the state itself. It dramatized the new post-Holocaust image of the Jew—assertive, proud, and tough, no longer dependent on the whim and caprice of history's tyrants.

Another important but less well understood political event occurred in the aftermath of the Six-Day War. A generation of young Jewish scholars in Middle Eastern affairs came to the fore. No longer was Middle East policy the sole province of largely Arabist scholars. Serious thinkers like Martin Indyk of the Washington Institute for Near East Policy and Steven Spiegel of UCLA gained prominence. Publications like *Orbis* and *Commentary* provided an avenue for scholars with a more pro-Israel orientation.

In the Bush administration, we are seeing the flowering of Jewish scholars entering positions of influence in the State Department and National Security Council involving Middle East policy. They feel no conflict between their Jewish identification and their sympathetic attitude toward Israel, on the one hand, and on the other their ability to fully serve the interest of the United States, nor should they. Key State Department policymakers such as Dan Kurtzer, Aaron David Miller, and

Dennis Ross, one of Secretary of State Baker's closest advisors, and Richard Haass, the Middle East specialist for the National Security Council, form the core of the Bush administration's Middle East team. When they meet with their Israeli counterparts, there is almost enough for a minyan!

So, too, at senior positions in the White House, from Mike Feldman in the Kennedy White House to Len Garment in the Nixon White House to my own position in the Carter White House, American Jews have been offered the opportunity of serving their country at the highest levels.

We have not entered public life as Jewish advocates. Indeed, Jewish advocates—or advocates for any particular interest for that matter—have far less influence in the American political system than those whose views are more balanced and objective. But these people all brought Jewish values and a sense of Jewish identity and history to their positions. In my work on the Arab boycott legislation, reinterprting U.S. visa requirements to permit tens of thousands of Iranian Jews to enter the United States as they fled the Khomeini revolution, helping convince President Carter to create a Holocaust Memorial Commission, developing a matching-grant program for Soviet Jewish immigrants, or pushing for more aid to Israel, I did what I believed was best for the United States, but from a strong Jewish identity.

There are some downsides to the heavy degree to which American Jewish identification is wrapped up in our organized involvement in the American political arena. One is that as a community we have exaggerated our influence. We have mistaken the political influence we have obtained through hard work, good organization, and playing by the rules of the American political system for political power. There is a very real difference. The only Jews in the world with political power are those in Israel. Only they have the capacity, within limits, to control their own destiny.

American Jews have influence disproportionate to their size on issues seen by the American political system as affecting their special concerns—issues like Israel and Soviet Jewry. In much the same way, blacks have a disproportionate influence on civil rights legislation because it is perceived as affecting them in a particular way. This is the essence of a pluralistic and tolerant democracy. But influence is not pure power, and we sometimes confuse the two.

On any issue of importance to our community we are constantly vying for influence with other groups and interests. Thus, for example, on the anti-boycott legislation, Jewish groups were balanced, on one side, with business interests, on the other, concerned that the legislation would restrict their access to Arab markets. On issues involving Israel and the Middle East there is an increasingly organized Arab-American community, certain elements of the press, and parts of the bureaucracies of the Pentagon and the Near East Bureau of the State Department taking positions contrary to those of the American Jewish community on behalf of Israel.

This brings me to a second concern. Because we feel—correctly—so passionate an attachment to Israel and so determined a belief that the flowering of the first Jewish state in two thousand years will not be crushed, we tend to see things politically in terms which are far too black and white. We are too eager to label people as anti-Israel simply because they may take positions at a given moment contrary to those we believe in Israel's interest without looking at the totality of their views. Thus, for example, the attacks from certain elements in the Jewish community against Senator Charles Percy, former Republican senator from Illinois and chairman of the Senate Foreign Relations Committee, are our case in point. I am a strongly partisan Democrat. I supported, and proudly so, Paul Simon against Senator Percy. But the vicious nature of the attacks by some members of the Jewish community against Senator Percy made it appear that he was Israel's archenemy. I was certainly concerned about his attitudes toward the Palestinians. But Senator Percy was not anti-Israel. So, too, I still see today negative comments in the organized Jewish community toward President Carter as if he were anti-Israel, if not anti-Semitic. This about the first President to bring peace between Israel and an Arab neighbor. For sure, President Carter had many disagreements with Prime Minister Begin over issues like the settlement policy in the West Bank. For sure he had to lean on Israel, just as he did on Egypt, to produce an historic agreement. But this in no way justifies the vilification that he has received.

The American political system is rarely made up of blacks and whites. It operates in shades of gray. Compromise is in the nature of our democratic system. We have a right to be advocates for our position but we must expect politicians to seek compromise. A senator or congressman who votes against our position on a sale of aircraft to an Arab nation should not be branded per se as anti-Israel.

In the Congress there are constantly shifting alliances and coalitions. There should be no permanent enemies. A person branded as an enemy may be needed as an ally on another critical issue.

A closely related but separate problem is the need for greater political judgment and discernment. We tend to speak at the same decibel level on minor issues affecting Israel as well as on major issues, which over time will make our community less effective on the really big decisions. We tend to expend as much energy on opposing arms sales to Kuwait as we do on more threatening sales to more hostile countries. If we go to the well too often there will be no water to drink when we really need it.

A good case in point is the speech by Secretary of State James A. Baker III to the American Israel Public Affairs Committee on May 22, 1989. This speech enunciated the Bush administration's policy toward Israel with greater detail and clarity than any other statement to date. It had many positive elements, the most important of which was its endorsement of Prime Minister Shamir's election plan as the key vehicle to commence the Middle East peace process. It called upon the Palestinians to end their dream of taking over all of Palestine and called for an end to terrorism and disturbances. He called on the PLO to abolish its charter calling for Israel's destruction. He asked the Arab nations to end their economic boycott of Israel, to "stop the challenges to Israel's standing in international organizations," to "repudiate the odious line that equates Zionism to racism," and to take concrete steps toward accommodation with Israel. Importantly, he called on the Russians to demonstrate by deed as well as word that they were ready to play a constructive role in the Middle East, by restoring "diplomatic ties with Israel," by behaving responsibly when it comes to arms sales, and by stopping the supply of sophisticated weapons to countries like Libya.

And, yet, many Jewish leaders overreacted to the speech because it likewise called on Israel to make concessions.

One paragraph in the speech seems to have set off the reaction:

> For Israel, now is the time to lay aside, once and for all, the unrealistic vision of a greater Israel. Israeli interests in the West Bank and Gaza—security and otherwise—can be accommodated in a settlement based on Resolution 242. Foreswear annexation. Stop settlement activity. Allow schools to reopen. Reach out to the Palestinians as neighbors who deserve political rights.

If I had been asked for advice on the speech, I would have written it somewhat differently and would have placed more emphasis on the terribly difficult decisions Israel will be called upon to make, given its security concerns. While Baker's speech was a message delivered bluntly, it is a restatement of U.S. policy since 1967, namely, that the United States supports the concept of trading land for peace in all areas occupied by Israel after the 1967 war, including the West Bank and Gaza.

The last concern with our political involvement is that we have too often premised our Jewish identity on an overly idealized and romanticized one-dimensional view of Israel. Our identification with Israel has been vicarious and arm's-length. We have set up an ideal in which Israelis are superhuman and their leaders always just and wise. In the process, we have set ourselves up for disillusionment. No country which exercises power in the real world, particularly a country like Israel, which must operate in the most vicious region of the world, can consistently take actions which comport with this idealized image. Israel is a nation state, and states must take actions which are oftentimes odious and uncomfortable.

Because our identification with Israel has been so limited and one-dimensional, focused on Israel in the political arena, there is the danger that when we disagree with the decisions of a given Israeli government, it can lead to disillusionment with Israel itself. It would be as if our identification with the United States were based on our agreement with a particular President or political party.

Permit me to conclude with the following thoughts.

First, we should continue our political activism on behalf of Israel and Jewish causes, tempered by a more realistic recognition of the operation of our political system. In dealing with the Bush administration, we should sensitize the administration to the difficulties Israel faces. We must make it clear that the intifada is not the Middle East equivalent of our 1960s civil rights movement. This is not an attempt by the citizens of a state to obtain their full legal rights. Rather it is a civil war of two competing national claims to the same territory. Just as Abraham Lincoln suspended that most basic of democratic rights, the writ of habeas corpus, during the American Civil War, so, too, many of the actions that Israel is forced to take to put down the intifada do not reflect a democratic ideal. This is all the more reason to seek a political solution. But Israeli conduct must be put into that context.

We must also continue to lobby the Congress and the administration for the security assistance and economic aid Israel needs. We must defend Israel when she is unfairly criticized or unfairly attacked.

But we need more discernment in knowing the decibel levels to use. We should not reflexively oppose every arms sale to every Arab nation. To the extent that the United States has more intimate ties with Arab countries, it is not necessarily at Israel's expense but indeed may be to her benefit if the United States can play a moderating role. We must know when to go to the mat and not be afraid to do so when the times require. But we must make sure we do not wear out our welcome.

Second, in dealing with the Israeli government we should sensitize Israel to the realities of American politics and to the limits of American tolerance. We do not serve Israel well if we give Israel a false assessment of what we can do to change the basic thrust of U.S. Middle East policy.

On those issues where we disagree with an Israeli government, such as the Lebanese invasion, very difficult choices are posed. For sure, speaking out publicly in the United States will be used by Israel's enemies against her. A divided American Jewish community is a weakened American Jewish community. But we can hardly expect a unified American Jewish community when Israel is itself divided about many of its recent decisions.

Israel in her fifth decade is strong enough to hear our unvarnished views. We should speak out when we disagree with Israeli policy, but we should do so in ways which are carefully calibrated to influence Israel while minimizing the opportunity—we cannot eliminate it totally—of unwittingly providing aid and succor to her detractors. Wherever possible we should speak out directly to Israeli political leaders and through the Israel press.

Op-ed pieces in the *Jerusalem Post* have more impact than those in the *New York Times,* with less negative reverberations.

But we can longer wall off Israeli politics from debate and discussion. As we have seen graphically in the past few months, in the wrenching anguish and debate between American Jewry and Israel over the possibility that the Law of Return would be amended to preclude Conservative and Reform converts from qualifying for automatic citizenship, what happens in Israel has a dramatic impact on our identity as Jews. The way in which the Jewish state acts on the world scene has a great deal to do with the future attractions of Judaism for us and for our children. The issue of whether Judaism has anything to say of relevance to today's problems is in significant, though not exclusive, measure dependent upon Israeli actions.

It would be supremely selfish for us to be involved only in a debate over "Who is a Jew," which directly affects only a dozen American Jews each year, and to stay on the sidelines on political issues affecting the very future of Israel and therefore the essence of Jewish life in the postwar era.

This imposes upon us special obligations to engage in that debate in ways which are sensitive to Israel's national security, and which come from an informed knowledge of the realities of the Middle East. But

Israel's future means too much to us and to our own identities as American Jews for the debate on the direction of Israel to go on only among those within Israel. For sure, our voice will be listened to less than those of its citizens, and this is as it should be. But we do have a contribution to make, and we should make it.

Third, and of greater importance than debating how we can best influence Israeli political decisions, is the need for developing a broader and deeper multidimensional relationship with Israel which goes beyond check writing or involvement in Jewish political issues. We need to make ourselves more a part of the life and times of Israel beyond her political struggles. Our identification must be with the country and its people, not just with Israel's government and its leaders.

There are straws in the wind. The American Reform and Conservative movements are beginning to develop roots in Israel. Today there are fifteen Reform congregations in Israel and over forty Conservative synagogues. Both movements have established kibbutzim and moshavim. There are eleventh- and twelfth-grade high school programs for American teenagers. More than seventeen hundred American Jewish college students are studying in Israel. There are summer camping experiences for young American Jews, unimaginable when I was growing up. A new Jewish Service Corps, Otzma, has begun for young men and women between eighteen and twenty-four. It is now possible to participate in a two-month pre-army program called Mirva. There is an older adult volunteer program called Active Retirees in Israel, run by B'nai B'rith. American doctors and dentists can spend short periods of time helping in deprived neighborhoods and in settlement towns. American Jewish psychiatrists have formed an organization which meets with their Israeli counterparts.

We can build on these important beginning to more closely wrap our lives together with Israel's and in turn enrich our Jewish identification against the strong currents of assimilation. Thus, for example:

- It is time that the United Jewish Appeal and other major Jewish organizations build into their Israel missions visits to the homes of Israeli families rather than stops at five-star hotels. American Jews coming on organized trips should have the opportunity of meeting with their professional counterparts. They should be people missions and not just one vast archaeological dig.
- It is unconscionable that on an annual basis Israel has only about $20 to $30 million in foreign investment. Project Independence is a disappointment. American Jewish businessmen and businesswomen

must do more to invest in Israel and to develop joint ventures with Israeli businesses.
- A new intermediary institution should be created by a joint team of Israeli and American businessmen to match appropriate businesses.
- Major Jewish investment bankers should be challenged to organize an independent investment banking house in Israel to help write business plans for Israeli enterprises, provide independent market research capability for Israeli businesses, and participate in raising equity capital for Israeli companies.
- An American-based diversified mutual fund of listed Israeli securities, called the Israel Fund, should be created, selling a significant percentage of Israeli stocks on the New York Stock Exchange in order to broaden access of Israeli companies to American sources of capital.
- Israel Bonds should increase its market-oriented bonds and move away from its "rachmanos" bonds, below market interest rates of return, which simply appeal to the charitable instincts of American Jewry.
- Private-sector business executive exchange programs should be undertaken to provide Israeli business executives with an opportunity to work in an American corporate environment for several months.
- American Jews should encourage the governors of their states to create joint economic enterprises with Israel modeled after the Texas-Israel Exchange and the Virginia-Israel Commission.
- Israelis feel increasingly isolated. There is no substitute for our physical presence, by short vacations and longer stays, by participating in conferences, by spending summers, by volunteering, by sending our children to camps and schools in Israel, and, if we are so moved, by aliyah.

Amidst all the change in the world, our relationship with Israel has not changed to meet the change in times.

The more American Jews we can get to Israel, and the more they are involved in Israel's life, the deeper will be their Jewish identity here in the United States.

But we must not kid ourselves. Even in the best of circumstances, present figures indicate we will be fortunate to ever get as many as 40 percent to 50 percent of American Jews to visit Israel. Thus, what we must do is use those who do visit Israel and are excited by the Zionist ideal to be the vanguard in spreading the message of Judaism's excitement, relevance, and meaning to a troubled world.

But in the end Jewish identity in the United States has to come not only from a deeper relationship with Israel, but from a deeper relationship with Judaism as a religion.

It has been said that Israel is the secular religion of American Jewry—and we must make the most of it. But more identification with Israel will not stop the forces of assimilation nor build a more authentic Jewish culture in America. Only if we make our religion, its practices, its history, its culture, its values, a central part of our lives will Judaism flourish and grow in America, and not become the retreat of an ever smaller core group of American Jews.

In Parshat Bamidbar, which we read last week in Numbers, we learned that the creation of the first Jewish community in the wilderness began when Moses assigned each tribe to a location around the Tabernacle and the Ten Commandments. The center of Jewish identity, now as then, must be religious teachings. It is these which impart the beauty of Judaism and the ethical and moral precepts which have made it timeless.

PART IV
Religion, Education, and Culture

The Role of the Synagogue in Jewish Identity

HAROLD M. SCHULWEIS

In order to measure the elusive character of Jewish identity with some degree of objectivity, social scientists tend to look at empirical data on public behavior. Questionnaires ask about membership affiliation with Jewish organizations, the extent of Jewish philanthropy, the frequency of synagogue attendance, the activity within Jewish institutions—the stuff of which eulogies and obituaries are made. This information seeks to provide relevant indices of identity. The question "who am I?" is related to another, "whose am I?." In this sense, belonging is prior to believing or behaving.

But what is missing in this objective assessment of Jewish identity is what Erikson called "the subjective sense of invigorating sameness and continuity," or what Carl Jung once referred to as "the innate idiosyncrasy of a living being." What is missing in the measurement are the private, personal dimensions of identity. And this methodological limitation has significant implications for the challenges confronting the institutions of Jewish life concerned with the cultivation and strengthening of Jewish identity. The commonly used type of evidence of Jewish identity is encountered in the *reshut ha-rabim,* the public domain: public Jews, led by public personnel, carrying out the mandates of the public agenda. Public Jews can be counted and computerized. They belong to synagogues, centers, federations, Zionist organizations, and defense organizations. Their acts are measurable and quantifiable. They pay dues, support building programs, serve on committees, task forces, commissions, boards, and attend meetings, conventions, banquets, and conferences. Such data are a boon for demographic surveys and statistics. Identity can be determined by the identification cards in the wallet.

But who are these Jews as Jews alone? Who are they after the last gavel has been pounded, after the Neilah service? Who are they stripped of their delegate badges, no longer solicitors or donors but individual Jews? Who are they as Jews after the shivah period, the minyan disbanded? Who are they alone on the hospital bed after the visitors have left their flowers? What Jewish resources do public Jews call upon in private, what Jewish wisdom, faith, conviction can they draw upon to walk them through the valley of the shadow? What is the character of Jewish identity of public Jews in the privacy of their homes? What Jewish songs do they sing, what poetry do they recite, what stories do they tell around the table, what Jewish wisdom is transmitted at home?

In modern times there is less and less correlation between the public and private Jewish personae. Peter Berger, in *Facing Up to Modernity* (New York: Basic Books, 1977), observes "the dichotomization of social life" in the process of modernization. This bifurcation applies to the Jewish forms of identity. Even among those who are Jewishly affiliated, a growing chasm exists between the public and private spheres, between the synagogue and school on the one hand, and the home on the other. Within the *reshut ha-yahid,* the home, the family and the individual are shriveled. The home has become the "interstitial area" left over from the public sphere. At home, the individual is left to his own devices "in a wide range of activities that are crucial to the formation of a meaningful identity, from expressing his religious preference to settling on a sexual life style." The sociologist Arnold Gehlen speaks of the "underinstitutionalization" of the private sphere. In our case it means that the Jewish individual and his family are ritually, morally, and culturally unsupported by the Jewish public organizations with which they may be affiliated. Perry London, in his important paper "The Psychology of Identity Formation" (1989), finds the search for adult identity "a problem of having to swim in a sea of choices in an almost normless and highly anonymous society." If there is any public supportive presence in the home, it comes from the commercial culture of the television media, as has been argued recently by Neil Postman. But between the public Jewish culture and the private Jewish home there exists an ever-widening "mechitzah."

The signs and symbols of that divide are all about us. The Passover seder has been moved out of the home into the social hall, words read by the rabbi, melodies sung by the cantor, food prepared by the caterer, and the Haggadah supplemented, compiled, and revised by the synagogue. The succah does not adjoin the walls of the private home but only those of the temple. We are socialists in our religious possessions. Nothing is privately owned. The lulav and ethrog are owned by the temple. The siddur, machzor, Bible, prayer-shawl, and skullcap are all public property. No names and dates of family births, deaths, and anniversaries are inscribed on the fly-leaf of the sacred texts in our public lecterns. Instead, they are stamped with the imprimatur, "Property of Valley Beth Shalom." Unintentionally, the public institution has robbed the family of its sancta, and the roles of parents have been preempted by the professionals of the public institutions.

This sort of expropriation is not the result of institutional cunning. The preemption is not protested by the laity. The individual Jew has willingly, even insistently, handed over more and more of his or her personal Jewish life to the synagogue. The individual Jew has adopted a passive-aggressive, hands-off role toward the Jewish way of life. The rites of passage, the most personal aspects of family life, are gladly surrendered to religious experts. Many are fearful of the synagogue and uncomfortable with its ways. An aliyah, much less a *hagbah, gelilah,* or *petichah,* is less a personal honor than an occasion for public embarrassment.

Graceless on the bimah, ritually and theologically incompetent at home, Jewish parents have turned themselves into referral agents on Jewish matters.

Children ask questions. When children ask questions about God or prayer or death or Bible stories or Christmas, parents no longer take it upon themselves to respond. They refer the children to experts who know better. Ask the rabbi. In this they are wrong. For when parents continually assume the role of referral agents, it is interpreted by the children not as a mark of parental modesty but as a confession of disinterest. It may well be that the fourth child of the seder, who does not know how to ask, feigns ignorance because he senses that his parents cannot and do not care how to answer. Parental ignorance is intuited as parental indifference.

No credentialed teacher can substitute for the emotional authority of the parent. Parents are gods to their children, particularly in their formative years. Parents create memories, the material out of which identities and fidelities are formed.

My *zeyda* came to the synagogue because he was a Jew. His grandchildren, if they come at all, come to the synagogue to become Jews. But the synagogue, for all its ambitions, will fail them if it thinks that it can be a surrogate for family and home. I am not "papa." The rabbi is not father or mother; the lectern is not the table; the synagogue is not home; the temple is not preparation for Jewish living at home. Adult education and temple lectures offer knowledge by description. And knowledge by description is far different from knowledge by acquaintance. The Jewish teaching and preaching of public institutions offer instruction with the instructor's hands tied behind his back. Try to teach someone how to tie his shoelaces without a physical demonstration. Speak out the instruction with your hands deep in your pockets, "Take the shorter lace in your left hand and press it down against the tongue of the shoe; then take the other lace in your right hand and cross it over and under the other lace . . . etc." The shoelace parable parodies meta-Judaism, the "aboutism" of lectures about festivals and about prayers and about Judaism as a way of life without entering the situation and venue in which Jewishness is lived and acted out. "For the synagogue," Franz Rosenzweig understood, "no longer acts as a member completing the body of a living life. The beadle no longer knocks at the house doors to summon us to shul."

Paradoxically, as the synagogue, its schools, its facilities, texts, and personnel are improved, the family has been disempowered. More articulate preachers, better lectures, better choirs, more elegant facilities, even better faculties will not increase or deepen the quality of Jewish identity. Attendance at services is a false mark of Jewish success. Attendance of the family around the table and the nature of the table talk are far more significant.

The frustration with public Judaism was expressed by the neo-Orthodox theologian Samson Raphael Hirsch when he wrote, "If I had the power, I would provisionally close all synagogues for a hundred years." And then, as if recognizing the shock such a proposal would provoke in the reader, he continued, "Do not tremble at the thought of it, Jewish heart. What would happen? Jews and Jewishness without the synagogue, desiring to remain such, would be forced to concentrate on a Jewish life and a Jewish home."

Hirsch's intention was honorable, but his solution was misplaced. The synagogue must not be closed. It must be reopened, restructured. What is required of the synagogue and the school and its projects is a perestroika, a reconstruction that would focus its energies upon the "underinstitutionalized" family, home, and individual. The focused goal must be the empowerment of the family, the design to help parents recover their roles as singers of songs and tellers of tales, to reclaim their generative powers to create memories, to explain and answer questions children ask. The goals of the synagogue should entail the personalization and decentralization of the public institutions. Its task is to cross over the private moat that separates the public Jewish world from the home as castle. The havurah has initiated that bridging of private and public places; its meetings at home are symbolic of the effort to open up the home to Jewish living. The havurah as a mediating structure is set in the right direction, but it now needs more focused direction toward *chizuk ha-mishpochah*—the empowerment of the family.

Toward this end, teachers and rabbinic seminaries and synagogues ought to cultivate *m'chanchei mishpochah*, family educators whose training is home-focused. This calls for a different pedagogy, a different ambience, a different teleology. The venue of family education is not the classroom of blackboards, desks, and auditorium. It is that of the chairs and tables of dining rooms, the art on the walls, the books and journals in the den, the aroma of cooking, the home as "safe haven from a heartless world."

Home Judaization requires more than bibliography. It entails a serious collegiality between Jewish professionals and laity, a collaboration that will match host families with teaching families, and target specific groups, e.g., singles, single-parent families, Jews by choice, whose home needs require special attention. Havuroth are halfway homes that lend themselves to the goals of family empowerment. *M'chanchei mishpochah* within the congregation are a cadre of morally serious Jews who are prepared *lilmod ul'lamed,* to learn in order to teach, to learn with rabbis, cantors, and gifted teachers how to transmit the choreography of a Sabbath or a festival, how to celebrate the family's rites of passage, how to enter the synagogue. Rosenzweig was on the mark when he noted, "Books are not now the prime need of the day. But what we need more than ever, or at least as much as ever, are human beings—Jewish human beings." Rosenzweig's insight in terms of our project means that Jews need Jews to be Jewish. However remarkable the intention of outreach programs, they sooner or later stumble over the failures of "inreach." There are few Jews secure enough to reach out to others. Outreach— with whom, outreach—from where? The targets are external, readily identifiable. Where are the internal resources, the powers within? We have the targets, but where are the archers?

In this regard, on the eve of Shavuoth, and the reading of the Book of Ruth, the frustrations of the outreach programs to proselytes are particularly pertinent. Consider the Ruth of modernity, a not atypical young woman who has attended public classes, been moved by the shiver of Jewish history, taught about the Jewish respect for the book and the centrality of the family. She who has been immersed in Jewish studies and the mikveh now comes to the home of her prospective Jewish in-laws on a Friday night. The home is finely furnished, the table exquisitely set. But she reports an evening bereft of benediction, a songless, graceless evening with pedestrian conversations about acquisitions and things. What is Jewishly distinctive about this family? If the definition of Jewish identity includes differentia, how is this Jewishly native-born family in the privacy of their home distinguished from any urban, upwardly mobile middle-class home?

The disappointment of Jews by choice who enter the un-Jewish homes of Jews by genes only to discover native Jews alienated from Judaism is illustrative of the failure from within. It is the estrangement of the born Jews, not the proselytized stranger in our midst, that cripples the best-intentioned outreach program. There can be no successful outreach without a meaningful inreach. The Ruth of modernity seeks to become a member of a Jewish family, not to be listed on the membership roster of the temple. The problematic character of outreach is not in Ruth's attitude, but in that of the Boaz and Naomi of modernity. Ruth is prepared to pledge, "Thy people shall be my people, thy God, my God." But where are the God and people of her beloved? Philip Roth confesses his childhood memories, "What a Jewish child inherited was no body of law, no body of learning, no language and finally no Lord."

We have had enough studies by now to convince us that schools can teach dates and geography, but not fidelity, attitude, character. Surveys and studies of religious schools (I have particularly in mind Ross and Greeley's *The Education of Catholic Americans*) agree that "a school cannot be expected to carry out a religious socialization process for which there is little sympathy at home."

Particularly in Judaism, where the family is the substructure of Jewish experience, theology, values, ethics, and philanthropy should begin at home. The vaunted idea of menschlichkeit was not transmitted by a lesson in ethics as surely as it was inculcated by the parental dictum *es past nisht*. The home boxes for Eretz Yisrael, orphan homes, and homes for the aged confirmed the adage that charity begins at home though it does not end there. I have said that the individual Jew has tacitly approved of the take-over of Jewish responsibilities by the synagogue. A half-conscious conspiracy between the laity and the institution has encouraged the usurpation of parental powers and the surrender of the home to the sanctuary. But occasionally one hears from lay people a cry of resentment that must be attended. "Don't tell me what I can do for Judaism; tell me what Judaism can do for me. Don't tell me what I can do for the synagogue, tell me what the synagogue can do for me. For me—in my aloneness, for me in my bewilderment and confusion, for me in my ineptitude and incompetency in raising a family."

That cry for attention calls for a more balanced view of Jewishness. For a variety of reasons Judaism has been viewed as if it were, to cite Spinoza, "a social organization," a polity to be supported and obeyed. Where public belonging is so exaggerated, private believing and private behaving are ignored. Whitehead's definition of religion as what one does with one's solitariness has been too quickly dismissed as irrelevant to Jewish religiosity. But while there is an individualism that separates itself from the community, hiding behind the skirts of the community is as threatening to Jewish identity. Heschel, for one, warned about the rabbinic neglect of the individual as Jew. "If we cannot pray alone, we will find it hard to pray with the congregation." Jewish interiority, subjectivity, inwardness, inreach, and the private sphere are all essential goals for the cultivation and meaning of Jewish identity. "If we meet no Gods, it is because we harbor none" (Emerson). But the gods we harbor are not born innate. The energies and competencies of the major public Jewish institution, the synagogue, must be cultivated, personalized, decentralized, and individualized. The substructure of Judaism, the family and home, must be strengthened if the superstructures of Judaism are to survive meaningfully and if Jewish identity is to mean more than simply registration. *Ayn bichlal ela mah she-befrat*—"There is nothing in the collective that is not in the particular" (Talmud Pesachim 66). Asked why she believed in God, the little girl answered more profoundly than she suspected. "I don't know. I guess it runs in the family." More than that runs in the family.

The Role of the Synagogue in Jewish Identity

RICHARD N. LEVY

The theme of our panel, "The Role of the Synagogue in Jewish Identity," is a troubling one. First of all, it is a sociological and not a religious title; second, it implies that the synagogue is only a means to serve the end of helping individuals find their Jewish identity.

Unfortunately, this sociological title is all too appropriate. The synagogue is too often judged by the manner in which it fulfills an individual's needs. But sociology and religion judge an individual's needs very differently. When my social worker friends speak of "meeting people's needs," they intend that the people themselves should define those needs. When rabbis speak of "meeting people's needs," we believe that it is Jewish tradition—or Torah—that defines what people's needs should be—even if people themselves are not always aware of them.

The board of a synagogue may believe that it needs more social events, more outreach to potential members; it may emphasize the need for a nursery school because that is a way of bringing in the young people whose children will tie them to the synagogue for a decade or more. But as the director of Hillel's Jewish campus work in this city, I daily see the failure of this definition of need: what Jews really need is to be seized by the power of their tradition, to be grabbed by challenges to the way they view the world, to be allowed to struggle with the reality of a God who cares about them, has needs for them to fulfill, has demands to which they need to say, "No, I won't," or "Yes, I will," or "I'm not ready yet, but I want to keep wrestling!"

I know many students whose families and synagogues made them bored with being Jewish—and, as we all know, one of the reasons why Christian missionaries can excite students and others is that the evangelicals care about religion; they care about the people they want to bring in; they know about people's spiritual needs. Religion is anything but boring to them.

Don't misunderstand me: on the one hand, there are many synagogues in this city that do wonderful things; on the other, all of us, in every

Jewish institution in this city, have a very hard time. Size and distance and the passion for privacy are problems enough; but the synagogue, which used to be a place that gave people a vision that raised them above the everyday, must in our town compete with a pervasive industry which gives people vision in Technicolor and Dolby sound, or on scanable channels. We live in a city whose roads and freeways stream with plush little chariots of air-conditioned cellular comfort, carrying us from grand, sweeping houses to even grander office buildings. The synagogue can seldom compete with these luxuries. Meanwhile, people in more modest dwellings feel they cannot compete with the owners of the sweeping houses, who often seem to own the synagogue as well.

And finally, the synagogue is a place that requires discipline to be effective: regular davening that lets us know what time it is, for we do not live in a country that runs on Shabbos time or Yuntiff time, or the changing time of the different Torah portions; the synagogue requires the discipline of regular learning—not an occasional star's lecture, or a rabbi's major sermon, but week-in, week-out wrestling with a teacher and friends over a text; and the synagogue also requires the discipline of regular attendance to its business and its members' welfare.

Such discipline is hard for anyone—but I think it is harder in Los Angeles. Our fabled sunshine, the delicious freedom provided by our climate, make it hard for anyone to willingly adopt a discipline—why should we? Why not play or shop or drink or make money or use drugs as much as as often as we want? Why should there be any artificial limits to our immediate desires? These questions are so pervasive, so seductive, that it is no wonder some Jews ghettoize themselves—moving into tight little communities in Fairfax, Pico-Robertson, or Venice to shut out the larger world and just be Jewish! Is it possible to be both Jewish and an actively participating citizen of Los Angeles's part of the world?

Some of those who are building shtetlach in Fairfax would like to live in an all-Jewish world; but the rest of us—Orthodox, Reform, Conservative, and Reconstructionist—are, I think, more inspired by Shimshon Raphael Hirsch's vision of a people inspired by Torah and the noblest products of Western life. The synagogue should be the place where we learn how Judaism helps us chart our way through the shoals of hard business choices, legal ethics, marriage and personal decisions; but at present it is primarily teachers from Aish Ha-Torah, Yeshiva University, or Chabad who fan out across the workplaces of this city to shine the light of Torah on the issues that occupy our professional or family lives. Their work is welcome—but it reflects the vacuum left by the synagogue in helping us understand how our tradition can inform every step of our lives. If we are to be true to Shimshon Raphael Hirsch's vision to live fully in both our worlds, these are the needs synagogues have to help people meet—on an individual basis. Were I the rabbi of a synagogue today, I would want to meet with as many members as would get together with me, to explore each of their religious and personal issues, to discuss areas where they felt their lives were lacking, and to try to develop a program to help them become more fulfilled religious human beings, following them through the year to give them encouragement and guidance, helping them develop the disciplines of study, prayer, and ethical reflection. This city is full of addicts to material freedom, both those satiated by wealth and those frustrated in its pursuit; the synagogue can help Jews learn the discipline that will keep material choices from ruling over them. To conquer the addiction to unbounded material success, not Twelve Steps do we offer, but Ten: the Torah discipline of Shavuot gives purpose to the unbounded freedom of Pesach. Indeed, the Mechilta even tells us that the Torah was given in the sunshine—for sunshine's purpose is not for tanning, but to reveal the truth to all whose eyes are opened to see.

Yet the synagogue should not limit its concern to the individual's personal life. It also must help its members fulfill their commitments to the Jewish people. There are synagogues in this city whose more active members are determined to bring other members—and nonmembers—into the beauty and majesty of Shabbat; who mobilize instantly around a member who is ill or in need of help. Most of you know the story about the person who asked God: "Why in ordinary times are there two sets of footprints following me, Yours and mine; but in hard times there is only one, and I feel so alone?" And God responded: "Ah, in the hard times I was carrying you." In a close synagogue community, it is our neighbors who enable us to feel God carrying us.

As a caring synagogue helps its members wrestle Jewishly with personal and professional decisions, so should it help them with tzedakah decisions. How much I should give to the synagogue, to the United Jewish Fund or to other causes should not be based solely on my income and the demands upon it; I believe such decisions should also be based on the principle, first stated in Proverbs, that tzedakah of money (or of time that might be spent earning money) enables us to shed all those material appurtenances that weigh us down, that anchor us dangerously to the world, fettering our soul in its quest to unite with its Source. The more we throw off the baggage of our possessions—the more our soul can breathe—the more fully and deeply do we come in touch with the Source of life. The question at the moment of a tzedakah decision should not only be "What do I owe my community?" but also "What do I owe my soul?"

"What do I owe my community," though, is also a religious question. What do I owe my people around the world—especially, these days, in Israel? There are settlers in the West Bank willing to kill people because they believe God intends for them to live where they do. Am I to counter that belief only with secular arguments, with issues of *Realpolitik*? Does my faith stop at the water's edge? If I share—as I do—that rabbinic belief which holds that while our claim to Eretz Yisrael is eternal, our right to settle and rule in the Land is determined by our people's behavior there, am I threatening that right when I remain silent in the face of Jewish injustice? Should not my synagogue help me solve that question? Should its members not be encouraged to speak up for all the views they believe will assure our right to an eternal claim on Eretz Yisrael?

And if these issues are not enough, if we are to follow Shimshon Raphael Hirsch's vision, does not the synagogue need to help us find our religious place among humanity as well? Synagogues in Los Angeles, I believe, should be places where we confront what Judaism has to say to the Buddhism of our neighbors in Little Tokyo and Koreatown, to the Catholicism of our neighbors in East Los Angeles and elsewhere, and to the varieties of Protestant Christianity practiced in south-central Los Angeles and Orange County—as well as to the Islam of the growing numbers of Arabs and black faithful who live in our city. This is not pious—and irrelevant—"interfaith" work: this is the work of Kiddush Ha-Shem, the proclamation of the holiness of the One God who rules the universe; it is the search for the reasons why one God has chosen to be revealed to our neighbors in so many different forms. This city will be governed more and more by its ethnic minorities, whose geographic and cultural distance from Jewish centers makes us invisible to each other.

As essential as day school education is for what I believe is the proper development of Jewish children, we must be aware that day schools tend to isolate us from our neighbors. When we add to day schools the increasing tendency of upper-middle-class Jews to send their children to non-Jewish private schools, we must face the fact that however valuable this trend may be for our children's academic advancement, it is forcing us to hide from the larger community. The synagogue can be a place to bring us out of hiding—to reach across the miles to other ethnic religious institutions so that we may understand who our neighbors are, and help them understand us. With the Temple destroyed, the synagogue could become the place from which we understand the world.

How might that happen?

For our grandfathers, one of the most precious things about a synagogue was that there was a seat there that belonged to them, a favorite spot to sit when they came in to daven. Even in our small minyan that meets in University Synagogue's little library, the regular members take the same chair every week. That chair—and the synagogue to which it belongs—is, like the Jerusalem Temple, an axis mundi—a stairway to the center of the universe which we can mount with our every step of discipline and creativity, our grief and our joy. When the synagogue becomes that kind of place, the grandest Beverly Hills mansion cannot hold a candle to it.

How can we let our synagogues be places where faith can seize hold of us, where we can be lifted to the realm of God—a realm in which we live every single day but to which we remain oblivious? We can start anywhere. But as a rabbi, I prefer to start with my colleagues. I would start with our need to be *shadchanim* between our people and God—and if we are unfamiliar with God, not sure whether we believe in God, not sure whether our people want us to acquaint them with God, we must do whatever it takes to explore the presence of God in our lives. We need to learn, to pray, to take hours of silence, to walk by the ocean, to learn to say the *berachot* in praise of sunsets and thunderstorms, trees in blossom, and people of learning. To say, with some of my Reform and Reconstructionist colleagues, "I cannot prove that God exists," is not enough; to say, with some of my Conservative colleagues, "One serves God sufficiently by doing mitzvot," is not adequate; to say, with some of my Orthodox colleagues, "One can serve God only when we do mitzvot the way we define 'Torah-true,'" is not helpful. We rabbis do not always bring our people closer to God; we sometimes push them away.

But of course we also know that congregants and boards of directors sometimes make it difficult for rabbis to develop the kind of closeness with God that will let us share it with our people. Some of them insist that the rabbi's primary role is as the CEO of the congregation—with the president acting as chair of the board. Some think the rabbi's primary role is to attract members—not through teaching, preaching, or concern about their religious development, but by presenting an attractive presence in the community, or through open houses for prospective members. Others feel the rabbi should be the congregation's chief fundraiser, or adept at telling stories to nursery school children. All of these roles, of course, divert the rabbi from those activities which would really challenge the members—children and adults: teaching, exhorting, davening, and acting religiously in the community. If a corporate model is necessary, I would suggest one in which the chair of the board is God, whose will the rabbi and the officers are all sworn to try to carry out.

What does it mean to build a synagogue in this city? I think, with the Kabbalists, it means to believe that every time we do a mitzvah we create an angel, and the more we help our people discipline themselves to pray, to study, and to do good deeds, the more we shall help create a City of Angels whose chariots will sweep us close to God: not only Jews, but all our neighbors on whom the sun so generously shines.

The Role of the Synagogue in Jewish Identity

DANIEL LANDES

I want to talk about the restructuring of the Orthodox Jewish community, basically its "shtiebilization," coming from the term *shtiebel*—the small, intimate minyan. What it comes down to is an apparently simple question: why do people come to my minyan? My parents' generation would never have tolerated sitting where my people sit, in the Hillel Hebrew Academy cafeteria, where near the *bimah,* one can invariably find a half-eaten peanut butter and jelly sandwich on Shabbos morning. Almost every Shabbos when there's a baby naming, a congregant's mother-in-law enters, sits down on the one seat that has a big wad of chewing gum, and remains glued to her seat. My parents would never have tolerated this.

My minyan, which has about 80 to 120 people on a given Shabbos, is the future, it seems, of the Orthodox synagogue. The large Orthodox synagogue of the past is a dinosaur. The only synagogues that will survive are ones that will be a collection of *shtiebels*. Beth Jacob Congregation, headed by the very fine Rabbi Abner Weiss, who gives me a free rein, has begun to do this. Beth Jacob is a synagogue in which there are six or seven minyanim on a given Shabbos. Ten years from now at Beth Jacob there will be eighteen different shtiebels, and that will be the only possibility of continued Orthodox renewal. If I'm right I'm right, and if I'm wrong I'm wrong, but I prefer the broad mistake in this talk tonight to the truth of a hundred qualifications.

Why the shift? What I have to do is go back with you, and I'm unencumbered by data or facts, to the Orthodox synagogue of my youth. I was bar mitzvah in 1963. At that time I think there were three major concerns that were articulated in synagogues around the country and which I felt not only at my service but at all the bar mitzvahs of all my manifold cousins and friends.

The first was the concern with modernity—how to become really American. How to be "with it" in dress, sports, and with style. On my bar mitzvah I received no *sefarim,* but I did receive eight red Perry Como sweaters which I wore successively eight days in a row before my mother discovered it, too late to return them. This was part of the Americanization process. Of course, more important than anything else was education—the possibility of getting into a good college in order to get into a good graduate school in order to have a respectable *parnosa* (livelihood).

The second concern was with tradition, and tradition meant something very specific within the Orthodox community: To marry within the faith, hopefully someone who was somewhat traditional, and to get the basic skills of Jewish life: lay tefillin in the morning, to be able to daven, and to keep fundamental observances, which were really Shabbos (not driving to shul on Shabbos was the norm—some places were a little bit more exacting) and observance of kashrut in the home and knowing what to order outside.

The third concern, the most difficult, was how to merge the first two concerns. How can you merge modernity with Orthodoxy? At my bar mitzvah (I have just come home from Chicago, where I saw my mother, so all these memories are coming back), my *droshah* was the same bar mitzvah *droshah* of every boy (and the bat mitzvah *droshahs* of the girls were basically the same). It was about *Birkat Efraim uMenasheh*, the blessings of Ephraim and Manasseh, the *brachah* that we give on Friday night to every Jewish boy. Ephraim represents the one who knows how to learn Torah, and Manasseh represents the one who is very worldly, who is involved with Joseph in running Egypt's government. We strove to be like Ephraim and Manasseh. Manasseh alone was not good enough; Ephraim alone, in those days, was certainly not good enough. One had to be a combination, a balance between Ephraim and Manasseh.

This precarious balance was defined in different ways in different communities, but it was always a balance between the two concepts. It thus became a real need to articulate an ideological position in which both could be maintained. Therefore Samson Raphael Hirsch's idea of *Torah umada*, of the putting together of Torah and secular wisdom, was our watchword. Individual Jews who in the twentieth century somehow seemed to represent that unification therefore became highly prized. One of the reasons for the great prominence of Rabbi J. B. Soloveitchik and Rav Kook in the Orthodox community is their delicate merging of these two philosophies. And what was the concretization of the ideal of being both Ephraim and Manasseh? Of course it was to be that lawyer who went to the Ivy League school but could still learn a *blatt* of *Gemorrah*.

Today these three concerns are not pressing concerns within the Orthodox community. In part, that is because of the success of the above models. I have two brothers. They both learn a *blatt Gemorrah,* they both went to the best universities, and they both spend most of their day defending the uptrodden for the finest law firms in the cities of New York and Chicago. It worked.

Then something else was discovered, and that was that one did not necessarily need an ideological formulation. This is still very hard for me to realize. I go to visit my cousins, my friends, and the guys I went to yeshiva with in New York. Last week I visited with a friend in his Wall Street investment-banking firm, and he said, "You know, let's go home to Boro Park, because there I can let my hair down." I said, "Let your hair down in Boro Park?" I didn't know what he meant. We went home, he took out his *peyes,* which were carefully hidden behind his ears, and he let his hair down. I said to him, "Don't you realize the conflict in your life, that here you are, this excellent investment broker, you're living in a goyishe society, now you're going back, you're raising your kids on a very traditional model? Don't you realize that this is not ideologically consistent?!"

But he doesn't need an ideological formulation for a synthesis between Judaism and modernity. Orthodox Jews don't even look for it today. All sorts of interesting combinations have occurred, because you can be successful in American society without figuring out ideologies and the philosophical niceties behind them. Jews live with these inner contradictions, and these outer contradictions, and they have absolutely no problems. They send their kids to the frummest yeshivas and they're not worried about it, because when the time comes they'll go to City College and then they'll get into a good law school. If they don't want to go to school, there are other ways of making a parnosa.

As a result, these three obsessions have disappeared. The outside world is no longer a threat for the Orthodox community. This is a broad generalization, of course. Yes, we have casualties. There are people who go off the deep end and leave us. But it is no longer a threat as a respected competitor, as an alternative model. This sense of competition is no longer part of the Orthodox Jewish consciousness. We know the outside society—and now I'm speaking within a *popular* Orthodox sense—we know the outside society to be one of degraded morals, one of entertainment which is not so enjoyable (of course we avail ourselves of it periodically, but that's just on a Saturday night), we know it not to be the attractive model that is going to snatch our children away. Therefore, the turn inward is no longer the result of the threat of the outside. Rather, if one wants to find meaning, and happiness, if one wants to find *nachas,* one will turn inside.

This is true even in the area in which I thought it never would occur. When I was growing up, Israel belonged to the Religious Zionists. If one did not have a Kookian vision, it was impossible to reconcile oneself to Israel and arrive at an ideologically correct way of going to Eretz Yisroel. At present, by contrast, all my friends' children, who study in the finest *shvartz* ("black-hat") yeshivas, whose ideology does not recommend the government, does not even recommend in a proper sense the viability of the democratic state, they feel Eretz Yisroel belongs to them. They even work on a moshav (communal settlement); they have a full Israeli experience. And do you know what? With their broken Ashkenazic Hebrew they learn to navigate Israel a lot better than their cousins who are spending their junior years at Hebrew University. There is nothing that's left out for them.

What, then, is the new ideological concern? I want to talk about how the Orthodox synagogue works when it works, and the ways in which it is not working. The new concern, the concern too, I believe, of my *baalabatim*, is a concern I can perhaps express in one word: authenticity. It's a heavily laden word. Let me not define it so much as describe how it works itself out. They want to have *authentic* Jewish lives. And therefore, they often go back to models which they don't necessarily have in their own families, or if they do, they're often romanticized. This going back to models of authentic Jewish existence means complete halakhic compliance and also having a proper ideology which is in consonance with Torah values. This is a real search and a real desire. This is true even within my minyan, which is a little bit different from other shtiebels, for we have certain stances which are distinctive. If for a moment any of my *baalabatim* felt that their experience in my minyan was somehow not authentic Judaism, as taught in the past by Hirsch or Maimonides, or did not involve a proper understanding of *Gemorrah,* they would leave it instantly. This authenticity has to be full, it has to be complete—tolerant of individual deviance, tolerant of individual lack, but on an ideological and ritual level complete, at the very least in its theory and in its goal.

I'll give you an illustration just in terms of the change in status and role of the rabbi within the Orthodox community. The rabbi, if he wants to be a leader, can pretend to be a leader. He can be a preacher if he wants to give a *droshah;* certainly a counselor is always important. But none of my colleagues of my age (thirty-eight) or younger can function within the Orthodox community today unless they have at least the pretense of being a *talmid chacham,* of being a *posek,* of being able to answer *shailos*. From the 80 to 120 people I have each *Shabbos,* I'm asked at least fifteen to twenty questions a week, and they run the gamut from the most mundane to the most exotic, from the most public to the most private.

What does a shul do? It not only reflects identity, but it actively creates it. It creates it, I believe, in five forms: (1) ideological, (2) ritual/cognitive, (3) ethical, (4) mythological and (5) a certain national identity.

First, the ideological belief, as I said earlier, is central. The prevailing question is, Who is a Jew? People consider seriously what the Rambam says in terms of the *ikarim,* dogmas. In fact, as I was sitting here, I was thinking, how can one determine what is the central dogma of a community at a given time?

Invariably, 95 percent of the *droshas* given, from *roshei yeshiva* to rabbis down to the *divrai Torah* given at Sabbath tables, have one or two messages repeated over and over again. These are the central dogmas of Orthodox Jewish life today. The first is the absolute authority of Torah, and the absoluteness of the Torah authorities. Second, amidst a general culture that talks about enhancement of the self, a constant Orthodox refrain is of the necessity of self-sacrifice. These two dogmas are ideological, consistent, and explored. I'll talk more about the downside of these principles later.

Secondly, the ritual/cognitive. There is a great literacy that one needs and the synagogues offer. The first is Hebrew literacy. It would be difficult for one to survive in the synagogue for more than a year if one doesn't know how to read Hebrew. There's also literacy of Halakhah, of basic Jewish concepts. And it's amazing what people can pick up when they assiduously apply themselves. I know I have certain *baalabatim* that are 90 percent wrong on every talmudic concept they have. But still, what am I going to say about that 10 percent that they're right about? After a while it's not a massive ignorance that builds up, but rather a massive knowledge and true knowledge. Finally, there is a literacy of ritual. One can't remain in my minyan—not that we kick them out, they just don't remain, they can't remain, unless they learn how to make Shabbos, how to make *yontif.* I can get up before Shabbos now, before *yontif,* and say Shavuos is coming, you have to make an *eruv tavshillin.* And they understand. It's a literacy of ritual.

The third way in which shul creates identity is the ethical life. The ethical life is really a grass-roots, interpersonal life. *Gemilus chesed,* doing a loving-kindness, are live words. There's a true support in time of family crisis. The ethical imperative and the creation of the ethical world are contained within the community itself.

The fourth dimension of Jewish identity is the mythological. The synagogue calendar dominates thinking. The cycle of the holidays renews the experiences of destruction, rebirth, and emancipation. The lifecycles of others also impact—the weekly baby naming, a bris, going to the house of shivah, this becomes a part of a person's life and death, and determines how they think and how they consider the week. Transcendence and immanence are not two separate dimensions; they interpenetrate each other.

The final identity concept that I want to talk about is that of peoplehood, a strong notion that the *tzibbur,* the community itself, is a microcosm of all Israel, and that as one participates within that community one is participating within the full range of Jewish life. The ethos, therefore, is very collective and family-centered. One of our problems is that we don't always know what to do with singles except to marry them off. And those who aren't married off (and it's certainly not always right to think this way), the dominant ethos casts as unfortunate. Those who for one reason or another do not choose to get married or can't get married become adopted by families and enter into families and enter into a family way of living, of support. She becomes *tante,* they become the good uncle. When it works out it works out very nicely.

Let me talk about when it doesn't work out, because I don't want to be accused of being an Orthodox triumphalist.

Let's go back to some of these categories. Ideology is often overheated. Actually, it's *always* overheated. Ideology has its own dynamic—pure, logical, consistent formulations create, perhaps, better defined communities; but they create even greater and greater division. I probably said I have ninety young people who come to my minyan on Shabbos; I know that I also have ninety people who won't go to my minyan on Shabbos, and that's part of their identity definition too.

I have this fellow who for a couple of months used to walk three blocks out of his way to walk by my shul to show that he's *not* coming to my minyan on Shabbos. His wife came to my study to say how terrible it was, and I agreed and thought she had come to make shalom; but she was telling me about her poor guy, he has to always demonstrate this *hashkofah* (ideological position); it's a *tirchah* (bother)! I called him up and I told him, "I recognize that you don't recognize me." He was appeased, I was appeased. We can now go on from there. But that's part of what ideology creates.

Localization within the Orthodox community can mean not confronting universal problems—for that matter, universal Jewish problems. Whom am I speaking about? The very terms I use, "overheated," "ideology," "localization," could be used as co-terms for the common charges against Orthodoxy, charges that I've heard often from Orthodox-bashers.

These are often charges of fanaticism and charges of obscurantism. Nonetheless, I think these are dangerous potentialities within the Orthodox community, especially now. This is a time of great power within the Orthodox community, great resurgence among the Orthodox, great feelings of happiness and optimism regarding the future of Jewish life. Therefore, while I'm not going to use or agree to those accusations of fanaticism and obscurantism, nonetheless I sense an overheated ideological framework and severely localized vision. It is a great misfortune, a great lack of developing the opportunity of what Orthodoxy at this present time can contribute to the larger Jewish community, and also to itself.

Part of the problem stems from the *problem* of authenticity. What is authenticity? In giving a *teshuvah* to those questioners, can I tell a person exactly what Torah expects at that moment? I have to tell you that many times I believe that's what is expected of me, and as a *rav* I do tell them. Authenticity, however, doesn't tell a person exactly what it is, inside, to be a Jew, and authenticity sometimes, and often within my community, has the danger of putting the lid on the creative internal development that was always part of the authentic Jewish response.

It was mentioned earlier that modern Orthodox rabbis love to tell horror stories of right-wing Orthodox rabbis, so I shouldn't disappoint that very astute observation. You heard earlier a reference to the four sons. It says that the Torah speaks *keneged arbaah banim,* "about four sons." So the Satmar Rav gave the following interpretation: He translated *keneged* not as "about" but as "against" four sons. Of course, he says, we understand why we don't like *she'eno yodeah lish'ol,* the one who can't ask. And none of us wants a son or daughter to be a *tam*—a simpleton. And certainly the *rashah*—the evil child—should be spoken against. But why do we say *keneged* in reference to the *chacham,* the wise son? The Satmar Rav says "The *chacham* was the worst of the four. Why? Because he legitimized the whole process of asking questions."

He didn't mean it as a joke, and that's a concern that I have about my community, that the search for authenticity will be a pointer, that it will give proper answers but such proper answers that the dynamic creativity within the community will be stifled.

I have much more to say but let me finish this way. What happens when it works? What happens when the community creates identity? As the two previous speakers said, shavuos comes, *Matan Torah* comes, the giving of the Torah, and then we read Ruth. Each speaker mentioned Ruth. What's the story of Ruth? The story of Ruth is the story of *chesed.* The story of Ruth is the story of loving-kindness: Ruth in relation to Naomi, Naomi gives back to Ruth, Boaz to both of them, the elders to the whole community. The *chesed* of the birth of King David finally represents the *chesed* that will come to the entire world with the coming of the Messiah.

That is how we understand the story. And that is how Maimonides defines who is a Jew. Of course when Maimonides does it, in the middle of the Laws of Forbidden Relations, he uses the negative: "Anyone who has arrogance, or anyone who has cruelty, or anyone who hates mankind, and doesn't do acts of loving-kindness, we have to suspect his lineage. Maybe he's of the Givon tribe—he's not one of the Jews. The Gibeonites were famous for their cruelty. Why? Because the signs, the identification marks of this holy nation, Israel, are what? *Byshanim,* they're shy. *Rachmanim"*—I don't have to translate *rachmanim*—"they have *rachmonis*; and they do *chesed*."

Years from now we will have to look in the mirror, we'll take out the pictures of our family, and we'll see the identification marks of our community. If we don't have these three identification marks, then none of us will be a Jew.

An Agenda for the Study of Jewish Identity and Denominationalism Among Children

DANIEL STEINMETZ

Explaining childhood from a poet's vantage point, Rainer Maria Rilke advised a young colleague, "Even if you found yourself in some prison, whose walls let in none of the world's sounds—wouldn't you still have your childhood, that jewel beyond all price, that treasure house of memories?" From this author's vantage point, as a researcher on relations among Jewish groups, childhood may be a potentially vast storehouse, but right now it is an unexplored one. It is the conventional wisdom that children accumulate a treasure house of memories, attitudes, and behaviors that affect their relations with other Jews (and other non-Jews) all their lives. It is commonly believed that the intermovement conflicts of adults are actually or embryonically present among children. Operating on these beliefs, practitioners have spawned curricula in "comparative Judaism" as well as programs to enhance *Klal Yisrael*-affirming attitudes. These policy paths make intuitive sense, but some may be taken without benefit of map or compass.

I am not aware of any systematic studies that let us know just how Jewish children feel, think, or behave toward other Jews. At present we don't know if the adult passions unleashed over the question of "Who is a Jew" were also unleashed among children. The single most cited example of children's intermovement conflicts is still the relationship between the protagonists in Chaim Potok's *The Chosen,* a novel involving two unusual children and two fathers distinguished by their scholarship and community influence during and after World War II. Our challenge is to study these issues at present as they affect large numbers of more typical children in more typical environments.

I will report on initial plans for a study of how children in Jewish schools relate to other Jews. The study will include a survey of several hundred children in Detroit's Jewish schools along with approximately 100 teachers and a dozen principals. The study's goals include:

1. Describing the character of intermovement attitudes and behaviors among children in Jewish schools, and developing methods others can use for the same purpose.
2. Examining factors associated with children's intermovement stances, especially factors growing out of the school environment, including the attitudes of personnel and the curriculum and programming.
3. Facilitating a process in which local schools and educational policymakers assess the performance of their own schools and evaluate steps they can take to affect intermovement attitudes.
4. Following up on the study with subsequent phases in which it will be disseminated for consideration and replication in other communities.

This project will be conducted at the University of Michigan's Project in Service, Training and Research (StaR) in Jewish Communal Development by the speaker and Armand Lauffer, who directs the project. It is sponsored by the Wilstein Institute and the American Jewish Committee's Jewish Communal Affairs Department in cooperation with the Detroit Jewish Welfare Federation and the Jewish Education Service of North America.

In the coming months survey instruments will be developed and agreements negotiated with the study sites. The survey is scheduled to start in the fall of 1989. Between now and then we will need to finalize our notions of how to engage educators and laity, how to measure intermovement attitudes and behaviors, and how to determine what features of the school environment should be systematically analyzed.

The first site for the study is metropolitan Detroit, a community of some 70,000 Jews. Over 6,000 students are enrolled in twenty-one Detroit-area schools operated by the Reform, Conservative, Orthodox, and secular movements, as well as a number of schools operated by a community-based nondenominational school system. About a fifth of those enrollments are in day schools.

Students in the classes best corresponding to ages eleven, thirteen, and fifteen will be surveyed with pencil-and-paper instruments. Those ages were chosen because many theorists of political attitudes focus on adolescence as a critical period for political thinking. However, others focus on earlier periods, and curricula aimed at teaching comparative Judaism tend to span that age range. Since the student survey wil be a pencil-and-paper questionnaire distributed to all students in a class, those grades in schools which best correspond to ages eleven, thirteen, and fifteen will be chosen.

The survey will be fielded in schools operated by the aforementioned movements and the community system. A mail-in survey instrument will also be distributed to all the teachers in the schools where students are surveyed. Finally, there will be in-depth interviews with the administrators of those schools.

The study will be developed in collaboration with a study advisory committee composed of educators, teachers, and lay leaders. They will be involved in decisions about the questionnaire, the study process, and dissemination. Their involvement should help the study be sensitive to concerns and needs, and later on their involvement should facilitate the dissemination of results and their use in making educational policy. To increase support for the project in participating schools, potential participants will be assured of input into plans for conducting and disseminating the study.

Many of our contacts have expressed a genuine conviction that the results will be useful in analyzing the problem and helping develop solutions. Most potential participants expressed a desire to get answers to questions they harbor about children in their schools and organizations. One Reform educator was curious to know more about how Reform students define their own Reform Judaism. An Orthodox educator was concerned to know more about the extent of extremism in Religious Zionism, which he is eager to counteract. It seems that the study will be just as intriguing to some key respondents for the light it will cast on Jewish identity.

All of this focus on schools may leave some observers uncomfortable because it seems to disregard the influence of other factors, such as family, peer socialization, and experiences in informal educational settings, such as camps, youth movements, and community recreation centers. These other factors are probably important, and in the best of all worlds they would also be examined at the same time. But resource constraints necessitate some narrowing of the focus, and schools are certainly one potentially important site for studying socialization into intermovement attitudes. Schools are an especially suitable point of departure because they are in the process of getting more attention and more financial support from federations and other community funding sources. At the same time, the community is becoming more interested in seeing how its educational expenditures can be used to promote intra-Jewish tolerance and cooperation. We hope to conduct additional research which will also examine the influence of informal education and the family. But for the moment the starting point is intermovement attitudes within schools.

The term "intermovement attitudes" is used broadly to cover affects, beliefs, and behaviors. The social-psychological literature has established that these factors do not necessarily go hand in hand. It is possible to cooperate in practice but to officially refuse to legitimate the beliefs of other movements. It is also possible to express positive feelings but refuse to cooperate in practice. Because of these inconsistencies there will be separate measures of affect, belief, and behavior.

Affects will be measured with open-ended questions about how comfortable children are when engaging in various activities with Jews from other movements. Students will also be asked what words come to mind when they think about the good and bad things about different movements. Many of their responses will doubtlessly be affective in character.

Beliefs about other movements include stereotypes about their characteristics and practices. Stereotypes distort perceptions about groups both because they are often inaccurate and because, even when they are accurate on the whole, they are often inaccurately applied to specific persons and situations. There may also be questions about the values of different movements.

Behaviors will be measured by asking questions about friendships and activities with Jews of different movements. Students will be asked the movement identification of their five closest friends, and their response to an invitation to attend a *bar/bat mitzvah* in another movement's facility. We will also examine their experiences in camps, youth groups, and other venues with children from different movements. This set of questions will constitute the measurement of attitudes. A larger set might be desirable, but for all practical purposes, a self-administered classroom questionnaire is limited to about 20 minutes.

Even this short battery will allow us to measure attitudes and determine where there is the most tolerance, or conversely, where there are the most negative feelings. The open-ended questions for adjectives describing Jews in other movements also will give us a better handle on the content of these attitudes. In addition these items will make it possible to begin exploring the relationships among these different manifestations of tolerance or intolerance.

We will attempt to account for such attitudes by looking at educational history, perceptions of the attitudes of teachers, school system, parents, extent of contact with children of other movements, and contact with non-Jews through non-Jewish schools or recreational programs, and neighborhood friendships.

The data on teachers and schools will be analyzed to determine whether there are relationships between student attitudes and the attitudes of teachers within individual classes or schools in the aggregate. The questionnaires given to teachers and principals will replicate the items given to children, thus making it possible to compare and contrast with regard to these values. In addition there will be questions about the school's curriculum and programs to affect intermovement attitudes, as well as questions on how staff and administration view the legitimacy of different movements and the prospect of cooperating with them on different issues.

It is too soon to fully specify the nature of the final research product, but it will encompass reports on the character of attitudes, reports on whether there was in fact a definable trend on the basis of age or movement of the school, and on the basis of other factors. Since dissemination and utilization are primary goals of this study, the results will be shared with the staffs of the participating schools and with the community-wide study advisory committee. If the results merit wider dissemination, they will be disseminated along with information for other communities on how they can conduct their own studies of themselves.

The vast, fissured terrain of intra-Jewish relations is refracted in the eyes of children. This project should help us clarify the ways in which children see and eventually reproduce this terrain. Hopefully, this study will offer answers to our questions and new tools for investigation and practice. We are optimistic that this endeavor will help us navigate our way through this terrain and find ways to bring different places in the Jewish world closer together.

Response to Daniel Steinmetz

HANAN ALEXANDER

Daniel Steinmetz raises interesting and important questions about the degree to which Jewish schools foster a sense of unity among Jews or, alternatively, emphasize more narrow ideological interests at the expense of intermovement tolerance. He has outlined in very broad strokes what a study proposal to explore denominational attitudes within Jewish schools would look like. The preliminary nature of his presentation offers an especially rewarding opportunity to a respondent because of the possibility that some of the questions raised might have a real impact on the final study design. In this spirit, I offer the following questions; first, concerning the focal issues which the study proposes to address, and second, concerning the method for addressing them.

The Focus on Denominationalism

1. Can we assume that all young Jews have denominational identities in an era when we question the degree to which young Jews identify with the Jewish people at all? Perhaps intermovement conflict is not a problem among the *amcha* of our people, young or old, but rather a problem among rabbis. As has often been pointed out, the question of "Who is a Jew?" may be code for the question "Who is a rabbi?" If so, then we should not expect to find much useful information about denominationalism by looking at adolescents in schools.

2. Is the problem of Jewish unity one of denominationalism, or rather a problem of the Orthodox (and the extreme elements among the Orthodox at that) vs. the non-Orthodox?

3. Does the author want to find out about the impact of the curriculum on Jewish youth? If so, is he concerned with what Elliot Eisner calls the "explicit curriculum"—what schools advertise that they intend to teach; the "implicit curriculum"—that which gets taught by the school culture and environment; or the null curriculum, that which doesn't get taught at all? Does he expect to see specific results from specific curricula? If so, which ones? Does he have any hypotheses concerning what kinds of attitudes he expects to find as a result of these curricula? If so, what are

they? Some interesting questions to ask in that connection concern the role of publishing houses such as Behrman, KTAV, and Torah Aurah in promoting tolerance among divergent Jewish groups, as compared with the role of denominationally sponsored curricula, such as "To See the World Through Jewish Eyes," published by UAHC,the Melton Curriculum of the Jewish Theological Seminary, and the publications of the Torah U'Mesorah movement. Other questions of interest might focus on the relative impact of supplemental and day schools in this connection.

4. It is not clear to me what is meant by the idea that this study will help provide a "map or compass" to schools, or that it will "facilitate a process in which local schools and educational policy-makers assess the performance of their own schools and evaluate steps that they can take to affect intermovement attitudes." Here, the author seems to have overstepped the bounds of empirical study. It is not a question for a psychological or sociological study whether or not anyone should do anything. To paraphrase the well-known educational philosopher Boyd Bode, a study may reveal that the number of burglaries has increased in a certain community. From this it does not follow, however, that the community should either increase the police force or encourage criminals. That depends entirely on the sort of community that is desired. For Steinmetz to make proposals to schools concerning evaluation standards in connection with intermovement tolerance would constitute an example of what the British moral philosopher G. E. Moore called the naturalistic fallacy of deriving a prescriptive "ought" from a descriptive "is." What is needed here is some careful philosophical analysis to develop an educational theory that reaches beyond denominationalism. Empirical data are useful, to be sure, in helping us to discover where we are and the paths we have followed to get there. It is up to conceptual inquiry, however, to take the lead in mapping out the road ahead. What, for example, is the degree of elasticity within any given ideology to which we can reasonably expect people to adhere, given some degree of integrity in their personal commitments?

Methodological Concerns

5. Why have schools been chosen as the first line of attack on this issue? I would have thought that movement affinities are much more powerfully developed in camps and youth movements. This point is emphasized, in this connection, by the concern with adolescents who tend to leave the school systems in droves after the bar mitzvah year but can still be found in the informal educational systems.

6. Why use a questionnaire format to address these issues? I would have thought that issues such as these call for a more qualitative approach, one that attempts to uncover the meanings that young people attribute to their experience. Open-ended, ethnographic interviews and participant observation will tell us much more about how young people understand themselves and other Jews than a short battery of questions. We would benefit from a much richer description of the attitudes of young people than whether they feel "warm, somewhat warm, neutral, somewhat cold, or cold" about youngsters who attend schools of other denominations.

7. In what ways does this study design fit into a tradition of scholarship either about the impact of schooling or the formation of identity. There is a considerable sociological literature concerning movement affiliation among adults. Does this study propose to draw on that literature? If so, how? There is a growing literature on the current state of teaching in Jewish schools. There have been studies in Boston, New York, and most recently by the schools of education of The University of Judaism and Hebrew Union College, together with the Bureau of Education in Los Angeles, concerning the state of Jewish teaching. From the Los Angeles study we have data about teachers who teach in several schools of different denominations, and about teachers who identify with one movement but teach for another. From the Schiff report in New York, we have information about the cognitive expectations of students in supplemental schools and the extent to which these are fulfilled. Professor Cutter and I returned only yesterday from the annual meeting of the Jewish Education Research Network at which we heard reports of a study concerning the state of nonformal Jewish education nationally. Here at the University of Judaism, I have conducted a study with my students in which we have tried to examine the role of ideology in the success of these programs. Jerry Friedman, who is with us today, and Gil Graff of the BJE have engaged in a study of good Jewish schools. The degree to which they have looked at the role of denominationalism in the schools is worthy of examination. Surely, these and other research programs are relevant to the Steinmetz project, and I urge him and his colleagues to reflect upon them.

Conclusion

At the Jewish Education Research Network Conference, Professor Lee Shulman of Stanford University commented on the importance of having scholars within secular universities take up the challenges of research on Jewish education. The efforts of Steinmetz and his colleagues at the University of Michigan represent a promising development in this connection, and the issues with which they are concerned are of great significance to fostering unity among our people in the years ahead. I hope that some of the questions I have raised will be helpful to them as they develop their instruments and process the results.

Response to Daniel Steinmetz

WILLIAM CUTTER

The Michigan Project addresses a major failing of our Jewish research system, namely, that we have rarely taken a close look at what Jewish children think of each other. Our approach has been either denominational, in which case we haven't been interested in what we think of each other, or "ecumenical," as in the case of the publishing houses, where it is prudent not to address the issue too openly. Thus today's paper is a reminder of our negligence. We might take this opportunity to look at other instances of "the other"—of outsiders and insiders—which we have also not examined: Jew vs. non-Jew, boy vs. girl, and so forth.

I have no doubt that the project will uncover numerous issues long overlooked, and I am certain that some of these will be unplanned outcomes. Both for its planned and its unplanned outcomes, much of the proposed research is welcome. We have, in short, not looked enough into our classrooms, and I welcome this opportunity to take a look.

However, I am bothered by a few questions that are suggested by Steinmetz's presentation and seem to me to color this study. I am ill-equipped to comment on quantification issues, and shall refer only passingly to questions of technical method.

1. The preliminary report indicates that "it is commonly believed that the intermovement conflicts of adults are embryonically present among children." While this may be true, I doubt that we can isolate the elements that constitute the relationship of youthful to adult attitudes. To do so we would have to presume a solution to the very next problem which the paper raises. Steinmetz says that "we have no idea just how Jewish children feel or think about other Jews." In fact, we have little idea about how they think at all. That is, how children process their evaluative and contrastive information is a mystery to adults. We know something about how they make contrasts from developmental psychology, but what we really don't know is what they do with the information. This is not a puckish nor a humorous deconstruction of Steinmetz's comment. I take quite seriously my experience with my son and his friends, which tells me that I cannot enter into their value systems when they are speaking about people who behave differently than they do.

2. Since the four goals of the project assume that there ought to be an amelioration of condition, there is an assumption that bad attitudes are lurking. Should an empirical study not first decide (my first point notwithstanding) whether those attitudes are really there? The associates of the project state that they are already worried about the problem. Will the study prejudice another kind of research: the kinds of revisions and redefinitions that other aspects of the Wilstein Institute's program encourage?

What is needed first is an examination of what we mean by "otherness" and how children might translate that notion. The role of otherness in identity formation, for example, seems a very important stage: children's sports teams, neighborhoods, commitments to Israel against one's friends' hostilities (as is the case with my own son). To what extent is one's own fragile identification forged out of the identity shaped by a mild competitiveness?

3. The Michigan project suggests that certain age levels are most critical for political thinking. But first we ought to find the keys for understanding the critical thinking that goes on at each age. The forms of address and discourse are certainly different when an adult is speaking with a ten-year-old and when he is speaking with a fourteen-year-old.

4. Related to this is the question of language on a broader scale. Can we presume to articulate or translate a person's imagination on the basis of our own figurative language? I suppose there are studies, and I even vaguely remember some. But the more I study the formation of language, the less confident I am that "arm" and "cold" mean the same thing to all people—and this is even less the case with children.

5. The relationships between student attitudes and teachers' attitudes will likely lead to entirely different sets of issues that need to be studied in any event. To what extent is the child's combative state of mind a factor in adopting or rejecting the values of his or her teachers?

7. I reject the idea that research constraints should limit this study to the classroom. And I apologize for the suggestion that there seem to be enough sponsors for this research to allow the study to move outside of the school. Restraint is, in any event, a poor determinant for where research ought to be conducted. And this is all the more so in an area such as this, where most children's attitudes seem to be developed on the street, in sports, and through the grapevines of children's fantasies and gossip. While Steinmetz does acknowledge these other factors, it would be my inclination to regard them as primary.

8. I suggest that if there are severe restraints on the study, the team focus on purely and narrowly empirical data: How many services from

other movements have you attended? When do you see people of other persuasions? Do you know how Orthodox (etc.) Jews feel about the following instances. . . . ?

9. Yet I acknowledge that comparative Judaism is a curriculum desideratum even though I can't prove this with data. It is interesting that the most extensive comparative Judaism textbooks come from private nondenominational publishers, such as Behrman House; and that probably says a lot about the harness our denominations find themselves in. But I believe that this study has not yet determined the distinction between the data it might discover and the data it wishes to uncover.

Jewish Studies in the University

BERNARD D. COOPERMAN

Over the course of the last twenty or thirty years, one of the dreams of modern Jewry has apparently been realized: Jewish culture has become a recognized and accepted part of the general university curriculum. Of course, the Hebrew Bible and, to an extent, the Hebrew language have always enjoyed a prominent place in Western education because of their position in Christian history, but in recent years we have seen a phenomenal rise in the number of courses dealing with postbiblical Jews, with their history, religion, and literature. Not only the content has changed; the orientation of these courses is radically different from what it was a generation ago. Jewish studies courses are now taught largely by and for Jews, and approach their subject from the point of view of a living Jewish culture seeking self-understanding, not from that of a Christian society interested in its, so to speak, "prehistory."

Jewish studies have become a "growth industry," and the signs of prosperity are everywhere. There is at least one, and usually more than one, full-time instructor in Jewish studies at almost every university in this country. The Association for Jewish Studies, the basic professional organization of academics in this area, counts well over 700 full members, that is, individuals who are employed in a recognized academic institution. Every major academic press in the country has an active list of Jewish studies books on topics ranging from Palestinian archaeology to the Holocaust, and from medieval philosophy to Yiddish literature. International conferences abound, new journals appear with alarming frequency, and weekends with distinguished scholars have become a necessary part of the synagogue calendar throughout the land.

From many points of view, these developments must be counted an unqualified success story. This is certainly true for the Jewish academics themselves. Not so very long ago the only jobs available to Judaica scholars were in afternoon schools, day schools, or, at best, Hebrew colleges. I myself was educated as a boy by a fine group of dedicated European-born teachers who all held advanced university degrees but were nevertheless forced to spend their days drilling ten-year-olds in how to translate *Humash-Rashi*. On the one hand, I wish such teachers were available for my children; on the other, I am grateful that I am not forced to make my living as they did. I and my colleagues can reasonably aspire to positions in universities and to all the benefits that come with such appointments—a decent salary, health insurance, sabbaticcal leaves, and, most of all, considerably enhanced status in the community at large. Proof positive of the change in attitude toward Jewish studies came to me just a few days ago at the wedding of one of my former students, who had gone on to a promising career with a large New York law firm. His mother confided in me that she was somewhat disappointed: she had hoped he would become a professor of Jewish studies![1]

The development of Jewish studies must also be counted a success from the point of view of the Jewish community. For one thing, it represents a tremendous net savings to the community. It is obviously far cheaper to give a million dollars or so to some university to establish a position in Jewish studies and let that institution worry about the day-to-day bills for classrooms and libraries, pools and gymnasia, building maintenance, secretarial help and office supplies—that is, in other words, the thousand and one things that are the really expensive elements in running a school and which otherwise would have to be paid for out of the already stretched resources of the Jewish community. True, we may be perturbed by the "alienation" of Jewish charity dollars to secular institutions, but I suspect that these funds would never have reached Jewish coffers in any case.

From a pedagogical point of view we may also greet this development with satisfaction. Present realities dictate that the vast majority of Jewish young people will attend secular universities where they will pursue areas of study largely removed from Jewish concerns. Most of these young people have only an elementary knowledge (if that) of Judaism, Jewish history, and Jewish thought; most have virtually no functional knowledge of Hebrew. When they think of Jewish things, they think in the very elementary terms that they remember from Hebrew/religious school or in terms of youth-group and synagogue experiences which aimed not at educating them but at generating enthusiasm and making them identify. Inevitably, many of these young people dismiss Judaism and their Jewish roots as simply unequal to the intellectual excitement and rigor of the university world. By making Jewish studies available at the university level, we have given these young people another chance to appreciate the positive and sophisticated aspects of Jewish culture. We have provided a forum within which our children can pursue Jewish subjects on a level beyond that of elementary school. We have legitimized these subjects and made them attractive by "neutralizing" the environment in which they are taught.

But as you may have guessed from my tone, I am not quite sure that developments are nearly as positive as I have so far described. For one thing, enrollment figures are still discouragingly low, and although I have no firm data, my impression is that they are getting lower.[2] Certainly we are failing to attract Gentiles to our courses; at Harvard even the four or five non-Jews who used to take my Hebrew or modern Jewish history courses have disappeared in recent years. It is difficult to pinpoint a reason for the drop-off in enrollment. Some would point to the decline in support for Israel: Israel is no longer "in," and few care about its history or culture. Others point more specifically to the recent unrest there, which has made travel to Israel less attractive: if students don't intend to spend a summer there, why learn the language? Sometimes we can point to structural features of university curricula which are totally beyond the control of students and Jewish studies faculty and which make our courses less attractive: the abolition of a language requirement, or increased "great books" requirements, for example, make our courses less useful to students trying to amass enough credits to graduate. Yet others point to the radically utilitarian attitude that supposedly prevails on university campuses. If you are bound for business school, you don't stop en route to smell the daisies or to study Maimonides, especially if the Maimonides course is not a guaranteed A. But whatever the explanation, the reality is that with rare exceptions Jewish studies courses do not attract large numbers of students. The field remains a "parochial" subject appealing primarily to the already converted. This is not in itself a condemnation of the enterprise; raising the level of discourse among involved Jewish young people is obviously to be desired.

But there is worse news yet. While it is undoubtedly true that we raise the level of our students' understanding of the Jewish past and present, it is equally true that the overwhelming bulk of our courses remain nevertheless at a quite introductory level. First of all, because there are very few majors in Jewish studies (after all, the field leads almost nowhere professionally), most students will take only one course with us over the course of their four years in college. Inevitably they will pick a broad survey course or an introductory language course.[3] In other words, the overwhelming majority of students in our courses will remain at the introductory level. So what? After all, this is true in all fields. Indeed, it is an underlying principle of American higher education that we aim to give students an introduction to many different aspects of human culture rather than encourage them to specialize in the European fashion.

Moreover, even an introduction at the university level is much more than was available previously. But in the case of Jewish studies we have reason not to be satisfied with a mere introduction. I and my colleagues are paying the price for the Jewish community's failure to educate its young. Every course in American history at a good university can assume that the students already know the basic outlines: who the colonists were, when the Revolution took place, what the Civil War was all about, and so forth. The student will be fluent in English and will have read widely in the cultural legacy of his country, whether the classics he was assigned in high school or the pop music she listened to on her radio. I, on the other hand, must assume that my students know next to nothing about the Jewish past, and that they are functional, and more likely total, illiterates in the language and culture of contemporary Jewish civilization. Many if not most students taking Spanish or French at college already have studied those languages for a number of years. Almost all students taking Hebrew start from *alef bet*. In the end, most of the Jewish studies enterprise is thus necessarily limited to a quite elementary level of instruction.

Still, you might say, even if the situation is not perfect, it is a definite improvement. But an improvement over what? Over total ignorance? That is obviously correct but also trivial. Also, the fact is that the rise of Jewish studies at secular universities has been accompanied by the demise or at least the serious decline of many Jewish-sponsored colleges and institutions of higher education. Did the one cause the other? I don't know. But I cannot help but briefly tell a personal anecdote. When I was applying to graduate school in Jewish studies, I made the grand tour of a number of institutions, hoping to speak to heads of programs and to learn into which program I would best fit. At one institution, the professor asked me an apparently innocent question: why was I interested in entering this field? I mentioned that I had a strong personal Jewish background and that I wanted to pursue this matter further at the academic level. To my astonishment, I was then mercilessly tongue-lashed for what seemed an hour. The purpose of the university, I was told, was not to solve my religious problems but to make me a scholar. Were I to get a Ph.D. the university would be declaring that I was competent, not religious. And so on. . . . Needless to say, I never finished filling out the application for that terrifying institution. But that is not the end of the story. Some years later, the same professor had become the head of a prominent, Jewish-sponsored institution, and at a major professional meeting he told his colleagues that it was only such Jewish institutions that kept alive the spirit and the content of Jewish civilization.

In fact the professor was right both times. The university is not devoted to promoting the ideals of Jewish civilization; it is, at least in theory, devoted to a dispassionate analysis of culture per se. And if we as a community put all our Jewish educational eggs in such a universalist basket, we run the risk of losing the kind of enthusiasm and commitment that created our culture in the first place.

Let me take this point a little further by moving from the level of the institution to that of the individual. To me and to others it seems clear that the rise of Jewish studies has meant the appearance of a cadre of academics who have in a real sense supplanted the traditional Jewish intellectual leadership. It is the university professor who is now regarded as the expert on Jewish law and lore, on Jewish history and Israeli politics, on the Jewish community and its future. (I have not heard of many synagogues that invited the rabbi of a neighboring temple to be the scholar-in-residence for a weekend.) And here is the danger: These Jewish academics—the major contact most of our young people will have with Jewish thought and history on a sophisticated level—owe neither institutional nor intellectual loyalty to any part of the Jewish community. Indeed, at least some of them are not even practicing Jews. I remember well a recent case in which Jewish money funded a new Jewish studies chair and the university offered the position to a man who had been, at least at one time in his life, an apostate! I do not believe that Jewish studies at the university level can, or should, be taught only by Jews. I do believe, however, that it is in the interests of the Jewish community to be sure that its children are educated by people committed to Jewish group survival. It must therefore question the value of Jewish studies courses in achieving that aim.

Of course, the vast majority of Jewish studies teachers are indeed personally committed to Jewish life and Jewish continuity in one way or another. Given the tremendous amount of background training required in many areas of Jewish life, it could almost not be otherwise. Only those with deep personal concern for the issues involved are likely to even think of entering such a demanding field. (There is a great deal of truth in the observation which I first heard from my friend, the historian John Marino, that medievalists are all lapsed Jesuits, lapsed Calvinists, or lapsed Orthodox Jews. And of course, this sort of lapse never implies unconcern.) The very high number of *hovshei kippah* among the members of the AJS is a good indication of the true state of the field. But self-selection can guarantee only so much. Gershon Hundert of McGill has recently suggested that a number of structural factors actually lead the Jewish academic—no matter what his personal orientation—to be uninvolved or only minimally involved with parochial Jewish concerns on campus.[4] Hundert suggests, in fact, that Jewish studies professors were "in the academy precisely in order to avoid becoming engaged."

But the issue is not merely linked to the individual professor. I would like to suggest that the very nature of Jewish studies is rooted in ambivalence. The attempt to apply the methodologies of the secular sciences as taught in universities to the traditional fields of Jewish studies dates back at least to the founding of the *Verein für die Kultur und Wissenschaft der Juden* in Germany in 1819. It is important to note that even then, at the very start of the nineteenth century, the bivalent nature of the endeavor was apparent. The high-sounding words and lofty ambitions of the young, university-educated German Jews who established this society point simultaneously in two directions, one inward and one outward. On the one hand, they were hoping to educate the Jewish people and purify Jewish tradition. This was not merely a philanthropic endeavor. As with all modern Diaspora Jews who live in some sense in a state of permanent but partial alienation from their Jewishness, these young intellectuals had to recreate the Jews and Judaism in their own image and thus make a place for themselves among their people. On the other hand, the founders hoped to disseminate information about the Jews among Gentiles and thus increase respect for Judaism. Here too, we should understand their goal in very personal terms: in effect, they were seeking to legitimize themselves as Jews in the eyes of their non-Jewish neighbors. Nahum Glatzer described the situation well when he pictured the Jewish scholar as "a *homo novus* in search of a home in a world that was not yet ready to grant him this privilege."[5]

As is well known, the Verein itself must be counted something of a failure. Many of the early members, including the jurist Eduard Gans and the poet Heinrich Heine, would soon convert to Christianity, at least in part to further their academic and professional careers. But this very "failure" highlights for us what has proven to lie at the heart of the effort to introduce Jewish studies into the university. This effort is not a "neutral" and "objective" support of scientific research; it is an integral part of the struggle to redefine Jewish identity in—and this is the essence—*purely secular terms*. In Jewish studies, Jewish intellectuals are seeking to legitimize themselves in their own eyes and in the eyes of their peers. Several scholars have recently written about the dual loyalties of Jewish studies professors, and of the mixing of the sacred and the secular in the field.[6] What I would like to stress is that the professor is not just personally torn between two worlds; his discipline is, of necessity, ambivalent, for it is ambivalence that gave it birth. If the growth of Jewish studies has made very little practical difference to Jewish life on the campus, as Gershon Hundert suggests, it may well be because of the nature of the field itself.[7]

It is always dangerous to define a phenomenon in terms of its roots. Surely the field of Jewish studies has grown beyond the problems of its founders over a century and a half ago. And of course it has, not only because methodologies have changed and new texts (in the broadest sense) have become available, but especially and inevitably because we have changed and therefore the questions we ask are different. Let me give just one example which may help to convey more concretely this change in historical approach.

I often ask my students to compare the spare, minimalist article on anti-Semitism in the *Jewish Encyclopedia* of 1903 with the much-enlarged, dare I say bloated, entry in the *Encyclopaedia Judaica* of 1972. Whereas the first restricted the term to a passing phenomenon in Hellenistic Egypt and a fringe political movement in late-nineteenth-century Europe, the latter article finds anti-Semitism everywhere! This changed perception of anti-Semitism is representative, I believe, of the impact on modern Jewish identity of the Holocaust and the rise of the State of Israel. At the beginning of the century, Jews were willing to believe in their neighbors' essential goodwill, and indeed had no choice but to do so. Anti-Semitism had to be a restricted phenomenon because otherwise there would have appeared to be no hope for the Jewish people. In our own day, to put the matter in very simplistic terms, Jews are not willing totally to trust their neighbors, nor, in a sense, do we have to. Ironically, therefore, we are freer than our predecessors to indulge our fears and find anti-Semitism in every heart and under every bush and rock.

That change in the view of Jews' relation to the world has also changed the task of Jewish historians and thinkers. A century ago, Jewish historians were busily trying to demonstrate the positive contributions of our people to those civilizations which had tolerated us.[8] Today, the agenda is obviously different—although I am still reprimanded by Jews who are offended when, in a lecture, I deviate from the old program and suggest that Jews may not have all been pious scholars, honest merchants, and upstanding citizens who were mercilessly persecuted by their fanatical and ignorant neighbors. Although I must admit that I find the present Jewish fascination with anti-Semitism both distasteful and essentially ahistorical, I am at least freed from the apologetic needs which dictated its historiography in the past. Historians are, like everybody else, creatures of their own time, and we ask questions of the past in order to find answers for the present. While our choice of a subject may often be serendipitous, historians must, of necessity, have an overall approach to that subject, for the questions we ask, for the type of answers we give. If not, we are nothing but antiquarians collecting random and meaningless facts.

What then is today's agenda? Some months ago, an Israeli colleague, a distinguished historian of Jewish thought, suggested to me that there is no hidden agenda to Jewish scholarship—especially in Israel. I disagree. While it will remain the task of another generation to offer a final evaluation of our motives as historians and of our success or failure in achieving our goals, it seems to me that certain tendencies are already becoming clear. More than anything else, it seems to me that we are engaged in searching for, and defining, an *authentic* Jewish culture.

To say that contemporary Jewish studies is a "quest for authenticity" may strike you as nothing more than inflated grandiloquence and empty rhetoric, but I mean something quite specific by it. Let me use my own field of historical study as an example. It strikes me as unsurprising that most of the Jewish history written here in America in the last generation occupies itself with the medieval and early modern periods, and that it focuses primarily on internal issues: the development of comunal organization, rabbinic thought, popular piety, mysticism, and so on.[9] To the extent that other concerns are dealt with—issues of Jewish participation in Western culture or the legitimacy and antiquity of a Jewish presence in a given region, to name two—they are treated in a new, and it seems to me more inwardly turned, manner. Why? I believe this focus has become dominant because it allows the historian to deal with a time and place when Jewishness was not hyphenated, when, rather, it stood on its own in its confrontation with outside cultures. Jews may have taken, and taken freely, from those cultures, but they did so from a position of strength. On the one hand, we refuse to dismiss Jewish culture as mere credulity, as mere traditionalism, as merely *minhag avoteinu be-yadeinu*. We insist that Jewish thought can and must be treated with the same sophisticated analytical categories which are applied elsewhere. On the other hand, we insist that the study of Jewish culture and society is an end sufficient unto itself. We speak not about the contributions of Jews to outside culture nor even, at least in the same way as we once did, of cultural symbiosis. (Scholem has warned us about symbioses which exist only in the minds of one of the parties.) Rather we speak of active polemic, of a Jewish society aware of its surroundings and in a constant confrontational, or at least dialectical, dialogue with them. The historian engaged in describing the tax structure of the medieval community or the site of a typical premodern Jewish family is just as much involved in the search for independent authenticity as the historian researching the pedigree of a halakhic or philosophical concept—all of these scholars are looking for an independently functioning Jewish world informed by and in turn shaping an autonomous Jewish culture.

What I have traced here is I suppose, less an agenda than a mood, less a programmatic statement than a description of the atmosphere within which Jewish studies are carried out. To me that mood and atmosphere seem positive, both personally and academically, and appear to have allowed for tremendous strides in the field. There are many reasons for the new mood, most importantly the existence of the State of Israel. And I have no doubt that so long as this mood and atmosphere continue, the pursuit of Jewish studies at the secular university will be "good for the Jews." But I cannot leave without a word of caution about the specific relation between Jewish studies and the formation of Jewish identity, the subject of our conference.

As I mentioned before, the vast majority of academics engaged in Jewish studies are themselves deeply committed to the continuity of Jewish life and values. It seems to me, however, that they perceive that commitment quite differently from many other, equally committed Jews; and the values of Jewish studies professors may often be at odds with the attitudes and positions of their rabbinic and communal colleagues. For instance, change is a given in the world of historical scholarship. For many Jews, whether Orthodox or Reform, change is something that applies only in the outside world, but never in the Jewish holy of holies. For the scholar, the past must be treated as critically as the present—anathema to the nostalgia buffs (whether Yiddishists or neo-Hasidim) who make up much of our audience. For the scholar, Jews' past ideological, spiritual, and political choices were conditioned by events and circumstances. That doesn't make them less valid, only more intelligible. Again, this is not a position easily shared by most of our community.

What I am suggesting, in short, is that contemporary Jewish studies represents a totally new kind of scholarship and intellectual endeavor—one radically removed from the rabbi's preaching. It is not my task as a scholar to advocate a specific philosophy or way of life which was practiced in the past; quite to the contrary, I try to structure my lectures specifically to challenge and contradict what I think are my students' assumptions about their past. That is not because I am spiteful or enjoy "playing with their heads"—although I suppose I am, and do. It is because it is my task to force them to think critically—about the Jewish past as about everything else. It is my job to stop them from accepting the pap and commonplaces that their society has taught them, to teach them how to stand outside their own society, and to teach them how to build their own identities as Jews and as human beings out of sound building blocks. If I do not accomplish that, I have failed.

I began my lecture by suggesting that Jewish studies has clearly achieved success. I suggested, however, that the success is far from complete, and I have tried to issue a warning to the Jewish community that Jewish studies should not be relied upon as the automatic answer to our pedagogical needs. I have ended by trying to find the essence of the aim of Jewish studies, and hence by trying to identify the manner in which Jewish studies will impinge on the identity and lives of our students. I would suggest that, to the extent that s/he is successful, the Jewish studies professor is an extremely dangerous person, for like all scholars s/he believes in the primacy of knowledge, the independence of the mind, and the obligation of individuals to think for themselves. The scholar is as much a threat to Jewish society as was Socrates to Athenian—and we all know what happened to Socrates.

I must end with one brief story. A course which I particularly enjoy teaching is a survey of modern Jewish history. In the course, I try to make the students understand and empathize with the agonizing and traumatic challenges which the modern world presented to the Jewish people. I try to show them how different Jews responded in radically different ways to the trauma of modernity—how Orthodoxy and Reform, the Bund and the Zionists, modern literature and the yeshiva all represent efforts to rebuild the Jewish identity after the old, "organic," and unselfconscious link with the past was irreparably shattered. My intent is to show them that none of these responses were necessarily "copouts"—that they were equally valid and equally tempting for different parts of the Jewish population. To the extent that some failed, it is the student's task to discover why. Several years ago a student brought me a copy of the text on which his rabbi in Chicago had based his Yom Kippur sermon. The text was a maudlin song by a Boston-based group called Safam. It told the story of horrible pogroms in Russia, of a grandfather loyal to tradition who had died, of a family that had forgotten its Jewishness. The song, of course, advocates a return to making Kiddush on Friday nights on the grounds that "who will be our zeydies if not we?" The sermon was apparently a big hit; not a dry eye was left in the house. Said my student: "Isn't this just what your course was about?" I didn't have the heart to tell this student who loved his rabbi that he had missed the point of my course completely. I couldn't tell him that unlike his rabbi I am not in the business of advocating nostalgia or a grandfather's religion. I couldn't tell him that I don't believe the past must be preserved merely because it is the past. I just flunked the kid.

Notes

1. The debate about the motives behind American Jewry's dedicated pursuit of a university education and entry into the liberal professions is of course old and to a large extent sterile. There is no way to divide between the desire for monetary comforts and the respect for education which are intertwined in the phrase "my son the doctor." It should be noted, however, that the effort to distinguish the two aspects is not without precedent. The *Beit ha-Levi,* R. Joseph Soloveichik, commented disparagingly, more than a hundred years ago, on those wealthy Jews who sought to marry their daughters to boys who were scholars. "It is clear," wrote Rabbi Soloveichik, "that Torah [i.e., learning] is an important value to [the father], but it gives no pleasure.... He wants his daughter... to enjoy this world with a carriage, etc." (*Beit ha-Levi* to Genesis 24:37–38). I don't know about the rabbinate, but a professorship of Jewish studies is definitely an acceptable job "for a Jewish boy."

2. A subject which deserves analysis, and which cannot, unfortunately, be treated in the present context, is the emergence of the yeshiva as an alternative model of Jewish higher education both in America and in Israel. Suffice it to say that at least in Israel the yeshiva world, which once provided the best candidates for graduate school, is increasingly able to hold on to its elite and give them acceptable jobs and status. A glance around the Jewish Studies Reading Room at the Jewish National Library will suffice to convince anyone of the increasingly Orthodox tenor of research in Jewish studies there. The relevance of this change to our entire perception of the present and future development of Jewish culture cannot be underestimated.

3. I am ignoring the question of whether the extremely popular courses in such fields as war in the Middle East or the Holocaust qualify for Jewish studies. I will point out, at least, that they add little to a student's understanding of Jewish civilization.

4. Gershon David Hundert, "The Impact of Jewish Studies on Jewish Life on Campus," *Association for Jewish Studies Newsletter,* 2nd series, 1 (Fall 1988): 6 f.

5. Nahum N. Glatzer, "The Beginnings of Modern Jewish Studies," in *Studies in Nineteenth-Century Jewish Intellectual History,* ed. Alexander Altmann (Cambridge: Harvard University Press, 1964), p. 45.

6. Arthur Green, "Jewish Studies and Jewish Faith," *Tikkun* 1 (1986); Susan Handelman, "The State of Contemporary Literary Criticism and Jewish Studies," *Association for Jewish Studies Newsletter,* 2nd Series, 1 (Fall 1988): 3–5, 16.

7. My own teacher, Joseph Hayim Yerushalmi, explored the implications of the

"ironic awareness that the very mode in which [the historian] delves into the Jewish past represents a decisive break with that past," in the last chapter of his *Zakhor: Jewish History and Jewish Memory* (Seattle: University of Washington Press, 1982).

8. See the insightful remarks of Bernard Lewis, "The Pro-Islamic Jews," reprinted in *Islam in History*, pp. 123–137, and idem, *History Remembered, Recovered, Invented* (Princeton: Princeton University Press, 1975), pt. III. In the field with which I am most familiar, nothing could illustrate this type of tendentiousness better than Moritz Gudemann's idealized picture of the relations between Italian Jews and their non-Jewish neighbors in his *Die Geshichte des Erziehungswesens und der Kultur der abendlandischen Juden* (1880–88). Gudemann, chief rabbi of Vienna, was reportedly instrumental in keeping the first Zionist congress out of his city because Herzl's nationalist goals undermined the Jewish effort at integration into general society.

9. Of course I am aware of, and do not mean to slight, the distinguished contributions of American Jewish historians in fields ranging from the biblical to the modern, but it seems to me that both *rov binyan* and *rov minyan* of efforts have been centered in the areas I have suggested. In this light, the changing emphases in the historiography of American Jews are quite interesting to watch. The situation is quite different, of course, in Israel, although not without parallels to the American scene.

Response to Bernard Cooperman

ARNOLD J. BAND

Cooperman's observations on Jewish studies in the university contain, as they must, much widely known information on the dynamic—and problematic—emergence of Jewish studies in the North American University in the past twenty-five years: the creation of positions and programs in almost all significant institutions of higher learning; the generation of a community of about 800 scholars with advanced degrees in Jewish studies; the intellectual ambiguities engendered by this phenomenon. He offers an interesting formulation of the nature of the Jewish commitment of these scholars and their "quest for authenticity"; he even suggests that this cadre of Judaica scholars has replaced the rabbis as the intellectual authorities of the Jewish communities. And yet something seems to be troubling him; and what troubles him, I suggest, is not well articulated or properly addressed. The following remarks, then, are my version of what I think Cooperman is trying to say.

He cites the paradoxical decline in the quality and quantity of students taking courses in this field despite the proliferation of positions. This, in itself, is a source of much anxiety, as it should be, but is rarely discussed in public fora. What both masks this decline from the eyes of the public and highlights it for the professionals in the field is the well-publicized proliferation in the past decade of endowed chairs which often cannot be filled by outstanding scholars, and the publication of many glossy newsletters touting the great achievements of little-known programs. This contrast of legitimate achievement and hype, so characteristic of much of American life, seems to contaminate Jewish studies as a field and undermine its claims to "authenticity." And this is indeed disturbing.

I would like to address these points in the light of my experience with the Association for Jewish Studies. I was a founding member, its president for three years (1972–75), and the editor of its newsletter until 1986. This professional experience put me in touch with many of the activities in the field over a significant period. I will ask the question: To what extent is the condition of Jewish studies an indication of something going on in the Jewish community? Obviously, if I am asking this question, I suspect that it is.

Some twelve years ago I began to note in my editorials in the *AJS Newsletter* that the number of undergraduate students was dropping, and that the surge of graduate students had peaked and would soon decline. These predictions were based on fragmentary yet hard evidence which I was constantly receiving from colleagues in the field. It did not surprise me that those remarks elicited no response when published. Only in the past three or four years have I begun to hear acknowledgments—still mostly in private—of the accuracy of my predictions. With few (questionable) exceptions, the numbers have dropped precipitously, as Cooperman reports on the basis of his Harvard experience. The fund of knowledge with which students come to our courses is embarrassing, and their Hebrew rarely qualifies them for second-year college status.

When I first wrote on this topic, I suggested three possible reasons for the drop. First, the birthrate in this country began to drop in 1964 and perhaps a bit earlier among Jews. This realization led to what I call "Band's Law of Education": you can't teach students who haven't been born. My demography might have been unscientific, but I think most sociologists would agree with me today on this point. Second, the American economy has changed since 1968: it is increasingly difficult to support a family on one salary, and Jewish parents, with their justifiable sensitivity to issues of security, both financial and physical, direct their children to "purposeful" pursuits. While these two suggestions have quantifiable bases, my third suggestion was merely speculative and was rejected out of hand in 1977: the mythic image of an invincible, pure Israel projected after the Six-Day War dissipated rapidly after the Yom Kippur War. Ironically, today, when the decline in student interest is cited, the decline in Israel's prestige is the first reason one usually hears.

To these three reasons I would now add one more. Until the early 1970s, there were two natural pools from which students came to Jewish studies: the children of Holocaust survivors or refugees from Europe in the 1930s, and the graduates of Orthodox day schools. The passage of a generation of history has eliminated the first group as potential Jewish studies majors or graduate students; the children of survivors are now in their late thirties. As for the graduates of day schools in 1989, they now find themselves as part of bustling communities of pious Jews, many involved in challenging aspects of high technology. While university-oriented Jewish studies may provide a few with the possible involvement that Cooperman calls "the quest for authenticity," most, I believe, feel perfectly fulfilled within their own societies, their families, and their work. America accepts them and encourages them, too, to become Yuppies.

This brings me to the second major point which, I feel, Cooperman makes. He offers a sophisticated characterization of the type of Jewish commitment found in the new generation of scholars: a quest for authenticity. Using the example of his fellow historians, he contrasts their attitudes with those of Jewish historians of the previous century and praises his contemporaries for avoiding the "contributionist" bias and focusing, instead, upon "the independently functioning Jewish world informed by, and in turn, shaping, an autonomous Jewish culture." Still, he appears to me to attribute a bit too much power to the new generation of scholars. "To me and to others," Cooperman asserts, "it seems clear that the rise of Jewish studies has meant the appearance of a cadre of academics who have in a real sense supplanted the traditional Jewish intellectual leadership." I would argue that in a society as diffuse as ours, one cannot situate the seat of Jewish intellectual power as easily as one perhaps could in the premodern period, when the corporate structure of the Jewish community still obtained. I wonder, furthermore, if it is indeed true that "it is the university professor who is now regarded as the expert on Jewish law and lore, on Jewish history and Israeli politics, on the Jewish community and its future." It is an intriguing idea, enormously gratifying to the ego of the professor, but is it true?

I find yet another irony in this contention. Cooperman speaks passionately of a quest for authenticity. A quest for authenticity implies, for me, a recognition that something close at hand is not authentic, and I would argue that what the professor finds inauthentic is not traditional Judaism, but the various manifestations of contemporary Jewish communal life. One manifestation of this inauthenticity is clearly the hype attending the creation of chairs in Jewish studies; another might be the popularity of courses on the Holocaust. This is the irony: Cooperman would have us believe, I suggest, that the university professor is now regarded as the intellectual leader of a community which the professor himself, wittingly or unwittingly, finds inauthentic. This, if true, would certainly be bad faith.

I have no idea which of the above-mentioned causes, or what other ones, are specifically responsible for the decline in student interest in Jewish studies, but I am certain that the ones I mentioned are contributory, and that the decline, therefore, is an indication of certain tendencies within the society in which we live. Anyone interested in Jewish identity should heed these signs. If we agree with Cooperman, as I do, that the emergence of this community of Judaica scholars is a positive development, we should be concerned for its welfare, investigate the causes of potential erosion, and do something, if possible, to counteract them.

It is precisely at this point that Cooperman fails to make the practical point which his paper suggests. Living in a society that presumes to be shaped by cost-accountants, one might easily arrive at the conclusion that given the decline in the number of students interested in Jewish studies, one should divert community resources elsewhere. To this possible conclusion I would like to offer the rebuttal which I am positive Cooperman would also want to make. To begin with, the cadre of scholars trained in Jewish studies in the past twenty-five years has immensely enriched Jewish life in this country. Though I would not go as far as Cooperman in stating that they comprise the new Jewish intellectual leadership, I cannot escape the evidence of my eyes: I look around me at this gathering, or at the faces in other assemblages within the Jewish community, and I see people whom I have known for years from meetings of the Association for Jewish Studies or whose articles I have read in a variety of academic or academically informed journals.

Aside from the evidence of my senses, there is historical experience. Jewish history is very long; it has its rises and declines; one never knows what will happen next or where it will happen. The emergence of this new cadre of Jewish scholars was totally unexpected. Just think: After the destruction of World War II, who would have predicted the emergence of an indigenous cadre of such scholars in this country? Even more: Who in the leadership of American Jewry in the late 1940s could think of such a possibility and plan for the future? The only visionary of this sort whose name springs to mind is Mordecai Kaplan, and he did not command a wide following. The Jewish community has inherited a sizable cadre of Jewishly committed yet independent scholars—of varying achievement, to be sure—for which it did not plan and in whose higher education it has invested relatively few funds. Belatedly, in the late 1970s, the organized community began to realize that this resource exists.

Finally, if the study of historical memory has anything to teach us, I would contend, it is that we should not try to shape future Jewish identity solely in the light of the most recent demographic statistics. A community which has awakened, however belatedly, to the realization that it should support Jewish studies in postsecondary institutions should not curtail its support because there are, at present, fewer students registered in courses now than there were ten years ago. None of us can predict what the numbers will be ten years from now, but we would all agree that a viable community must have an intellectual elite to assess, preserve, and disseminate the lessons of the past.

Response to Bernard Cooperman

STEVEN J. ZIPPERSTEIN

Bernard Cooperman's insightful paper examines three themes: the role of Jewish studies in shaping the commitments of Jewish students; the Judaica scholar's role in the community; and the identity of such scholars. I must admit that what most impressed me about his presentation was the way in which it confirmed a suspicion that I've had for some time—Harvard *is* different from UCLA. There on the Charles is a place where, or so Bernard tells us, university professors feel they are paid decently, are accorded status even in the Jewish community, and—this is what amazed me above all—where the mothers of graduating law students wish their children had become Judaica professors! I've long felt that regional and local factors are insufficiently acknowledged in Jewish history—indeed, my book on Odessa Jewry addresses this very theme—but rarely have impressions been more vividly reinforced.

It is Bernard's last theme, the identity of Jewish academics, that I would like to discuss here.

Bernard is right, of course, when he identifies the very enterprise of Jewish studies as embodying a fundamental ambivalence—a tension between commitment and criticism, attachment and detachment, belonging and the distance essential for responsible scholarship. Such tension is, as Yerushalmi suggests, heightened by the conflict between drastically different epistemological understandings of the general Jewish public and Judaica scholars on the one hand, and on the other hand, the consciousness of the latter being shaped by a cyclical worldview that stresses repetition, essential sameness, that rejects the prospect of change.

Judaica specialists experience this tension in a particularly vivid fashion, since the decision to enter this field is frequently, as Bernard observes, shaped to a large extent by abiding extra-academic attachments. Indeed, in any graduate history program in the United States, for example, the vast majority of students and faculty work in the American or European fields. The world, as reflected in our history departments, is still the Western world, and France, England, Germany, perhaps above all France (my department has seven French historians, one-tenth of the faculty), represent fields of paramount importance. Even a moderately self-conscious graduate student is aware of these institutional realities, and the decision to embrace a so-called small field—less widely accessible, often less prestigious, considered more likely to be narrow and parochial—such a decision is rarely accidental. It is something of an existential choice.

I thought of this recently during a lunchtime conversation with a colleague. I remarked that several members of our department were at work on biographies—a mutual friend of ours on Van Gogh; I mentioned that I was writing about Ahad Ha'am. "Ah, Van Gogh," he replied. Ahad Ha'am elicited not a word. The encounter reminded me of a quip of the great Yiddish poet Glatshtayn: "What is a Yiddish poet? A Yiddish poet is someone who must read Auden, But Auden need not read him."

People I know who are young, smart, ambitious and have gone into Jewish studies have done so, at least in part, to live their lives in a secularized, pluralistic *beis medresh*. For me such a time is best represented by the dark, noisy YIVO Institute library, but many such rooms—and many of our private studies—nourish our Jewish souls in ways that neither synagogues nor federations nor even egalitarian minyans can. Our books are naturally written, above all, for academics. But we also hope that they will have some wider resonance now or later; that they will help shape a Jewry less obsessed with horror, or less moved by rank nostalgia, less impressed with Monty Hall—a Jewry more like us. Bernard Cooperman says that people like ourselves constitute "as much a threat to Jewish society as . . . Socrates," that our primary task is to challenge the status quo, to unsettle, to leave our listeners—our people—uneasy.

Perhaps so. But does this function as gadflies satisfy our needs as Jews? What does membership in Jewry mean for those who spend most of their time apart, critical, hugely skeptical—as we are and must be?

As I read Bernard's draft, I reflected on Berdichewsky's image of a restless man, his image of himself, beside a table cleared of weekday books and covered with a white Sabbath cloth. He is sitting alone and restless—unable to proceed with his daily chores and yet equally unable to attach himself to a larger community of Jews. (Here, as is so often true of Berdichewsky, images speak more coherently than arguments.) Are we to live as Jews primarily by flunking hapless young men or women who return from rapturous evenings with their rabbis and prove themselves unable to understand what we've taught them? Please understand me: I expect that I, too, would have failed the student. But this student enjoys something that many of my colleagues do not and for which we hunger: a community in which he and his family come to cry and laugh, to celebrate without critical distance and skepticism. And I find it inadequate to live my Jewish life primarily by chastising the likes of him.

I say this, of course, not to chastise Bernard but, rather, to admit that this is precisely how I, and most of my closest friends who are also Judaica scholars, live as Jews. We engage in *limmud Torah* far from any community, except for one's community of academic peers. The extent to which we are involved in communal affairs is to wring our hands, to roll our eyes in disbelief, to correct errors that we know full well will be repeated again and again.

It is true, I would suggest, even for many of my Orthodox colleagues. Take, for example, a recent session on contemporary Orthodox Judaism at the Association for Jewish Studies which, I admit, I didn't attend but which was described to me. Here a *frum* panel regaled a mostly *frum* (and very large) audience with tales of ultra-Orthodox excesses, bigotries, and just plain silliness. One felt, or so I was told, that here was a sort of annual alternative minyan, a hevrah or, to be more precise, a therapeutic community experiencing a form of release far from their *ba'lei batim* in the genteel cocoon of the Copley Plaza. Here, some may say, is the last bastion of modern Orthodoxy; here also is a group of academics who feel Jewishly most at home with one another.

Long gone are the excited crowds of would-be *maskilim,* the artisans and *ba'lei batim* eager to commune with scholars, to hear the latest *vort* from Yehoash or the historian Tcherikover on the steps of Vilna's YIVO; those women and men who pinned pictures of Dubnow on their walls and read his *Weltgeschichte* with the avid attention that their fathers had shown the *Ein Yakov*. But then, who would have predicted four years ago that a sufficiently large, intelligent readership existed to sustain a very thoughtful, demanding "thick journal" like *Tikkun*? And *Tikkun* is only the most visible of an array of such publications (at Yale and elsewhere), some short-lived, but nonetheless with great vitality and an impressive total readership. Popular images of Jewish life still evoke among many literate people the clubbish, parvenu hilarity of "Goodbye, Columbus," but a sort of moderate but discernible *teshuva* seems to be taking place in the same circles—not the sort that would necessarily please Chabad but one with perhaps greater long-term implications. For example, my department hired two feminist historians this past year, one of them a Marxist theoretician. Among the first things both did upon moving to Los Angeles was to join synagogues; one also registered her son in a Conservative day school. Or look at Todd Gitlin's highly intelligent and engaged memoir of the 1960s—it is infused with strong and clearly stated Jewish attachments. These are random and unscientific examples, but there seems to exist a large number of intellectually engaged, skeptical, committed Jewish people, eager for direction, hungry for learning, nominally attached but not wholly satisfied with establishment Judaism and ready for a second opinion. Perhaps most of them are Camp Ramah graduates or day-school *apikorsim*, but they constitute the closest that we are likely to come to the sort of crowds, the intelligent lay readership, that so nurtured Jewish culture at the turn of the century.

Rank nostalgia, I can hear Bernard muttering. I'm not so sure that he is wrong. At the same time, the awful aloneness in that now classic tract of Yerushalmi's *Zakhor*—that brilliant, lonely plaint of a historian whose very culture belies the need for his scholarly enterprise—repels me, frightens me. A scholar's life is brutish and lonely; *Gemeinschaft* is a modernist fantasy, you may be saying. The tensions that I've described may be inevitable, even salutary and useful for our work. But I'm not convinced that community is unachievable, and the success of *Tikkun* reinforces my impression that an educated public exists that already finds Monty Hall crass, that sickens when confronted with maudlin sermons, and is nonetheless eager to be a part of the Jewish world. A call to *teshuva* this is not: Rather, it is just a private admission by one insufficiently committed Judaica academic who would like to establish closer links between his studies and his Jewish life. My suspicion is that such desires are not wholly idiosyncratic.

Popular Fiction and the Shaping of Jewish Identity

ARNOLD J. BAND

The prodigious achievements of American Jews in the area of fiction since World War II are one of the phenomena commonly cited as evidence of the integration of Jews into the mainstream of American life. No account of the historical experience of American Jewry during this period is complete without the evocation of the triumvirate: Bellow, Malamud, and Roth. Just what identifies these writers as specifically Jewish, however, is usually a source of perplexity, even embarrassment, for the critic and historian. I cite the eminence of these writers and the attending problem of definition, not to reopen this tired discussion, but rather to identify a problem which has intrigued me for some time.

Contemporaneous with the works of Bellow, Malamud, and Roth—or of such authors as Ozick, Doctorow, or Halpern—one finds a group of books of less critical acclaim but of clearer Jewish resolution, books which have enjoyed enormous popularity and have had a significant impact on American Jewish life. Leon Uris's *Exodus* immediately leaps to mind and is, perhaps, archetypical, but there are others of equal significance: *Marjorie Morningstar, Fiddler on the Roof, The Chosen*, and Wiesel's *Night*. While these books differ markedly one from the other—*Fiddler* is a musical, and some of these works have had greater impact as films than as books—I think we could all agree that all these works contributed significantly to the identity articulation and agenda setting of the post–World War II American Jewish community. While these are not projects initiated by the organized Jewish community and its variegated institutions, these works evoked responses from both the affiliated and unaffiliated portions of the community. As such, they have been historical events of major import and deserve our serious study. Tentatively, I will call this subgenre "American-Jewish popular fiction" and include in it a wide variety of types, even a musical comedy like *Fiddler on the Roof*, whose popularity and impact are undeniable.

We can examine only a sample at present, and my selection has to be rationalized. As I began to marshal my evidence, a striking pattern began to emerge. Herman Wouk's *Marjorie Morningstar* appeared in 1955; Leon Uris's *Exodus,* in 1958; *Fiddler on the Roof,* a joint composition (Stein, Bock, and Harnick), in 1964. In less than a decade, three of the most significant samples of this genre were issued to great popular acclaim and commercial success. While one can think of other examples from the same period, or from the past two decades, the limited timeframe affords us a tight control; the reasonable distance from our vantage point, 1989, allows us the proper perspective.

The commercial success of this genre, its market orientation, has generated much of the negative criticism it has inspired and has surely blinded us to its significance for the formation of the contemporary American Jewish identity. Once we overcome our initial naive impulse to reject as art whatever makes money, a vast territory is opened for exploration as the ground for cultural history. And it is precisely the market orientation which should suggest the proper model for our exploration: the motion picture industry, also a primarily Jewish empire, as Neal Gabler has so cogently argued in his *Empire of Their Own: How the Jews Invented Hollywood* (1988). While the dynamic period of Jewish empire and image-building in Hollywood which Gabler describes ends shortly before the period which concerns us, the operational patterns of the years between 1910 and World War II are still very much with us and suggest ways of understanding the social functions of the three works we will examine here.

Gabler begins his study with a series of paradoxes which enable him to ask the questions leading to his analysis.

> The American film industry . . . the quintessence of what we mean by "American," was founded and for thirty years operated by Eastern European Jews who themselves seemed to be anything but the quintessence of America. . . . Their dominance became a target for wave after wave of anti-Semites. . . . Ducking from these assaults, the Jews became the phantoms of the film history they had created, haunting it but never really able to inhabit it. . . . What deepened the pathos was that while Hollywood Jews were being assailed by know-nothings for conspiring against traditional American values and the power structure that maintained them, they were desperately embracing those values and working to enter the power structure. Above all things, they wanted to be regarded as Americans, not Jews; they wanted to reinvent themselves here as men. The movie Jews were acting out what Isaiah Berlin, in a similar context, has described as an "over-intense admiration or indeed worship" for the majority, a reverence that, Berlin also noted, sometimes alternated with a latent resentment too, creating what he called a "neurotic distortion of the facts." Hollywood became both the vehicle for and the product of their distortions. (pp. 1–2)

The Jews also had a special compatibility with the industry, one that gave them certain advantages over their competitors. For one thing, having come primarily from fashion and retail, they understood public taste and were masters at gauging market swings, at merchandising, at pirating away customers and beating the competition. For another, as immigrants themselves, they had a peculiar sensitivity to the dreams and aspirations of other immigrants and working-class families, two overlapping groups that made up a significant portion of the early moviegoing audience. The Jews were their own best appraisers of entertainment. "They were the audience," a producer told me. "They were the same people. They were not too far removed from those primitive feelings and attitudes." (p. 5)

But in order to understand what may have been the chief appeal of the movies to these Jews, one must understand their hunger for assimilation and the way in which the movies could uniquely assimilate that hunger. If the Jews were proscribed from entering the real corridors of gentility and status in America, the movies offered an ingenious option. Within the studios and on the screen, the Jews could simply create a new country—an empire of their own, so to speak—one where they would not only be admitted but would govern as well. They would fabricate themselves in the image of prosperous Americans. It would be an America where fathers were strong, families stable, people attractive, resilient, resourceful, and decent. This was their America, and its invention may be their most enduring legacy. (pp. 5–6)

Though the American Jewish community has changed markedly between the pioneering days of the movie industry and the post–World War II period we are considering, the social and psychological dynamics of the Zukors, the Foxes, the Mayers, and the Warners can serve as a convenient guide to our understanding of those writers who were also seeking to capture a mass, perhaps mostly Jewish, market in the entertainment industry. We should not forget, for instance, that American writers appealing to a large audience must have in mind the possibility of selling their product to Hollywood, where large royalties are available. Precisely because of this market orientation, we can apply reception theory and ask such questions as: For what kind of audience was the author writing? What did he assume about the Jewish cultural background of the audience? What shared values could he take for granted? Was his goal primarily entertainment, or did he have a specific message to convey? What did the audience find appealing in the work: the characters? the plot? some notions about Judaism?

A second set of questions is: Did the work become a cultural event that elicited discussion and perhaps action? Did it modify the reader's notions about a certain aspect of contemporary Jewish life? Did it seek to confirm or subvert certain "Jewish values" held by the audience? Often, we shall discover, these two sets of questions overlap.

The works we have chosen to explore cover a wide range of Jewish concerns: options of behavior in the open society *(Marjorie Morningstar);* the ideals embodied in the creation of a sovereign Jewish state *(Exodus)* and its Holocaust background; nostalgia for the shtetl *(Fiddler on the Roof).* Our study of these particular works should therefore yield interesting information concerning their contribution to the formation of Jewish identity in America over the last few decades.

Exodus

Leon Uris's *Exodus,* both as book (1958) and as film (1960), clearly ranks as the archetype of the genre under consideration. Its impact on the American Jewish attitude toward Israel since its publication is incalculable. Initially, it projected an image of a country an American Jew might care to visit as a tourist, inspiring tens of thousands to search in the real streets and kibbutzim of Israel the selfless, dedicated, loyal, intelligent, attractive Ari Ben Canaan of their fantasies. More significantly, it molded and dominated the shared image of Israel that persisted from 1958 probably until the Lebanese War. (It was used, in Russian translation, as a consciousness-raising device in the 1960s and 1970s.) As such, it is certainly a major document in modern Jewish history and, once properly treated, can tell us much about the audience which embraced it and was, in turn, shaped by it.

The book—and the film—gave the American Jew of the period the identity-confirming epic that gave coherence to the turbulent world of the 1950s and 1960s. It presented the emergence of the State of Israel as a saga of drama and success, and rooted it in modern Jewish history, especially in the Holocaust. It thus gave meaning to the Holocaust and allowed for its assimilation in the course of events. Though the story was richly plotted with its tense, exciting moments, and peopled with a varied cast, the message was unambiguous and simple: the line of historical development was envisioned as inevitable and just. Jewish history was portrayed in bold colors as a smashing success, and there is nothing so validating to an American as a sense of being on the winning team. The American Jew, furthermore, discovered in the 1950s that he was a member of one of the three accepted American religious denominations in Eisenhower's America (cf. Jonathan Sarna's paper in this volume) and could take great pride in his allegiance to this winning team of attractive, air-brushed Hollywood figures, while feeling not the slightest threat to his American loyalties. *Exodus* was conceived as an American epic, a Western set in the Middle East with John Wayne played by Ari Ben Canaan and the bad Indians cast as Arabs, the duplicitous "city folk" as the English led by Bruce Sutherland, a closet Jew.

In commenting on his novel, Leon Uris remarked that "all the cliché Jewish characters were left on the cutting room floor." The cliché characters he referred to were obviously the conflicted individuals, the knights of alienation of Bellow and Malamud, let alone Kafka, who made the Jewish literary hero paradigmatic of the hero of modern fiction. What Uris has actually given us is a new set of cliché characters, all more acceptable to the middle-brow Jewish audience he was aiming to please. The Ben Canaan family, formerly the Rabinsky family, shook off its exilic characteristics when it settled on the soil of pre-Israel Palestine, just as the David Levinskys rid themselves of their "green" East European notions and habits when they settled into their American settings. They are attractive precisely because they are unlike the stereotype of the East European Jew prevalent in the mind of the Jewish audience. Like the children of David Levinsky, Ari and Jordana Ben Canaan maintain through all adversity a healthy view of the world and their place in it, unclouded by doubts and ambiguities. They and the kibbutz society they embody and energize comprise a new world that can heal the scars of such survivors as Karen Clement or Dov Landau—or even the American Gentile nurse, Kitty Fremont. The latter, the stereotypical shiksa, the fantasy of American Jewish males, learns to understand and even love these determined Jews who make bold to tame the wild west of mandatory Palestine and build in it a homeland, even a state of their own. *Exodus* thus conforms to the great American tradition of novels of the frontier.

Uris correctly gauged the needs of his intended audience, their desire for an uplifting epic which would validate their sense of themselves as American Jews, predominantly middle-class, appreciative of a fictional world which would allow them to be proud spectators, enthusiastic tourists, but never demand anything of them nor subvert their sense of well-being as Jews who had made it in America. On the other hand, the book coalesced and reinforced the often disparate tendencies that were turning Israel into the "civil religion" of significant portion of American Jews (cf. Stephen Cohen's paper in this volume) and in the process granting to Israel the moral and political hegemony over world Jewry. Uris's book enhanced those aspects of philanthropy and tourism which characterized American Zionism in the 1950s and 1960s; it probably prepared the way for the next phase, political lobbying, which developed in the 1970s.

Marjorie Morningstar

In turning from *Exodus* to *Marjorie Morningstar,* we move not only from one writer (Leon Uris) to another (Herman Wouk), but to a significant change in focus. The scope of *Exodus* was epic and distanced: it concentrated on the struggle for the establishment of the State of Israel and, though written for an American—predominantly Jewish—audience, the action and characters never directly involved American Jews. Marjorie Morningstar, her family and friends, her lover, Noel Airman, and the man she finally marries, Milton Schwartz, are emblematically American Jews. Their attitudes and aspirations are those of American Jews of the first post–World War II generation; the book is suffused with the dim realization that these Jews are a new, more self-assured breed, the children or grandchildren of David Levinsky. Poverty and the neighborhoods of initial immigrant settlement are behind them. Their exodus is not from the Egyptian bondage to the Promised Land, or even from the Lower East Side to the Upper West Side, but from Manhattan to Mamaroneck.

This journey, despite its interruptions and divagations, is presented approvingly, even triumphantly, a major cultural statement which differs markedly from the critique of Philip Roth's *Goodbye, Columbus,* published only five years later (1960). The existential dilemma is that of American Jewry; the Jewish dramas being played out in Europe or Palestine are essentially irrelevant to the life of the heroine, Marjorie Morningstar, whose life in the novel spans the crucial years 1933–1954. The question is not how one builds a sovereign state or recovers from the trauma of the Holocaust—the paucity of reference to events outside of America is striking—but rather how one lives as a Jew in an open, affluent society. The process of redefinition, furthermore, is charged with none of the anguish so characteristic of Hebrew or Yiddish fiction of earlier generations; Marjorie Morningstar never feels that in some sense she, too, once fled the Egyptian bondage and stood at Sinai.

As a fictional type, Marjorie relates not to Anne Frank or Hannah Senesh or Golda Meir, but to Emma Bovary and her many literary sisters, daughters of the middle class who fantasize in their adolescence— sometimes a very prolonged adolescence—about a more intriguing world than that of their parents or husbands. And just as Emma attempts to find her escape from the humdrum life of provincial France through the reading of romantic novels, Marjorie aspires to the life of the Broadway stage and the Hollywood screen. Her Hollywood fantasies attract her to Noel Airman, a scriptwriter, more a mediocre fabricator of marketable fantasies than the anguished artist who represents a stance critical of the middle-class culture that Marjorie imagines she yearns to flee. Noel is conventionally, predictably bohemian, as are his sojourn in Paris and his seduction of Marjorie. Their stereotypical bohemianism and romance attest to the domestication of the traditional novelistic topoi within the American Jewish novel. Wouk, nonetheless, cannot let himself go all the way, and hence his success with his suburban Jewish audience. Marjorie initially denies her social background, dreams dangerous dreams, and eats forbidden foods, but finally returns to her people, not on Central Park West, but in its postwar transmogrification, the New York suburb with all its typical assumptions and appurtenances. Marjorie, we should remember, entered the American Jewish consciousness before the emergence of the feminist movement and the figure of the JAP. While we cannot expect her to strive for feminist ideals, we can entertain the possibility that she contributed significantly to the popular and usually invidious image of the JAP.

Unlike Philip Roth, whose polemics with representatives of the American Jewish establishment are well documented, Wouk affirms the practices and values of American Jewish life as he found them in the 1950s. Intrigued by the emergence of a new, self-assured Jewish community in the post–World War II era, he chronicles its rituals and public festivities, thus legitimizing them as a normative aspect of Jewish life. While he does not hide the sumptuary excesses of Jewish weddings and bar mitzvahs—they look worse in the film than in the book—he envelops them in a warm tegument of family togetherness which seems to absorb and atone for all vulgarity. The Hollywoodish names taken by the two principals in their assimilatory process (Morningstar was Morgenstern; Noel Airman was Saul Ehrman) and the professions they choose to catapult them above and beyond their class, both aspects of the entertainment industry, suggest that Neal Gabler's argument regarding the Jews who "invented Hollywood" applies here too. The ideal Jew portrayed in *Marjorie Morningstar* is not the rootless intellectual, the stranger within the gates, but the happy citizen at home in Mamaroneck, the Jew living the American dream which he himself invented.

Fiddler on the Roof

Herman Wouk has his heroine dream of a career on Broadway and in Hollywood, but he could not have imagined her aspiring to star in a musical nostalgically celebrating the life of the shtetl as imagined in *Fiddler on the Roof*. That was not part of her American dream. Ironically, the three authors who collaborated in the composition of *Fiddler* (Joseph Stein: book; Jerry Bock: music; and Sheldon Harnick: lyrics) did conceive of such a musical less than a decade after the publication of *Marjorie Morningstar,* and succeeded in producing not only a Broadway hit but a movie, a record album—and even new materials for Jewish weddings, bar mitzvahs, summer camps, and religious schools. The shtetl and "the world of Sholom Aleichem" as rendered in *Fiddler* is an integral part of the Jewish cultural repertoire in America (and elsewhere), understood by Jews and non-Jews as something authentically Jewish.

Its Jewish "authenticity" is precisely what intrigues us here, since *Fiddler* is obviously a collaborative, commercial production designed to please an audience with beguiling tunes and colorful scenery all carefully calculated to conjure up, before an audience which had never seen a shtetl, the image of a shtetl which never existed. The peculiar nexus between vicarious experience and the sense of authenticity commands our attention. To argue that *Fiddler* appealed to Jews merely because of its catchy tunes and modish ethnicity seems to fail to assess the needs and nature of the intended audience. The stated intentions of the playwright, however, can shed some light on the intriguing questions about the audience.

In his introduction to the musical (*Best Plays of 1964–65,* pp. 118 ff.) Joseph Stein offers the standard assertion that "the problem of adaptation was to remain true to the spirit, the feeling of Sholom Aleichem and transmute it for a contemporary audience." The details of this adaptation bear close scrutiny.

> First, the play required the establishment of an overall focus and point of view. Hidden within the stories was the sense of a breakdown of the traditional cultural forms and beliefs of "the *shtetl*," the village community, under the buffeting of social change and hostile forces, finally leading to disintegration of that society. We decided to make the crumbling of tradition, illustrated by the daughters' love stories and other developments, the theme of our play.
>
> Then a fresh story needed to be created, to hold the isolated tales together. This became the saga of the community within which Tevye and his family functions: a tightly-knit, rigidly-structured community, surrounded and constantly under attack, finally breaking up and scattering to different parts of the globe. Historically, of course, this was accurate. This was the period of great Russian-Jewish immigration to America. . . .
>
> Tevye himself had to be changed somewhat to make him more effective in

our play. Sholom Aleichem's Tevye, richly amusing and colorful, was a more humble, more passive character than he is in our play; he was typical of his community, but certainly not its spokesman. To make him the moving force in our story, it was necessary to give him more strength, while keeping the shadings of his character intact. . . .

And to give the story a meaning for our times, we brought to the foreground an element implicit in the Tevye tales . . . the hostility, the violence, the injustice practiced by a ruling majority against a weak minority. We wanted in this to point up the internal strength, the dignity, the humor of that people and, like minorities today, their unique talent for survival. (p. 119)

The amalgam of cultural rejection and appropriation is fascinating. We American Jews, we are told, are clearly different from the shtetl Jews from whom we are descended, since our parents—or even our grandparents—came to this secure land from that land of "hostility, violence, and injustice." Those people, that Tevye and his daughters, were a bit peculiar, but they were warm people, sang beautiful tunes, and danced with genuine joy. Tevye, in fact, is somewhat problematic as a character: he was a bit too passive, "typical of his community, but certainly not its spokesman. To make him the moving force in our story, it was necessary to give him more strength." The stereotypical shtetl Jew we imagine we know was fine in his place and time, but he could never keep an American musical moving. We American Jews do have this vitality and initiative, since, after all, we are really no longer a weak minority—"like minorities today"—but part of the majority, even quintessential of the majority. We have made it here because of "the internal strength, the dignity, the humor of that people, and . . . their unique talent for survival."

The symbol of the musical is, of course, "the fiddler on the roof" taken from Chagall's paintings, which, it is assumed, is a recognizable Jewish icon. The surrealistic image of the fiddler hovering above the straw roof of a shtetl home had appeared as the artist's wry portrait of himself as shtetl fiddler in Chagall's paintings early in the century, but by the 1960s it was less a charged artistic image than a logo for "the world of Sholom Aleichem." In his first speech addressed to the audience, Tevye comments on this familiar emblem:

A fiddler on the roof. Sounds crazy, no? But in our little village of Anatevka, you might say that every one of us is a fiddler on the roof, trying to scratch out a pleasant, simple tune without breaking his neck. It isn't easy. You may ask why do we stay up here if it's so dangerous? We stay because Anatevka is our home. And how do we keep our balance? That I can tell you in a word—tradition!

In one word we have the secret of Jewish existence throughout the ages: tradition—sung by the villagers as they enter, filling the stage with their colorful community. As the musical unfolds, we learn that "tradition" is the all-embracing but totally undifferentiated notion for the way all Jews lived "there"—as opposed to "here." Because of tradition, "everyone knows who he is and what God expects him to do." We are never really told what this magical practice is, what gives it authority or coherence; we are assured, nevertheless, that it certainly worked "there," and that we "here," in America, obviously don't have it. When you have tradition or "keep the traditions" you are authentic, surely worthy of admiration, if not emulation. And yet, in no way is it suggested that tradition is something we American Jews might care to adopt outside the hall of the musical—or those musical-like occasions of our communal lives like weddings or synagogue socials. *Fiddler on the Roof* thus allows us to have our authenticity and enjoy it vicariously by keeping the areas scrupulously compartmentalized. Again, we are invited to be comfortable, appreciative spectators of a life-style we do not live. Our present mode of existence as middle-class citizens of America is never challenged, but is, rather, fully validated.

Some hundred and fifty years ago, the early proponents of *Wissenschaft des Judentums,* the first modern scholars of Judaism, realized that the belief in the Sinaitic imperatives which gave both legitimacy and coherence to Jewish life was no longer effective for many Jews confronted with Enlightenment ideals. True to their times, they sought to substitute an awareness of Jewish history, historical self-consciousness, for the eroding faith. Their meticulous research was designed to give the Jews a history like the history the Gentiles had, with personalities, periods, and movements. In brief, they tried to create for the mostly German-speaking Jews of the nineteenth century the basis for a new identity, one consonant with "the world as they found it." Whether or not they succeeded or how many people they actually reached are questions still debated by historians.

It might at first seem rash to compare the highly serious efforts of Zunz or Graetz with the seemingly trivial, market-oriented works of Wouk or Uris. But once we ask the basic question, What shapes the identity (in the sense of self-image) of a Jew in the post-Enlightenment period?, we are compelled to treat *Exodus, Marjorie Morningstar,* and *Fiddler on the Roof*—and dozens of other works of this genre—with the same scholarly respect as a truly epic work like Graetz's *History of the Jews*, which reached a select audience both in its German original and in its translations. Any doubts we might entertain about the significance of these works—particularly in their film versions—should be readily dispelled by our realization of the image-making power of these mass media as described by Neal Gabler. And while my initial analysis of these works has yielded a picture of American Jewry which is far from flattering, I would argue that the existence and importance of this fictional genre is indisputable.

Job's Children: Post-Holocaust Jewish Identity in Second-Generation Literature

ALAN L. BERGER

Post-Holocaust Jewish identity demands a response which somehow incorporates awareness that the grotesque and horrible deaths of millions were the result of their having been born. The Jewish people, as Elie Wiesel attests, was the only group "ontologically threatened" by the Nazis. Knowledge of this situation makes Jewish identity a complex phenomenon eliciting a variety of responses. Simply put, is remaining a Jew worth the potential risk? Not only to oneself but to one's children and grandchildren? In responding to these questions, moreover, one must assess whether the classical paradigms of covenant and chosenness address the post-Auschwitz generation. If these paradigms are no longer plausible explanations of reality, what constitutes authenticity in contemporary Jewish identity? While many have addressed these issues, the voices of now-adult children of survivors command particular attention as they are one of the very few groups of Jewish Americans who self-consciously reflect on the content and meaning of their Jewish identity. Through films, novels, plays, poetry, and short stories, the second generation attests not only to their parents' continued survival, but suggests as well certain theological directions taken by American Judaism.

Job's tale as paradigm

The tale of Job is paradigmatic for those who seek to confront the ways of God with man and to ponder the possible meaning of unwarranted suffering. Throughout the ages, the experience of this mysterious figure has served to console and fascinate humanity. Rereading Jewish history in light of Auschwitz, Wiesel calls Job "our contemporary."

A little-known pseudepigraphic text, the Testament of Job (1st cent. B.C.E.—2nd cent. C.E.), presents a reinterpretation of the Job figure which is significant for understanding second-generation Holocaust literature. The text reports that a dying Job gathers his ten children—born after the deaths of their half-brothers and sisters—and tells them of his misfortune and his perseverance. His advice, in keeping with the piety of the times, is traditional in nature: remember God, help the poor, assist those in need, and marry within the faith. While lacking the grandeur and epic sweep of its biblical predecessor, and relatively unsophisticated in its concern for theodicy, the Testament's importance is threefold: Job's children are, in effect, "replacement" children,[1] the survivor tells his children the tale of his suffering; and, finally, he urges their own Jewish steadfastness after the catastrophe. In a somewhat similar spirit, the names which the biblical Job gives his second set of daughters, Jemimah, Keziah, and Keren-happuch, are highly symbolic. One commentator interprets these names as follows: Jemimah derives from *yom* (day) and implies brightness. Like the light of the sun, Jemimah will brighten things. Keziah, a fragrance, is to waft out over the world; and Keren-happuch, a horn of eyeshadow, is to shine like a gemstone called *hapook*. Each of the names implies an outgoingness.[2] The children are to have an impact on the world. The survivors' suffering is to be transformed into a salvific message for everyone. While not each of the second-generation novels reaches out in terms of social action, many in this generation are in the helping professions—physicians, teachers, therapists, and all testify in order to inform, and possibly save, the world.

In our own time, seeking to establish the relationship of the Jobs of Auschwitz to succeeding generations, the theologian Eliezer Berkovits reminds his readers that "we are not Job and we dare not speak or resound as if we were. We are only Job's brother."[3] In contrast, the historian Deborah Lipstadt, in a moving piece entitled "We Are Not Job's Children," reminds students of the Shoah that they are not even Job's brother. At best they are, she writes, his "nieces and nephews."[4] Both Berkovits and Lipstadt, despite the difference of their familial metaphors, rightly warn against substituting standards of nonwitnesses for those who passed through the Shoah's fiery gates. But there is a generation of children of survivors who, like the children of Job of antiquity, have received their parents' testament, and whose actions reveal how Jewish identity is assumed and expressed by the generation living after a catastrophe. Their writings reveal a multiplicity of messages; that the Holocaust remains an unmastered and now intergenerational trauma,[5] that the second generation may in fact constitute a new social type[6]—going out to improve the world much in the manner suggested by the symbolic reading of Job's daughters' names, and that the question of Jewish identity is now being addressed by a generation who knows that this time Isaac's life was not spared nor was a ram put in place of the Jewish people.

This essay initially discusses Jewish identity in light of the phenomenon of the second-generation witness. Selected examples of this writing are then scrutinized with a focus on the psychosocial and theological implications of the second generation's assumption of post-Holocaust Jewish responsibility. The paper concludes with a meditation on the ramifications of this generation's quest for post-Auschwitz Jewish authenticity.

The second–generation witness

Second-generation witnessing is done both despite and because of the Shoah. The experience of their parents, in spite of its great variety (some were in camps, some were in forced-labor brigades, some in hiding, and some fighting with partisans), attests to God's increasing hiddenness in the affairs of man. Therefore, second-generation Holocaust writing constitutes a search for Jewish affirmation which embodies recognition of Emil Fackenheim's contention that "a Jew today is one who, except for an historical accident—Hitler's loss of the war—would have either been murdered or never been born."[7] Authentic post-Auschwitz Jewish identity, argues Fackenheim, requires nothing less than a "mending of the world."[8] This mending, moreover, is accomplished by both secular and religious people. Pre-Holocaust boundaries between sacred and secular have been replaced, according to Fackenheim, by a new distinction between authentic and inauthentic responses to the Shoah. The former recognize the epoch-making nature of the event, whereas the latter attempt to either avoid, deny, evade, or flee from the Shoah's singularity.[9]

Furthermore, the second generation's quest for Jewish authenticity reveals dimensions of what Irving Greenberg calls the "voluntary covenant," which, he asserts, characterizes the third great cycle of Jewish history.[10] The voluntary covenant is one in which the very hiddenness of God requires that man assume greater responsibility for maintaining the divine-human relationship. Basing his contention on the rabbinic model of response to catastrophe, Greenberg argues that the message of the Temple's destruction is that "God had hidden to call Jews to greater responsibility."[11] With the Shoah, God is even more hidden, resulting in a "more drastic call for total Jewish responsibility for the covenant."[12] This covenant underscores that, for both Greenberg and Fackenheim, pre-Auschwitz categories of what constitutes religious and secular behavior are no longer applicable to the human condition.

Seen in this context, second-generation writings comprise a quest for Jewish authenticity after a catastrophe of biblical proportions. Although it is important to note that its authors have a wide variety of attitudes toward traditional Judaism (some are observant, others are not, certain authors have intermarried), collectively these writings reveal a search for authentic post-Auschwitz Jewish identity in America. Yet there is an irony in second-generation literature. The most important event in the life of this generation occurred before any of its members were born. Nevertheless, the members of the second generation view themselves as "keepers of their parents' Holocaust accounts."[13]

From a literary-psychological point of view, second-generation authors refrain from defining Jewish identity by attempting to imagine events of the Shoah. Rather, this generation deals with the destruction's continuing impact on the survivors and their children. The second generation, therefore, relates to the catastrophe of European Judaism in an intensely personal fashion. In fact, Wiesel contrasts the Holocaust concern of the second generation to that of other people who want to study the Shoah. Concerning the former, Wiesel writes "You want to study that event in its most human dimension. For you, the war has a face—the face of your father, the face of your mother, her eyes on Shabbat or after Shabbat."[14] Consequently, Jewish identity in second-generation literature is frequently expressed in existential rather than in classical or halakhic terms.

In the last five years there has been a proliferation of novels and short stories by and about the second generation which reflect both its psychosocial and theological concerns. Focusing just on the novels, examples which come immediately to mind include Thomas Friedmann's *Damaged Goods* (1984), Elie Wiesel's *The Fifth Son* (English trans., 1985), Art Spiegelman's *Maus* (1986), and three which appeared in 1987: Barbara Finkelstein's *Summer Long-a-Coming*, Carol Ascher's *The Flood*, which is, properly speaking, a novel by a daughter of refugees, and Julie Salamon's *White Lies*. Each of these novels presents a different dimension of the search for post-Auschwitz Jewish identity. Some view their Jewish identity in a particularist manner, while others distill universal lessons from the Holocaust.[15] All the novelists, however, are united by their identity as members of the second generation. For many, the Holocaust is the author's point of entry into Jewish history. This results in the central characters' discovery of their own post-Auschwitz Jewish vulnerability. Theologically, these novels reflect the tenuousness of post-Auschwitz covenantal Judaism while simultaneously revealing the necessity of its continuity, albeit in a modified form. In terms of Jewish identity, all the second-generation authors discover in their own lives—at first through listening to their parents' stories and then through their own readings and reflections and personal experiences—that the post-Shoah generation reflects—in Fackenheim's terms—the result of an historical accident. Consequently, for the second generation, the Holocaust is both an historical event and, as Robert Prince observes, "a psychological event that provides themes and metaphors around which personal identity is organized."[16]

A biographical note

Second-generation authors seem to be compensating for their parents' inability to communicate in English. The public silence of the survivors is now, for example, being supplanted by the testimony of their offspring. Thomas Friedmann, born in Hungary, is a professor of English. Art Spiegelman was born in Stockholm and edits *Raw* magazine, while the American-born Barbara Finkelstein is a free-lance writer. Julie Salamon is the film critic for the *Wall Street Journal*, and Carol Ascher, who was born in England, is both a novelist and a researcher at Teachers College of Columbia University, where she focuses on minority education. Professionally, these second-generation members are journalists, teachers, and writers.[17]

Wiesel, the Nobel peace laureate, is perhaps the best-known of the witnessing writers. His position on witnessing is dialectical in nature. For example, while Wiesel feels that to reduce the experience of Auschwitz to words is to betray that experience, he also feels a "compulsion" to witness. Wiesel also carefully differentiates between Holocaust survivors and nonwitnesses. And yet, on the other hand, he observes that even those not present during the time of night have a responsibility to testify. "One can," Wiesel writes, "step inside the fiery gates twenty-five, fifty years later."[18] The fact that he has written a second-generation novel attests to the importance which Wiesel attaches to the witnessing mission of this generation. Significantly, Wiesel dedicates *The Fifth Son* to Elisha, his own son, and to all children of survivors. This fact, coupled with the rapidly dwindling number of survivors, and his increasing literary focus on America, may be seen as Wiesel's way of symbolically passing the torch of remembrance to the second generation, especially those living in America.

Considering the examples

Second-generation literature confronts the reader in an intense way with the relationship between innocence and identity. Like the biblical

Job's children, the contemporary children of Job attempt to reflect on their identity in the aftermath of unjust suffering. The situation is well stated by the late Terrance Des Pres, who wrote:

> Like it or not, we are involved beyond ourselves. To be in the world but not of it, to recover innocence after Auschwitz, plainly, will not work. The self's sense of itself is different now, and what has made the difference, both as cause and continuing condition, is simply knowing that the Holocaust occurred. We are in no way guilty but we do not feel blameless. We live decently but not without shame. We are entirely innocent but innocence, the blessedness of simple daily being, no longer seems possible.[19]

Des Pres' observation spotlights the existential drama of the second generation in its attempt to grapple with post-Auschwitz Jewish identity within a covenantal framework.

Among the recent second-generation novels in America, I have chosen three written by women writers in order to compare the contemporary daughters of Job to their counterparts in antiquity. The novels of Barbara Finkelstein, Julie Salamon, and Carol Ascher each illumine certain themes of post-Shoah Jewish identity manifested by the second generation.

Summer Long-a-Coming, [20] like *Damaged Goods* and *Maus,* is set against the turbulent decade of the sixties. Finkelstein's novel skillfully weaves together the strands of personal and collective Jewish identity by merging the trauma of the Holocaust past with the experiences of the American present. The Szuster Family live on a New Jersey poultry farm where the survivor parents, Rukhl and Yankl, isolate and insulate both themselves and their three children; speaking Yiddish, observing traditional Judaism, and constantly mourning their lost family members. Sheiye, their oldest son, whose birth in an Austrian displaced-persons camp is replete with a messianic portent, accidentally kills his nine-year-old sister Perel. The tale, which is narrated by fifteen-year-old Brantzche (Brenda) Szuster, unites psychological and theological themes of post-Shoah identity.

Finkelstein's novel reveals the powerful impact of the Holocaust upon identity formation, stressing (much in the manner suggested by Perry London's paper) the variety of ways in which the trauma can be communicated. Her identity as a child of survivors initially confuses and threatens to consume Brantzche. Her mother not only "scares" Brenda. The young girl wishes to remove the burden of her mother's past. Often, prior to sleeping, Brantzche has a fantasy that she rolls her mother into a ball and throws this ball back to Holocaust Poland. Her parents' silence about their Holocaust experiences and their inability to understand or accept their children's unhappiness leads Brantzche and Perel to imagine various horrors and sufferings which serve only to intensify the communication problem between survivor parents and their children.

Like many survivor families, the Szusters have various rituals of commemorating the Holocaust. Foremost among them is lighting yahrzeit candles. Watching this seemingly endless ritual has a profound effect on her second-generation identity. Brantzche notes that:

> We had a cabinet full of empty yurtsaht glasses, enough to hold dozens of drinks at a banquet. To me, yurtsaht represented yet another Jewish holiday whose celebration was whimsical and whose meaning was indecipherable. I would not have been surprised to learn that no one else on earth knew a thing about this candle, and assumed that my father had designed a new holiday to remind us that we were Jews. (133)

Lighting these candles has, however, emerged as a central Holocaust commemoration ritual among the second generation and stands in place of the mounds of corpses, piles of shoes and eyeglasses, and mountains of human hair which are icons of the survivor generation.[21]

Tales of survivors are the touchstones linking the generations. This communication is, however, a complex phenomenon. While the children of survivors are young, they may hear only fragments of their parents' tales. Moreover, the Holocaust past may be communicated in nonverbal ways. For example, photos of murdered half-siblings may be displayed, as in the case of Spiegelman's *Maus*. Spiegelman recalls that during his childhood an enlarged photograph of his murdered brother was prominently displayed but rarely spoken about.[22] The Holocaust past may also be referred to by means of indirection. Friedmann's *Damaged Goods* portrays a scene where Jason Kole, the American-born son of survivors, is told by his father that he "need not say the blessing for the first born the morning before Passover." Moreover, children of survivors may learn more about their parents' experience from other survivors than they do from their own parents. This is instanced in the case of Wiesel's *The Fifth Son*, whose son of survivors, Ariel, contends that the tales of Bontchek, a survivor friend of his silent father, "fuel" his own imagination.

Survivor tales in *Summer Long-a-Coming* are told both directly to the children, in abbreviated form, and in great detail to a professional researcher at Israel's Yad Vashem. Both versions profoundly impact on

Brantzche's own identity as a member of the second generation, an identity which undergoes several stages. Initially, she is angry both with her parents and with God. Her parents berate their children for any expression of unhappiness. Comparing her own Holocaust past to the apparent comfort of her children, Mrs. Szuster observes, "Kinder, kinder . . . what would you do if you had no parents and you had to live together in the woods?" The Szusters and the Spiegelmans, in fact, exemplify survivor parents who are "so preoccupied with the unending mourning process and problems of starting a new life in a strange country that they are unable to relate to their children's needs."[23] These needs are instead viewed by parents as "draining their already limited emotional resources."[24]

Brantzche's understanding of her identity as a member of the second generation slowly begins to dawn following Perel's accidental death. Like Job, Brantzche must wrestle with the meaning of pain and the suffering of innocents. As she reflects on this millennial problem, Brantzche articulates an awareness of Jewish vulnerability. She observes that:

> Up until that moment, my parents' tales of survival had done little more than fuel my self-emancipation fantasies of entrapment and escape. At best, staying alive was a question of odds, of monitoring the whereabouts of a predator, and side-stepping it in the nick of time. With Perel gone, I had the sickening realization that survival meant coming out the victor by chance, not by destiny or individual cunning. The Szusters were merely like the other creatures on the farm—chickens, earthworms, dogs—who, on suspending their vigilance for a second, succumbed to a greater, more confident power. (203–204)

Brantzche's rumination, which reminds us of Des Pres' statement, is a recognition of the common vulnerability she shares with her parents. Reaching maturity, Brantzche is able to begin to fathom the dimensions of her own identity. She regularly listens to and reflects on the meaning of her parents' Yad Vashem tapes. These tapes, sent to her by a survivor friend, compel Brantzche to realize that the meaning of the Shoah and the continued suffering of its survivors will forever be beyond her grasp. She is "thrown into despair," realizing that she "had never understood anything. Certainly, I had never known who Rukhl and Yankl Szuster were." Brantzche, however, refuses to yield to despair. Rather, she attempts to transform despair by endless reading about the Holocaust. This literary encounter with the Holocaust is a theme found in many second-generation novels and serves to emphasize the fact that the Holocaust is the touchstone of reality for this generation.

Theologically, Brantzche accuses God but does so from within. She is like Jeremiah of antiquity when, reflecting on the devastation that has followed the family, from the European Holocaust to the death of Perel, Brantzche wonders if her father "questioned whether the small joys of living would ever compensate for the destruction that had tailed him from Uchan to Long-a-Coming. It had all been reckless destruction, as if God had faltered in His capacity to distinguish between the wrongdoers and the blameless" (212).

But Brantzche's questions are not shared by her survivor parents. Despite the destruction of Yankl's European family, her father continues to believe in God "because I have no one else to believe in."

By novel's end, Brantzche lives in New York City, while in her early thirties, and unmarried. Her parents have moved to Israel. While unable to accept the God of the Sinaitic covenant, she voluntarily affirms her second-generation identity, listening incessantly to Rukhl and Yankl's Yad Vashem tapes. Brantzche's behavior exemplifies Greenberg's observations concerning the voluntary nature of covenant adherence in the post-Holocaust world, and the irrelevance of the pre-Shoah distinction between sacred and secular. While not religious in the formal sense of the term, Brantzche is determined to read, write, and talk about the destruction of European Jewry. This type of faith may in fact be the only appropriate kind for an age in which God is so hidden. Moreover, as a daughter of survivors she articulates the special connection between survivors and their children, observing: "Like them, I live without hope of settling scores yet love life unreasonably, and will until the day I die—even though I cannot reclaim what I have lost" (262).

The most compelling testimony to the Holocaust's imprint on Brantzche's identity is seen in her commitment to memory of the tragedy. This commitment is, moreover, undertaken in the face of a hostile or, at best, neutral cultural environment. Brantzche contends that "qualities like Moma and Papa's fortitude and patience were dispensible values here, like memory . . . outdated and ineffective in an age of time-saving, convenience commodities" (301). Children of survivors appear imbued with a mission that distinguishes them from both their Jewish and non-Jewish contemporaries.

Julie Salamon's *White Lies* defines second-generation identity by relating the Holocaust to American culture in the seventies. Unlike Finkelstein's novel, which views second-generation identity through psychosocial and theological lenses, Salamon's work concentrates on the Shoah's second-generation societal legacy. The novel tells the story of Jamaica Just, a features reporter for a newspaper whose assimilated Jewish managing editor criticizes her for insisting on "taking everything so personally" (102). Jamaica receives three interconnected assignments which underscore her second-generation identity: a piece on second-generation teenaged welfare mothers, one on children of Holocaust survivors, and a feature story on the so-called news junkies—compulsive writers of letters to the editor.

Assigned to write about her experience as a member of the second generation, Jamaica reflects that she has spent years "anguishing over this pivotal event of her life, and the fact that it had taken place before she'd been born." Jamaica's sense of isolation is intensified each time she encounters other Jews "who were made uncomfortable by the ugly scar on her past" (33). She then asks the question which haunts the contemporary children of Job. Had anything really happened to her? Her "memories" of the Holocaust, like those of Jason Kole, Art Spiegelman, and Brantzche Szuster, are tales she has heard from her parents. But Jamaica has no choice, "she wanted to forget but it was her birthright to remember. Lucky her, Chosen of the chosen" (28). She accepts the assignment.

Jamaica's second-generation identity distinguishes her not only from other Americans but from other Jewish Americans. Sammy, her American-born husband, whose parents spent the Holocaust years on an American Air Force base, remembers the funny stories his parents told about life on the base. Jamaica, on the other hand, confesses her childhood belief that all Jewish parents spent the war either in concentration camps or in hiding" (34). The second generation's identity is ineluctably shaped by their parents' experience of the Shoah.

Jamaica Just, like Brantzche Szuster, spends her youth in vicinal isolation. Surrounded by non-Jews, she remembers how the Shoah continued to single out the Jews. Once, for example, in the fifth grade, her "only partly anti-Semitic" teacher asked the class to trace their genealogy. When the young girl asked her father about their family tree, Dr. Pearlman responded cryptically, "Ours has been pruned." Not comprehending her father's cynicism, Jamaica copied her teacher's family tree, "leafy with ancestry," and could not understand why, when she showed it to Eva, her mother began to cry. Both of these events underscore the nonverbal manner by which some survivors sometimes transmit their Holocaust experience. Jamaica, like Brantzche, begins to comprehend her second-generation identity as she matures. Unlike Brantzche, Jamaica attends college, where she attempts to define the distinctiveness of her legacy. She is made physically ill by reading Jerzy Kosinski's *The Painted Bird*, which reports "the Jews going to slaughter." Refusing this as inaccurate and offensive, Jamaica instead offers a poignant midrash on the Shoah's meaning in the life of the second generation. She thinks: "Those Jews aren't nameless, pitiable beings to me, yesterday's swollen bellies, a 40-year-old newsmagazine cover. They are my mother, my father, my uncles, my aunts, my cousins. They are me" (37). She knows that the Shoah destroyed human beings, not numbers. Furthermore, the second generation views itself as imbued with a mission to perpetuate an identity which was nearly obliterated. Consequently, this generation is far from being simply students of an increasingly remote event in history.

Jamaica's identity entails an obligation which, in the first instance, requires her to pass on the Shoah's lessons to her yet-to-be born children. In fact, among second-generation novels *White Lies* communicates most explicitly the necessity of teaching the Shoah's meaning to the third generation. Jamaica shares with the reader her goals for that generation.

> I want my children, when I have them, to know what happened during World War II. I don't want them to think their birthright is privilege and ease. I hope they have those things. I have. But I want them to know that such things are a matter of luck and circumstances and should be appreciated. My Mother, too, was a child of privilege for the first eighteen years of her life. I guess I will make my children feel guilty, even though that isn't my intent. (44)

In short, Jamaica, like the biblical Job's daughters, wishes to instill social responsibility as a response to disaster. Her determination is based on her distillation of the Shoah's universal lessons. Jamaica summarizes these lessons for the third generation. For example, she hopes that her future children will be sensitive enough

> to learn what I think I've learned. I make an effort to be decent because I have some understanding of what happens when decency doesn't exist. I try to keep aware of what the government is doing because I have some understanding of what happens when governments turn evil. I try to be good to my family and friends because I have some understanding of what it's like to have family and friends taken away.

Jamaica learns another lesson as a member of the second generation. She rightly distinguishes second-generation literature both from survivor accounts and from novels written by nonwitnesses when she observes, "most of all I understand that I have only some understanding of these things, which is quite different from experience."

Unlike the Szusters, Jamaica's parents are secularists. Nevertheless, Dr. Pearlman inculcates his daughters in the Jewish way. His response to Jewish identity reflects the reaction of many in the Jewish community who, although secularists before the war, "enter" Jewish history through the Shoah.[25] Jamaica, like Brantzche, comes to the realization that in Europe Jewish birth was a sentence of death. Dr. Pearlman's embrace of Jewish identity is, however, complicated. On the one hand, he bought his daughters a comic book version of the Hebrew Bible replete with records, and insisted that his wife light Friday night candles so that, Jamaica recalls, "our Presbyterian surrounding wouldn't obliterate the yellow stars engraved on our souls." On the other hand, he encouraged his daughters to think of themselves first as Americans and then as Jews.

Salamon's novel, like those of Finkelstein and Spiegelman, recalls a traumatic death which serves to personalize the mystery of theodicy. Jamaica's high school friend dies in an auto accident. Echoing Jeremiah, she asks why the innocent suffer. Her survivor mother, who has seen innocent suffering on a vast scale, remembers that in the death camp she felt detached from mass death. "I felt," she says, "like I was floating above it all, like I wasn't there" (179). In Auschwitz, she concludes, one did not see the dead, but rather "one could smell" their burning bodies. Her seriously ill father gives a series of unresponsive answers to Jamaica's question about why her friend had to die. Angry over his apparent indifference, Jamaica asks her father if he would think differently had her friend been Jewish. Reaching maturity, Jamaica adopts a universalism which flows specifically from her Jewish identity thereby affirming Wiesel's view that the more Jewish one is, the more universal are one's concerns.

Unlike Brantzche, Jamaica hears many survivor tales, both from her mother and from Jules Marlin, the news junkie. Eva shocks Jamaica by claiming that the evil Doctor Mengele saved her life by choosing her to live and her mother to die. Revealing the perversions of the death camps, Eva contends that this was a favor because Jamaica's grandmother could never have endured the camps. Going further into the death camps' corruption of the human image, Eva tells Jamaica of an especially senseless "selection" which claimed the life of a healthy young Jewish woman. Less than a week later, the victim's sister lost her mind and their mother died. After that episode, Eva began hating Mengele. Eva tells these tales while she and Jamaica await an open tennis court. In this way, Salamon reveals the hovering presence of the Shoah. In both *White Lies* and *Summer Long-a-Coming* the very understatement of survivor testimony underscores the incomprehensible dimension of the Holocaust's legacy.

Jamaica learns that Jules Marlin came from her parents' hometown, and that his brother was Dr. Pearlman's best friend. Jules had loved her father's first wife, who, with her infant daughter, was murdered in Auschwitz. Jules's disclosure serves to explain Dr. Pearlman's unpredictable fits of anger as well as the intense arguments he and Eva had in Hungarian. Jamaica remembers being so frightened by these arguments that she hid in the closet. Like Art Spiegelman, Jamaica Just bears the emotional burden of a murdered European sibling whom she never knew.

A passion for justice serves further to link Jules and Jamaica. His unending stream of letters to the editor demonstrates a deep anxiety about a society which he views as morally askew. Jules and Jamaica can, in fact, be understood as personifying what Wiesel has termed "mystical madness,"[26] a single-minded devotion to care in a world characterized by cruelty and indifference. For example, readers' responses to her Holocaust article indicate that most people no longer want to hear about the Shoah. Jamaica explains why Jules, and she herself, seem out of step with American culture. She contends that this is "only because you are still capable of feeling outrage" (247). Her comment is reminiscent of Wiesel's position that while in the early days he used to shout in order to change man, he now shouts in order to prevent man from ultimately changing him.[27] Jamaica's shout is a reminder that injustice still pervades the world, and that redemption has not yet occurred.

The Shoah's universal meaning emerges most clearly, however, in Jamaica's concern for Lonnie, the second-generation welfare mother. Jamaica wants to write about an individual "bravely trying to fight the system." But there is more. She herself identifies with Lonnie. Attempting to explain her position to Sammy, Jamaica contends:

> It's hard to explain. I guess I have this image of myself as a martyr once removed, that somehow I've been victimized by the Holocaust even though that was my parents' show, not mine. In a weird way, I guess I "related" to Lonnie, stuck where she is because of her parents. (71)

Jamaica's second-generation mission consists of her attempt to alleviate suffering no matter where it is found. Second-generation identity in *White Lies* is clearly expressed through a sense of social responsibility. Both Jamaica and her older sister Geneva work for the betterment of humanity; Jamaica through her writing and sense of compassion, and Geneva through her vocation as a physician. Jamaica's concern for others may be seen as a form of secular messianism. One should note here that *White Lies* contrasts clinical understandings of survivors to the personal knowledge of the second generation. For example, Jamaica detests the mental health profession for its uncaring and unknowing attitude toward survivors.[28] Geneva, on the other hand, is more like Art Spiegelman. Both have difficulty with their Jewish identity and both receive professional counseling. Geneva's analyst interprets the Justs as perpetual victims eternally preparing for another Holocaust rather than as survivors of an epoch-making event who live in a world largely indifferent to their experience. Jules Marlin's letter-writing is, for instance, analyzed as a harmless form of "undoing" that reveals neurotic but not psychotic tendencies. These professional opinions reveal a total lack of understanding concerning survivors and the second generation. Nevertheless, despite societal indifference, Jamaica is determined to bear witness to the Shoah by restoring human dignity.

Carol Ascher is the daughter of refugees who left Europe as counselors on the last children's transport *(kindertransport)*. Her novel, *The Flood*, differs in significant ways from the other works we have considered. First, it is written by a child of refugees rather than survivors. Next, the timing and setting are different. She describes 1950s Topeka, Kansas. Finally, Ascher's is the one novel in which a child attempts to distill the Shoah's lessons. Yet the novel illustrates, much in the manner of *Summer Long-a-Coming* and *White Lies*, the distinctive quest for post-Auschwitz Jewish identity in families who have been seared by the Shoah's flames.

Ascher's novel tells the tale of the Hoffmans, secularist Jewish refugees from Austria who live in Topeka among a remnant community of European Jews, most of whom work in a psychiatric hospital. David and Leah are the parents of two daughters, six-year-old Sarah, and Eva, a precocious nine-year-old, whose Jewish identity is formed amid the tumultuous backdrop of both human and natural upheavals. Mordecai, an associate of David Hoffman's at the Menninger Clinic, is a religious Jew and a refugee from Prague. The two psychiatrists disagree on every topic, ranging from the Shoah's meaning to the purpose of psychotherapy. As they argue over the recent upheaval of Jewish history, American race relations are on the verge of being profoundly transformed by the Supreme Court's landmark *Brown vs. Topeka Board of Education* decision, which abolished school segregation. There is, as well, a natural calamity in the form of severe flooding which uproots many people, including the rascist Terwilliger family, who stay with the Hoffmans for the duration of the flood.

The Flood is one of the few Jewish American novels which brings to light the lives of refugees.[29] In so doing, the reader is made aware of the fact that refugees, like survivors, remain out of place in America. Eva, the novel's narrator, reminds her readers just how different from midwestern Americans her parents are. For example, in the midst of a rural population which relies for the most part on physical activities and manual labor, Dr. Hoffman is an intellectual. Moreover, the Hoffmans and their refugee friends are lovers of culture. Eva's father and a survivor couple meet regularly to play chamber music. There is the language issue as well. Although Mrs. Hoffman derides German as "Hitler's language," she frequently lapses into her native tongue. Eva's father, for his part, constantly feels the outsider. Called out at 2:00 a.m. to help sandbag the banks along the flood-swollen river, he cynically observes, "It's a chance to show I'm a useful citizen, don't you think?"

Eva's quest for the nature of her Jewish identity is fueled both by her parents' European experience and the American flood. Moreover, as a young girl, her views of identity and responsibility are shaped to a great extent by the discussions she hears between her parents and her own talks with Mordecai. Although neither David nor Leah Hoffman is observant in the traditional manner, they, like the Szusters in *Summer Long-a-Coming* and the Justs in *White Lies,* wish to imbue their children with a sense of Jewish identity.[30] The nature of this identity is, however, very far from the davening and lighting of yahrzeit candles stressed by the Szusters, nor is it composed of the type of tales told by Mrs. Just and Jules Marlin. Instead, Eva Hoffman's Jewish identity emerges from the matrix of her mother's recollection of children in the English refugee camp, and the caldron of anti-Semitism and racism in Christian America.

Ironically, an experience in a local church, whose basement serves as a collection point for flood relief, triggers Mrs. Hoffman's anxiety concerning Eva's Jewish identity. The young girl's infatuation with the beauty of the church prompts Leah to observe that Eva does not "understand what it means for someone not to know they are Jewish." She tells her daughter that there were two types of Jewish children in the refugee camps in England; those who had no idea of what their Jewish identity meant, and those who did. Only those "who had been given a religious or Zionist training, or who knew they were Jewish by other means were all right." In other words, although these children suffered too, "they had some real understanding of why they had come to this strange place." Eva reports that her mother's story made her "feel dizzy and weak in the knees." The crucial subtext undergirding Leah's observation is that Jewish identity prepares one for Jewish destiny. This is a lesson which the mother is especially anxious that her daughter learn in an indifferent and, at times, hostile, American environment.

Eva also learns from her mother a type of practical Jewish theology. For example, in response to her daughter's naive enthusiasm ("wouldn't you like to go to a church like this?"), Mrs. Hoffman, weeping, not only says that it "doesn't look very religious," she also exclaims that "I believe more in what they are doing downstairs" (collecting supplies for flood victims). Ascher's novel is, in fact, a literary embodiment of Irving Greenberg's contention that the crucial post-Shoah religious act is "recreating the image of God" through recreating and restoring human life and dignity.[31] Pre-Holocaust distinctions between religious and secular are, as noted earlier, now bereft of meaning. It is human behavior rather than theological preachment which is decisive. In Greenberg's words, "to leap in and pull a child out of a pit, to clean its face and heal its body, is to make the most powerful statement—the only statement that counts."[32] *The Flood* is at its best in revealing the unpleasant but common coexistence of religion and prejudice: Christian ministers who preach for segregation, churchgoing people who are anti-black, the Terwilligers, who "give the Lord His due" (pray before eating) but who are anti-black and anti-Semitic. These are powerful images which serve to underscore Greenberg's contention that post-Shoah religious life consists of an entire range of apparently secular acts, e.g., giving material aid to victims of the flood, housing an evacuee family, fighting for social justice, all of which serve to restore human dignity. This is the lesson of Jewish identity which Eva learns.

Like Job, the refugees in *The Flood* are confronted with the problem of the suffering of innocents (*zaddik ve-ra lo*). Mordecai explains the issue to Eva by telling her of the different Jewish theological responses to the Shoah. His own father had been a Hasid, a pious Jew who praised God even when entering the gas chamber. Mr. Hoffman, on the other hand, is a theological empiricist. He sees what was done to the Jews in Europe and observes how the blacks live in America and says, even if God exists, I could not pray to a deity who permits these things. Mordecai's father embodies the view of centrist Orthodoxy, which faults man and not God for the Holocaust. This position is best seen in the works of Eliezer Berkovits and Michael Wyschogrod.[33] Mr. Hoffman, for his part, typifies the view of the death-of-God theologian Richard Rubenstein, who, with Elisha ben Avuya of antiquity, contends there is neither "Judge nor judgement."[34] Mordecai's observation that both positions may be correct underscores the complexity of things. He adopts Job's position, telling Eva that the question of evil and suffering is unanswerable. People, asserts Mordecai, "have to live with the pain of what [they] see every day."

The novel explores many forms of evil and suffering, and of prejudice. The Holocaust and the flood are obvious examples of the former. Anti-

Semitism and anti-black feelings exemplify the latter. Mrs. Hoffman compares the plight of Jews in Europe, flood victims, and blacks in Kansas. Like Jamaica Just, she believes that anyone who suffers deserves help.[35] But the complexity of the Jewish situation is revealed by Mrs. Hoffman herself, who embodies a Jewish version of blaming the victims for the crime of the criminals. She, like many allegedly "enlightened" Western European Jews, is critical of Hasidic Judaism, contending that it made no attempt to accommodate to secular culture, thereby incurring the wrath of the murderers. This position rests on the demonstrably false assumption that the Nazis could have been dissuaded from their fanatic attempt to eradicate the Jewish people.

Jewish identity when filtered through the eyes of a nine-year-old child lacks the perspective of history. Wrongs can be set right. For example, after a series of episodes and statements which reveal the prejudice of the Terwilligers' young daughter, Eva dumps a portable swimming pool on the child's head. Temporarily running away from home, Eva sees an old black man retrieving items from the receding flood waters and offers to help him. These symbolic gestures are statements of social concern and human empathy. The novel's title also has important bearing on Eva's Jewish self-understanding. Ascher offers several interpretations of the flood. Epigraphically, she employs Theodore Roethke's observation: "Surround yourself with rising waters: the flood will teach you how to swim." This psychological understanding is contrasted with the biblical view, which sees the deluge as a divine punishment. Interestingly, the two characters who maintain this position, a racist preacher and a crazed inmate of the Menninger Clinic, serve as foils. Mordecai, on the other hand, utilizes the biblical tale differently. He emphasizes not its destruction, but the fact that God renewed the covenant by sending a rainbow. It is now up to man to save humanity. Consequently, Jewish identity in *The Flood* consists of an effort to brighten things through attempts at social justice. Eva Hoffman emerges as a contemporary Jemimah. Her impact on the world, like that of her "sister" of antiquity, will be one of elevating and ennobling the human condition.

Conclusion

This study reveals several dimensions of Jewish identity in second-generation Holocaust literature. Theologically, this writing exemplifies what Greenberg denotes as the "magnetism of the broken covenant."[36] By this he means that the covenant, like God, shares Jewish fate. "The Torah," he writes, "is not insulated from Jewish suffering."[37] Citing Reb

Nachman of Bratzlav's well-known dictum that "nothing is so whole as a broken heart," Greenberg extrapolates that after the Holocaust, "there is 'no faith so whole as a broken faith." He completes the logic of this position in writing that there is "no covenant so complete as a broken covenant."[38] In literary terms, these writings are important for their sense of moral purpose and mission, and echo Wiesel's contention that contemporary writers must write with the Holocaust as background, and that the task of the writer is not to entertain but to disturb and to instruct.[39] This moral edge clearly distinguishes the second generation from other American authors, Jewish and non-Jewish, who either are nonwitnesses or whose purpose in writing is frequently self-serving. Names which come to mind here include Philip Roth and William Styron. While the literary quality of second-generation novels is uneven, these works are crucial as testimony written by those seeking to articulate an authentic post-Auschwitz Jewish identity. Moreover, these works constitute part of the data for those seeking to understand the complexity of this identity.

Second-generation Holocaust literature "remembers" an event not personally experienced, as, in Wiesel's words, "how to deal with evil and the memory of evil . . . how to remain generous in a cold, cruel, cynical society."[40] Moreover, in terms of the dynamic of Jewish American culture, these writings constitute a search for identity undertaken from within the tradition. Unlike the characters of other Jewish American novelists, those created by the second generation are defined not by the outside, Christian, world, but rather by reflecting on the continuing impact of the Holocaust on their own lives. It is the covenant and not Christianity by which the second generation defines itself.

Elie Wiesel summons the unifying motif of the second generation's search for identity. He writes: "I am Jewish because I am Jewish. And not because my existence is a problem for those who are not."[41] As the Shoah gains increased literary attention, it is accompanied by inevitable distortions and trivialization. This is the price paid for bringing to public attention the catastrophe of European Jewry. Consequently, we now see novels like Frederick Busch's spoof of the second generation, *Invisible Mending*, which won a Jewish book award, and, more recently, Erich Segal's *The Doctors*, which features a black medical student who is the son of survivors (he is adopted). Amidst this literary nonsense, second-generation writings may prove to be the leaven in the lump of American Holocaust fiction.

In psychosocial terms, if it is true that Holocaust survivors constitute a new first generation,[42] then this new second generation is behaving in ways distinctively different from the earlier second generation of Jewish Americans. Far from upholding Marcus Hanson's sociological law which contends that the second generation wishes to forget the ways of the first generation, children of survivors embrace their identity by remembering rather than by assimilating. While outwardly "American," children of survivors grapple with distinctive memories of their parents' tales and rituals of remembrance. For the second generation, the world-historical event of the Holocaust is filtered through their family lens.

In regard to classical Jewish paradigms, second-generation novels frequently either do not specifically mention God or are angry with Him. Lack of overt reference to God in this literature, however, reflects neither theological denial nor indifference. Rather, these writings tend to confirm Greenberg's insights concerning the broken state of the post-Auschwitz covenant. These novels may be seen as an attempt to re-fuse the covenant even while quarreling with God. This quarrel is, however, maintained by those who remain within the tradition even while they modify its teachings. This phenomenon is well known in Judaism and ranges from the Bible through Hasidism. After Auschwitz, however, this quarrel assumes new urgency. Both Wiesel and Greenberg articulate the need for this stance as a vital component of post-Holocaust Jewish identity.

Following the model of Job, each of the novelists emphasizes an aspect of the biblical figure's experience: anger, quarreling with God, and fidelity to values. The second-generation novelists' theological quarrel with God, while assuming many forms, is intimately linked to their sense of themselves as Jews. As with Job, second-generation authors live in an existential quandary. Their parents' tales reveal the inappropriateness of American culture to meaningfully address the issues of post-Auschwitz Jewish existence, while at the same time the second generation is raised according to the standards of a vanished European Jewish culture. Moreover, all of the second-generation novels are concerned with theodicy. A traumatic death or disappearance occurs in the works of Friedmann, Wiesel, Spiegelman, Finkelstein, and Salamon, reminding the reader of Des Pres's observation concerning the post-Holocaust loss of innocence. Finally, like their predecessors in antiquity, the contemporary children of Job are concerned to testify and share their testimony with the world. Children of survivors may indeed constitute a new social type who, like Job's children, reflect on their identity in a manner which permeates the world in an attempt to move humanity away from the edge of disaster.

In terms of policy, second-generation novels constitute a vast and, thus far, little-used resource for determining the role of the Holocaust in shaping Jewish-American identity across denominational lines. Examining this data can also help clarify the dimensions of contemporary Jewish response to catastrophe. In what ways does such response follow classical models? How does the second generation differ? What type of covenant do these novels reflect? What are the components of post-*Shoah* Jewish identity? Analysis of these novels can also shed light on the current controversies concerning the place of the Holocaust in Jewish history and theology, while revealing the nature of Jewish existence in America.

Notes

1. Accounts of this phenomenon are widespread in the literature. To mention only a few, I note Martin S. Bergmon & Milton Jucovy (Editors) *Generations of the Holocaust* (New York: Basic Books, Inc., 1982), Helen Epstein *Conversations with Sons and Daughters of Survivors* (New York: G. P. Putnam's Sons, 1979), Eva Fogelman "Therapeutic Alternatives for Holocaust Survivors and Second Generation," in *The Psychological Perspectives of the Holocaust and of its Aftermath*. Edited by Randolph L. Braham, (Boulder: Social Science Monographs, 1988), Robert Prince *The Legacy of the Holocaust: Psychohistorical Themes in the Second Generation* (Ann Arbor, Michigan: UMI Research Press, 1985), and Elie Wiesel "Survivors' Children Relive the Holocaust," in *The New York Times*, Sunday, November 16, 1975 (Op. Ed. page).

2. See Metzudat David and Metzudat Zion in *Mikra'ot Gedolot* on Job 42:14. (New York: Abraham Friedham, n.d.), p. 53b. I am grateful to Rabbi Neal G. Turk of Congregation Ahavath Achim in Fairlawn, New Jersey for initial discussion on this matter.

3. Eliezer Berkovits, *Faith After the Holocaust* (New York: KTAV, 1973), p. 5.

4. Deborah Lipstadt. "We Are Not Job's Children," in *Shoah* 1:4 (1979), p. 16.

5. It is interesting to note that Jewish thinkers who occupy very different positions on the Jewish theological spectrum and who disagree on the Holocaust's covenantal impact, all assert that the trauma of the *Shoah* is intergenerational. Consequently, thinkers as diverse as Eliezer Berkovits, Emil Fackenheim, Irving Greenberg, Richard Rubenstein, Elie Wiesel, and Michael Wyschogrod see the Holocaust as casting an enormous shadow on future Jewish life and thought.

6. The pioneering work here was done by the late Dr. Shammai Davidson, an Israeli psychiatrist who viewed the second generation in much broader terms than other clinicians. Davidson's unpublished notes and manuscripts on this matter are currently being edited by Professor Israel W. Charny of Tel Aviv University.

7. Emil Fackenheim. *To Mend The World: Foundations of Future Jewish Thought* (New York: Schocken Books, 1982), p. 295.

8. This is the title of Fackenheim's most systematic work on the impact of the Holocaust on Jewish thought. See above, footnote seven.

9. *Op. cit.,* chapter seven, "Unauthentic Thought after the Holocaust."

10. Irving Greenberg. *The Voluntary Covenant.* (New York: CLAL—National Jewish Resource Center, 1982), p. 11. Greenberg's new book *The Jewish Way: Living the Holidays* (New York: Summit Books, 1988) persuasively argues that contemporary Jewish observance of the holidays manifests both God's continued hiddenness and the Jewish peoples' espousal of the voluntary covenant.

11. *Op. cit.,* p. 320.

12. *Ibid.*

13. Irena Klepfisz, a second generation member born in Poland, has written a book of meditations entitled *Keeper of Accounts* (Watertown, Massachusetts: Persephone Press, Inc., 1982). One of Klepfisz's meditations in particular focuses on the role of the second generation in keeping memory alive. She writes:

> Yes. It's true. All true. I am scrupulously accurate. I keep track of all distinctions. Between past and present. Pain and pleasure. Living and surviving. Resistance and capitulation. Will and circumstance. Between Life and death. Yes. I am scrupulously accurate. I have become a keeper of accounts. (p. 85)

The cadence and juxtapositions in Klapfisz's words are deeply imbedded in the Hebrew context reminding one of the *Unesane Tokef* prayer which is recited in front of the ark on Rosh HaShannah and Yom Kippur. At these times congregants petition God, the ultimate keeper of accounts, asking who, in the coming year, shall live and who shall die. Who shall prosper and who shall wither. On a symbolic level, the keeper of accounts is one who has an obligation to see that justice is done.

14. Irving Abrahamson. Editor. *Against Silence: The Voice and Vision of Elie Wiesel,* (New York: Holocaust Library, 1985), Volume III, p. 321.

15. See Alan L. Berger "Ashes and Hope: Second Generation Literature of the Holocaust," in *The Holocaust: Reflections in Art and Literature.* Edited by Randolph L. Braham (Boulder: Social Science Monographs, 1990), pp. 97–116.

16. Robert M. Prince "A Case Study of a Psychohistorical Figure: The Influence of the Holocaust on Identity," in *Journal of Contemporary Psychotherapy* (11:1, Spring/Summer, 1980), p. 44.

17. For an interesting and helpful assessment of the relationship between the use of English and choice of profession in the second generation see Stephen M. Pincus "Emerging Voices: The Literature of Children of Holocaust Survivors." Unpublished Alternative Honors English Thesis. The University of Michigan. May, 1989. pp. 46–47.

18. Elie Wiesel. *One Generation After.* Translated by Lily Edelman and Elie Wiesel (New York: Schocken Books, 1962), p. 168.

19. Terrence Des Pres. "The Dreaming Back," in *Centerpoint* (4:13, 1980), p. 14.

20. The present discussion of *Summer Long-a-Coming* and *White Lies* is a revised version of some earlier ideas which appeared in my essay "Ashes and Hope." See above, note fifteen.

21. The absence of these icons is a noticeable feature in Claude Lanzman's magisterial film *Shoah: An Oral History of the Holocaust*. Lanzman's focus is, like that of Elie Wiesel, on the dialectic between tales of survivors and silence.

22. David A. Gerber. "Of Mice and Jews: Cartoons, Metaphors, and Children of Holocaust Survivors in Recent Jewish Experience: A Review Essay," in *American Jewish History* (LXXVII:1, September, 1987), p. 167.

23. Jack Nusan Porter. "Is There a Survivor's Syndrome? Psychological and Socio-Political Implications," in *Journal of Psychology and Judaism* (6:1, Fall/Winter, 1981), pp. 45–46.

24. *Ibid.*, p. 46.

25. On this point see Alan L. Berger *Crisis and Covenant: The Holocaust in American Jewish Fiction* (Albany: SUNY Press, 1985), Chapter four.

26. Abrahamson. *Op. cit.*, Volume III, p. 232.

27. Wiesel. *One Generation After*. p. 72.

28. On this issue see Cynthia Ozick's short story "Rosa," (*The New Yorker*, 21 March, 1983, pp. 38–71) and Elie Wiesel's "A Plea for the Survivors," in his *A Jew Today* (Translated by Marion Wiesel, New York: Vintage Books, 1979), pp. 218–247.

29. Lore Segal's *Other People's Houses* (New York: Harcourt, Brace, and World, 1964) is the model for this genre. Segal, a child refugee from Vienna who left on a children's transport, poignantly describes her experiences in England.

30. Ascher recalls that as a child her religious education "was pretty much limited to not denying my being Jewish, at the same time as being rather ashamed of those who were conspicuously Jews." Both she and her sister are intermarried, although Ascher observes that her marriage to a non-Jew has "somehow heightened my Jewish feelings, and given me the awareness that the responsibility for Judaism in the family is mine." Ascher's comments appear in the *American Jewish Archives: The German-Jewish Legacy in America, 1938–1988, A Symposium* (XL:2, November, 1988), pp. 381 and 382.

31. Irving Greenberg has written extensively on this theme. His early programmatic essay on this theme is "Cloud of Smoke, Pillar of Fire: Judaism, Christianity, and Modernity after the Holocaust," in *Auschwitz: Beginning Of a New Era?* (Edited by Eva Fleischner. New York: KTAV, 1977), p. 41.

32. *Ibid.*, p. 42.

33. For an exposition and critique of this position see Alan L. Berger "Holocaust and History: A Theological Reflection," in *Journal of Ecumenical Studies* (25:2. Spring, 1988), pp. 202–205.

34. *Ibid.*, pp. 197–198.

35. Ascher reports that her mother became active in helping Vietnamese refugees after American troops pulled out of that country. Echoing earlier statements, her mother said "Whoever is a refugee, I have to help." Ascher, *Op.*

cit., p. 376. This attitude is reflected both by Mrs. Hoffman and Eva in *The Flood.* Ascher in fact reports that she has been "surprised by how deeply the stream of my German-Jewish refugee background runs through my writing. *The Flood* expresses fictionally many of the themes of identity, assimilation, and responsibility in the new land . . ." Ascher, p. 383.

36. Greenberg. *The Jewish Way.* p. 322.

37. *Ibid.*

38. *Ibid.*

39. Elie Wiesel. "A Personal Response," in *Face to Face: An Interreligious Bulletin.* Special issue on "Building a Moral Society: Aspects of Elie Wiesel's Work." (New York: Anti-Defamation League of B'nai B'rith, Spring, 1979), Vol. VI, p. 36. Wiesel's observation deserves full citation. He writes: "If the role of the writer may once have been to entertain, that of the witness is to disturb, alert, to awaken, to warn against indifference to injustice—any injustice—and above all against complacency about any need and any people. If once upon a time words may have been used by tellers of tales to please, they must be used today to displease, to unsettle." Wiesel's criteria are incisive for evaluating any literature which purports to be about the Holocaust. Against this background, the second generation writers can be viewed as accepting the legacy of the Holocaust and of their parents' testimony.

40. Abrahamson, *Op. cit.,* Vol. 1, p. 164.

41. Elie Wiesel. *One Generation After.* (Translated by Lily Edelman and Elie Wiesel, New York: Random House, 1970), p. 164.

42. Jacob Neusner. *Death & Birth of Judaism: The Impact of Christianity, Secularism, and the Holocaust on Jewish Faith.* (New York: Basic Books, Inc., 1987), p. 266.

PART V
The Economics of Jewish Identity

Keeping the Cost of Living Jewishly Affordable

J. ALAN WINTER

Since time immemorial, Jews have been known to complain, *shver tzu sein a yid*, "it is tough to be a Jew." However, the recent content of that time-honored complaint is often new. No longer need it refer to physical or psychological hardships. Nowadays, the complaint often refers to the financial difficulty Jews encounter as they seek to live as Jews in contemporary society, to the problem of affording the cost of living Jewishly. The aim of this paper is to provide Jewish institutions with suggestions on how to determine whether the complaint is valid and how to render the cost of living Jewishly affordable if indeed it is.

Obviously, as Cohen's studies in New York and Boston (1983, p. 92; 1988, p. 107) and that of Rimor and Tobin in a northeastern metropolitan area (1988) suggest, the higher one's income, the easier it is to decide that one can afford to live Jewishly. Nevertheless, Lazerwitz and Harrison's analysis of the 1971 National Jewish Population Study (1979, p. 663) found differences related to income to be small. Clearly, the factors other than income are also important, as Rimor and Tobin (1988) found in their study of the correlates of contributions to Jewish organizations. For example, some, regardless of their income, find no level of contribution to a federated campaign acceptable because they do not wish to support the agencies it funds. For others, virtually any level of day school tuition they are likely to face is worth the sacrifice required to educate their child Jewishly. Still, no matter how deep the commitment to living Jewishly, the sages tell us, *im ain kemach, ain Torah*, "if there is no bread, there is no Torah." If one cannot afford to maintain a desired standard of living, few, if any, funds may be available to meet the cost of living Jewishly.

Furthermore, insofar as Jewish survival is dependent upon participation in Jewish institutional life, rendering the cost of affiliation and the use of services provided by Jewish organizations affordable is essential. Moreover, since the contributions of those willing and able to pay virtually any level of dues or fees is apt to be insufficient to meet an organization's needs, adjustments which attract others less willing or less able to pay may be needed if the organization is to remain viable. That is, Jewish survival, both individual and collective, may be dependent on the adjustments which organizations make so as to render affiliation with them and use of their service affordable. In hopes of contributing to that survival, this paper first discusses how to determine whether the cost of the Jewish affiliation or service in question is affordable; and then, what an organization can do about it if it is not.

The Affordability of the Cost of Living Jewishly

The affordability of the cost of living Jewishly, as I have noted elsewhere (Winter 1985), can be regarded as dependent on three factors: (1) the cost of the services or affiliations which define living Jewishly; (2) the level of discretionary funds, i.e., the funds available after providing whatever is necessary to maintain one's desired standard of living; and (3) the rate at which discretionary funds are used to meet the cost of living Jewishly as opposed to other purposes. The last two factors clearly involve setting priorities and making trade-offs. Consequently, the affordability of any given level of living Jewishly is a relative amount, not an absolute figure. It is relative not only to family income but, more importantly, to how the family unit chooses to use that income for Jewish and other purposes. In other words, the affordability of living Jewishly is determined by the value of doing so, not just its cost. Nevertheless, as I shall endeavor to show below, it is possible to discuss how to estimate the affordability of living Jewishly.

The Cost of Jewish Services and Affiliations

The total cost of whatever services and affiliations define "living Jewishly" depends on two factors: (1) what items are included in the definition, and (2) their individual cost. The determination of what items to include depends, in turn, on a series of decisions or choices to be noted below. The cost of individual items can, of course, generally be determined by contacting the agency or organization in question. However, average or national costs are more difficult to come by. In my admittedly limited experience, national organizations frequently have either unreliable information or none at all as to the dues or fees charged by their local constituent organizations. A survey may, then, be required to determine national or average costs of the service or affiliation in question. Further difficulties may be encountered if the item in question is a contribution, e.g., to a federated campaign, rather than membership dues or fees for services rendered. There is no ready formula for determining an acceptable amount to be contributed. Again, an appropriate community survey may reveal the average contribution. Such averages are, of course, more meaningful if they are adjusted for relevant characteristics such as age, occupation, and family composition. In any event, as difficult as it may be to determine the cost of a given component of living Jewishly, it may be even more difficult to decide just what components to include.

Clearly, the cost of Jewish living should include the activities or affiliations which define what it means to live Jewishly in contemporary society. Thus, the cost of synagogue membership replete with its building fund would be included, as might a contribution to a federated campaign. However, membership in a Jewish country club or health club might not be. Second, the list may or may not be restricted to costs which are encountered on a regular, annual basis. For example, while the cost of day school tuition will likely be included where incurred, the cost of such special events as a bar/bat mitzvah or trip to Israel may or may not be included. Some decision also has to be made as to whether or not to include incidental and/or "start-up" costs of a Jewish life—for example, as to whether or not to include the costs of subscriptions to Jewish periodicals or of a mezuzah, menorah, and seder plate. Finally, a decision has to be made as to whether or not to include the total cost of a component of Jewish living which may also be obtained under non-Jewish auspices. For example, the entire cost of a Jewish day camp may be included, or only the difference between that cost and the cost of a non-Jewish camp. Similarly, a decision may have to be made as to whether to include the entire cost of kosher food or only the difference between its cost and that of an equivalent diet of non-kosher food. In any case, once the items to be included in the cost of living Jewishly have been identified, and after their individual costs have been established, the next step, determining the level of available discretionary funds, can be taken.

Determining the Level of Discretionary Funds

Fundamentally, there are two methods of estimating the discretionary funds available within a family budget to meet the cost of living Jewishly. The first, as illustrated in Table 1, is to use a prescriptive budget, i.e., to use a budget which some authoritative body (here a Bureau of Labor Statistics expert committee) has designated as sound, and to note the discretionary funds it contains. Such a budget might, although the illustration in Table 1 does not, set such funds as high as the biblical standard of a tithe.

The second method, illustrated in Table 2, is to use a descriptive budget, i.e., one based on actual expenditure patterns, and again to note the discretionary funds it contains. Such a budget might show, as the illustration in Table 2 does, that about 2 percent is devoted to discretion-

Table 1
Estimated Prescribed Budget for a Four-Person Family: Intermediate Standard of Living, January 1987[a]

Item	Percent of budget	Dollar amount[b]
Basic family consumption	95	$32,650
Food	20	6,880
Housing	27	9,280
Transportation	11	3,780
Clothing & personal care	6	2,060
Medical care	5	1,720
Social Security & Disability	8	2,750
Personal Income Tax	17	5,840
Other expense, e.g., insurance dues	1	340
Discretionary funds	5	1,720
Gifts & contributions[c]	2	690
Other consumption[d]	3	1,030
Total Budget	100	$34,380

Source: Colien Hefferan, "Family Budget Guidelines," *Family Economic Review* 1987 (4): 1–9.

[a]Percentage estimate family budget allocations updated to spring, 1987 prices and then current Social Security and income tax regulations and rates (cf. Hefferan 1987). Figures rounded to nearest percent.

[b]Total dollar amount is based on estimates derived by a 1978 committee of experts convened by the Bureau of Labor Statistics. It represents a median-level expenditures in a two-parent, two-child family (cf. Hefferan 1987). Dollar amounts adjust the 1984 figures reported by Hefferan to January 1989, rounded to nearest $10, according to *CPI Detailed Report: January, 1989*, p. 77.

[c]Percentage for gifts and contributions based on Sholl (1986).

[d]Other consumption includes recreation, education, reading matter, tobacco, alcoholic beverages, bank charges, children's allowances and miscellaneous expenses away from home.

ary funds. Such a figure is consistent with Rimor and Tobin's (1988) study of Jews in a northeastern metropolitan area, which found that only 1 or 2 percent of one's income is contributed to Jewish organizations or philanthropies. Scholl (1986, p. 12), using the interview portion of the continuing Consumer Expenditure Survey conducted by the Bureau of Labor Statistics, notes that in 1981, gifts to individuals and organizations outside the family averaged 2 percent of before-tax household income. Interestingly, while the amount given increases with household income, the proportion declines from 4.1 percent for those with annual incomes under $5,000 to 1.9 percent for those with incomes between $15,000 and $20,000 to 1.8 percent for those with incomes over $40,000. The rate for those with a college education is 2.4 percent of annual income, and it is 2.3 percent for those with course work beyond the bachelor's degree. Jews, of course, are quite apt to have at least a college education, if not more.

Each of the two methods, the prescriptive and descriptive, offers advantages and disadvantages to those seeking to determine whether the cost of living Jewishly is affordable. The main advantage of using a prescriptive budget is that it is apt to reflect sounder principles of consumption and finances than might be common practice. Thus, policy decisions based on it can be seen as supportive of sound budgeting practices, whether common or not. Unfortunately, the only prescriptive budgets I have been able to locate to date are outmoded, reflecting 1960–61 spending habits (see Mason and Butler 1987). However, recent studies, to be noted below, mitigate the outmoded character of available prescriptive budgets.

The primary advantage of using available descriptive budgets is that they are more recent and reflect more contemporary spending habits. However, they may reflect habits Jewish organizations would be uncomfortable supporting, e.g., a relatively high outlay for tobacco and/or alcohol. Moreover, I doubt that anybody knows how the spending habits of Jews compare with those of the rest of the American population. Consequently, the use of a descriptive budget based on the spending habits of the total American population may be misleading when applied to Jews. It might be wiser to undertake the appropriate study and determine a descriptive budget for Jews in the United States.

In any case, prescriptive budgets were routinely published by the Bureau of Labor Statistics (BLS) until 1981. The BLS budgets represented three hypothetical lists of goods and services designed to reflect lower, intermediate, and higher standards of consumption, respectively, and were based on the assumption that the family involved consisted of a

Table 2
Estimated Descriptive Annual Budget for a Consumer Unit Headed by a 35–44-year-old, January 1989

Item	Percent of Budget		Dollar Amount[a]	
Basic family consumption	88		$32,350	
Food		14		5,050
Housing		14		9,460
Transportation		15		5,340
Clothing & personal care		5		2,020
Health care		3		1,110
Social Security, retirement, pension		5		1,890
Taxes		19		6,950
Other: insurance, dues		1		530
Discretionary funds	12		4,450	
Gifts & contributions		2		860
Other consumption		10		3,590
Total Budget	100		$36,800	

Source: David E. Bloom and Sanders D. Korenman, "The Spending Habits of American Consumers" *American Demographics* 8 (3): 22–25.

[a] Dollar amounts are from Bloom and Korenman 1986), to the nearest $10, updated to reflect the Consumer Price Index of January 1989 as reported in *CPI Detailed Report: January, 1989*, pp. 77–78. Percentage figures are calculated from the dollar amounts. The Bloom and Korenman figures are based on the Consumer Expenditure Survey, 1982–83.

[b] Other consumption includes entertainment, education, reading, tobacco, alcoholic beverages, and miscellaneous expenditures.

thirty-eight-year-old husband employed full-time, a nonworking wife, a thirteen-year-old son, and an eight-year-old daughter. Since 1981 there has been no ongoing statistical series designed to define a standard budget for American families. However, the Community Council of Greater New York does irregularly publish standard budgets based on expenditure patterns and costs of families in New York City. Moreover, it is possible, using information for various metropolitan areas published in the monthly report of the Consumer Price Index, the *CPI Detailed Report*, to adjust for the differences between any given community and New York. Thus, the updated New York budgets can provide a basis for a descriptive budget for the community in question. However, it should be easier to use the guidelines provided by Hefferan (1987).

Hefferan's guidelines make use of the recommendations of an expert committee established by the BLS in 1978. The expert committee devised a budget that would reflect the median level of expenditure for a two-parent, two-child family. Hefferan (1987) has calculated a revision of the recommended budget for the median level of expenditures based on prices in the spring of 1987 and the then current Social Security and income taxes. The resulting budget is expressed in percentage amounts devoted to given budget categories rather than in absolute dollar amounts (see Table 1). Furthermore, Hefferan (1987, p. 3) cautions that the revised budget "be used very judiciously." Despite the updated prices and tax figures, it still represents 1960–61 spending habits and an increasingly atypical two-parent family with a nonworking wife. However, Gieseman and Rogers (1986) do provide estimates, based on the BLS Consumer Expenditure Survey, to help determine the average differences in spending between one- and two-earner households. They also report annual expenditures classified by household income quintile, age of reference person, region, and household size. In any case, the discretionary funds in the Hefferan budget amount to some 5 percent of the total. These funds are typically used for such items as reading matter, recreation, tobacco, and alcoholic beverages. A further study by Scholl (1986) indicates that about 40 percent of that, or 2 percent of the total budget, can be said to be devoted to cash gifts to individuals outside the immediate family and to contributions to religious, educational, political, or other organizations—a figure, by the way, comparable to that found for contributions to Jewish organizations in the Rimor and Tobin (1988) study noted above.

The most recently available descriptive budget that I have examined is presented by Bloom and Korenman (1996). Their analysis (see Table 2) is based on the Consumer Expenditure Survey which is still conducted regularly by the BLS. The survey consists of two parts: (1) a diary in which respondents record spending on inexpensive, frequently purchased items; and (2) interviews which discuss purchases of relatively expensive items. It leads to a similar conclusion, viz., that approximately 2 percent of the budget (here that of a consumer unit headed by someone thirty-five to forty-four years old, comparable to the thirty-eight-year-old household head of the prescriptive budget just discussed) is devoted to charitable contributions.

In sum, based on either descriptive or prescriptive budgets for the American population as a whole, or on a study of the Jewish population in one metropolitan area, it would appear that it is reasonable to assume that a family unit will use between 2 and 5 percent of its income for discretionary items, including those which define the cost of living Jewishly. The rate at which they do so, i.e., the proportion of discretionary funds devoted to Jewish living, is the matter considered next.

The Use of Discretionary Funds to Live Jewishly

It would, of course, be comforting to assume that all of the discretionary funds available to a Jewish family will be used to support the cost of living Jewishly. For example, it can be hoped that contributions are made to a federated campaign or dues paid to a synagogue before money is spent on alcohol, tobacco, entertainment, or some other discretionary expenditure. If such is the case, then using Hefferan's (1987) figures noted above, a Jewish family with an annual income of $40,000 will have some $2,000 of discretionary funds available, including $800 for synagogue dues and contributions to a federated campaign or other causes. However, there is no evidence that the hoped-for 100 percent use of discretionary funds to meet the cost of living Jewishly is a reality. Moreover, there is good reason to believe that such is not always the case. Rather, as Ritterband and Cohen (1979) show for contributions to non-synagogue Jewish causes, it can be expected that the rate at which funds will be used for living Jewishly will vary with Jewish commitment. Specifically, they found that those with the highest Jewish commitment contributed about twice as much as did those with a moderate commitment and about four times what those with the lowest Jewish commitment contributed. Thus, if the most committed families are assumed to use all (100 percent) of their discretionary income to meet the cost of living Jewishly, those who are moderately committed can be expected to use half (50 percent), and the least committed, one-quarter (25 percent). Again assuming a $40,000 income, the most committed family would then have some $2,000 to meet the cost of living Jewishly; the moderately committed, $1,000, a bit more than average; and the least committed, only $500, less than the average usually devoted to charitable contributions. Moreover, if the cost of living Jewishly includes $800 in synagogue dues and religious school tuition, a $100 contribution to a federated campaign, and an additional $100 or so in Jewish community center dues or other items, i.e., about $1,000 in all, then while the most committed could well regard the total amount as "affordable," i.e., as within the range of the $2,000 they are willing and able to pay, the moderately committed might feel "pinched" in that the cost is at the $1,000 limit they are willing to spend; and the least committed would likely conclude that even the synagogue dues exceed the $500 they can "afford," given the standard of living they wish to maintain and the discretionary expenditures they want to make for items other than those involved in living Jewishly. It would remain, then, for the Jewish community either to do what it can to render the cost of living Jewishly more "affordable" in the eyes of those who are not highly committed to meeting it or to run the risk of alienating them from the Jewish community still further. Clearly, the Jewish community has a stake in trying to induce as many as possible to conclude that the cost of living Jewishly is indeed "affordable," i.e., in encouraging them to meet such costs without undue sacrifice in their standard of living. I will close with some thoughts on how that might be done even if the Messiah tarries.

Keeping the Cost of Living Jewishly Affordable

Given the framework employed here, two general strategies are apparent to enable a Jewish community to render the cost of living Jewishly "affordable" in the eyes of those who do not now believe it is. They are: (1) decrease the cost of the service or affiliation in question for those who do not regard it as affordable; and (2) create an atmosphere which will encourage those concerned about the costs to use a higher proportion of their discretionary funds for Jewish living.

Both strategies assume that minimizing the financial consequences of income differences will have a significant impact on Jewish affiliation rates. However, as Cohen notes (1983, p. 92), "Differences in income relate to differences in class and cultural style." For example, even if the strategies discussed below render the cost of living Jewishly affordable to a given family, they still may feel uncomfortable attending a synagogue where they park their very used station wagon between a new sports car on one side and an even newer convertible on the other, and where conversation at the Oneg turns to Caribbean vacations well beyond their reach or colleges they do not even dream of sending their kids to, and everybody else seems to prefer tennis and golf to football and baseball. Families uncomfortable with such differences, or others associated with income, may not affiliate with a given organization even if it does all it can to make membership financially affordable. Moreover, more than money may be at the root of reluctance to join. Social differences associated with differences in income may also pose a problem that organizations wishing to increase their membership may have to address. However, such problems are beyond the scope of this paper.

In any case, the first strategy noted above for rendering Jewish living affordable, that of reducing fees or dues, may involve additional financial burdens on Jewish organizations already likely to be operating on tight budgets. However, failure to make Jewish living more affordable to more Jews may undermine Jewish survival in America. In any case, reduced costs to the families involved may result from one or more of three programs: (1) subsidies or scholarships; (2) a "give-or-get" standard; and (3) reduction in costs.

Subsidies or scholarships may, of course, be underwritten by the organization in question with or without help from other funding sources such as the local federation. Financial assistance from the local federated campaign might, however, be regarded as controversial in that providing it may be seen by some as diverting funds otherwise destined for Israel. Moreover, even those who agree, in principle, that more federated campaign funds be used to subsidize local organizations, can still disagree as to which organization can appropriately receive such subsidies. For example, most would argue, I think, that synagogues should "pay their own way" without use of federated campaign funds. I assume there is little doubt such would be the case when synagogue membership dues are the issue, but many may also oppose the use of federated funds even for the support of synagogue schools, e.g., to subsidize Sunday school enrollment. It is also possible that many will object to subsidies for day school tuition on the grounds that such enrollment is optional, and something of a "luxury." I certainly heard many such objections when I served on the local-allocation committee of my federation. There are, it appears, some who interpret the *ve'ahavtah* reference to *veshenanta levanecha* as establishing their individual obligation to provide for the diligent teaching of their own children, and not a corporate responsibility to ensure that all Jewish children are taught Torah.

Furthermore, even if there is agreement that a given fee or dues be subsidized, whether by a central funding source or the organization in question, there are still some rather knotty issues to resolve before a program can be put in place. For example, there is the issue of what constitutes need, i.e., what a given family can or cannot afford. The basic points to be raised in order to resolve such an issue are outlined above, viz., (1) determining the cost of the service or affiliation in question; (2) the level of discretionary funds available; and (3) the rate at which discretionary funds are to be made available for the cost in question. The first is, of course, easily determined by the organization in question. It should know what it "normally" charges. However, determination of the second and third points involves some difficult issues.

For example, if subsidies are to be income-dependent, the organization must devise some procedures for determining the income of a family seeking subsidy. How to make such determination while balancing due respect for the privacy of the family involved with the organization's need to know the family's (private) income can be very demanding. Of course, an organization can simply take the applicant's word on what their income is. However, such a system is clearly open to question, especially on the part of the full-paying members, who may want to be sure no "freeloaders" are subsidized.

In any case, even where the family income is known, the problem of deciding the amount of its funds that should be devoted to the cost of living Jewishly still must be faced. That amount depends, of course, on two factors: (1) one's income, and (2) the standard of living one hopes to maintain. Clearly, it is easier to maintain a moderate standard of living with a given income than a higher standard. Thus, those who wish only to maintain a moderate standard of living have more funds available for meeting the cost of living Jewishly at any given income level than do those who wish to maintain a higher standard of living. For example, a family with an income of $40,000 can easily maintain a moderate standard of living as defined by either the prescriptive or the descriptive budget (Tables 1 and 2, respectively). However, such an income would likely not suffice if the family wishes to maintain a higher standard of living. Thus, the same $40,000 leaves one family, that desiring a higher standard of living, little or no money for the cost of living Jewishly, and another, wishing only a moderate standard of living, over $3,000 for such costs without reducing any other expenditures. It is likely that any organization would be reluctant to subsidize the dues of a family earning $40,000 which could "afford" its dues and still maintain a moderate standard of living. Nevertheless, the family may feel strongly that it is entitled to live at a higher standard, as in fact many Jews do, and that it is quite justified in claiming it cannot "afford" the cost of affiliation without some help. In other words, those who decide who is to receive a subsidy must decide what standard of living it is reasonable for the organization to help potential members support. If it is reasonable to support a higher standard of living, then the income level of those subsidized will be higher than if only a moderate standard of living is supported. Of course, if only those able to live at a lower standard are to be helped, the income levels that will be subsidized will be lower still.

Unfortunately, deciding what standard of living or, for that matter, what income level renders one eligible for support does not answer all the questions facing an organization that undertakes a subsidy or scholarship program. It must also decide at what rate the available discretionary funds are to be used to meet the cost of living Jewishly. For example, it must decide whether a family which has $1,000 in discretionary funds should be given help to meet the $800 dues noted above because it wishes to spend only half of its discretionary funds on the synagogue and put the remaining $500 in a fund for its child's college education or to pay for a needed vacation.

Finally, even after the organization decides on what choices it will support with regard to the use of discretionary funds to meet the cost of living Jewishly and other discretionary spending, there is still the question of whether it is to help underwrite other costs of living Jewishly. For example, a synagogue may or may not include the cost of day school tuition when deciding who is to be permitted to join with reduced dues. It is certainly conceivable that a given synagogue will decide not to reduce dues for those who enroll their children in day school, on the grounds that doing so is tantamount to subsidizing the day school at the expense of its own religious school.

The provision of either scholarships by the organizations involved or subsidies from some central funding source, then, may create its own difficulties. Thus, a second strategy for reducing costs may be employed, viz., a "give-or-get" policy. That is, those who wish to use or affiliate with the organization in question but cannot afford to give money, i.e., pay its dues or fees, may instead help it to "get" the funds it needs by assisting in activities designed to help the organization meet its costs. The donation of professional, clerical, or other services which help reduce the organization's costs may or may not be counted toward the amount to be "gotten." Time spent on fundraising activities should surely be counted. In any case, some schedule must be devised to establish the dollar value of the time or services that are provided in order to help the organization meet its costs. Unfortunately, many of those least able to "give" money are single-parent families which also have the least free time or other resources to help the organization "get" what it needs to reduce costs or raise its income.

Finally, since neither subsidies nor a give-or-get program may be feasible, a third program, one which I suspect is rather common, may be employed, viz., reducing the operating costs of the organizations in question, thereby reducing its need for funds and possibly hard-to-afford dues or fees. However, since the largest part of the budget is apt to be the salary and benefits of its own Jewish professional staff, cost-cutting has its own risks. Such professionals, after all, are likely to use their Jewish peers in other professions as a referent group. Since these peers are among the most affluent Americans, the temptation to leave the field of Jewish communal service would only be increased should the salaries of professional Jewish communal workers, educators, rabbis, etc., be held down. Low salaries for Jewish professionals could very well reduce the pool of those willing to enter or remain in the field of service to the Jewish community.

Each of the three proposals for reducing the costs of using services or affiliating with Jewish organizations, scholarships, subsidies, and cost-cutting, has its own drawbacks. Moreover, each is rather difficult to administer. Little is known, I believe, about the extent and operation of any of these programs. Clearly, it would be wise to conduct appropriate studies to identify the difficulties encountered by such programs and the factors which influence their success or failure. Given their inherent problems, however, the attractiveness of a second major strategy, viz., increasing the proportion of funds devoted to living Jewishly, is obvious. It is equally obvious that doing so entails short- and long-term strategies for strengthening Jewish identity. That is, as Ritterband and Cohen (1979) suggest on the basis of a 1975 study of Boston-area Jews, "the more the more" theory is a good basis on which to build a strategy to encourage Jews to support Jewish organizations. The theory holds that Jews who take one aspect of Jewish life seriously tend to respond in like manner to other aspects, including tzedakah, or philanthropy. Further support for the theory is found in Rimor and Tobin's (1988) study of Jewish philanthropic contributions in northern New Jersey. Specifically, they conclude that "the religious aspects of Jewish identity are highly associated with one another as are the civil aspects of Jewish identity" (p. 32). Moreover, their data suggest that both as a long- and a short-term strategy, "building religious identity through increased synagogue attendance and membership ultimately will have strong effects on (federated) fundraising campaigns." Unfortunately, neither Ritterband and Cohen nor Rimor and Tobin discuss how to go about building the religious identity which they see as basic to Jewish philanthropic behavior. Indeed, even with this conference, not enough is known about how to go about increasing Jewish identity and about how to link a strengthened identity to the realization that one may have to pay for the privilege of actualizing it, i.e., give money to support the Jewish institutions and organizations in which it is actualized. Thus, however *shver* (hard) it is *tzu sein a yid,* (to be a Jew) it is likely to be *shverer* (harder) still to know how to convince others not only that they can afford to be Jews, but that there is great value in doing so.

References

Bloom, David E., and Sanders D. Korenman. 1986. "The Spending Habits of American Consumers." *American Demographics* 8 (3): 22–25, 51–54.

Cohen, Steven M. 1983. *American Modernity and Jewish Identity*. New York: Tavistock.

———. 1988. *American Assimilation of Jewish Survival*. Bloomington: Indiana University Press.

CPI Detailed Report: January, 1989. Washington, D.C.: U.S. Department of Labor, Bureau of Labor Statistics.

Gieseman, Raymond, and John Rogers. 1986. "Consumer Expenditures: Results Form the Diary and Interview Surveys." *Monthly Labor Review* 109 (6): 14–18.

Hefferan, Colien. 1987. "Family Budget Guidelines." *Family Economic Review* 1987 (4): 1–9.

Lazerwitz, Bernard, and Michael Harrison. 1979. "American Jewish Denominations: A Social and Religious Profile." *American Sociological Review* 44: 656–666.

Mason, Charles, and Clifford Butler. 1987. "New Basket of Goods and Services Being Priced in Revised CPI." *Monthly Labor Review* 110 (1): 3–22.

Rimor, Mordechai, and Gary A. Tobin. 1988. "Is a Good Jew a Contributing Jew? The Relationship Between Jewish Identity and Philanthropy." Conference on Jewish Philanthropy, CUNY, June. Mimeo.

Ritterband, Paul, and Steven M. Cohen. 1979. "Will the Well Run Dry? The Future of Jewish Giving in America." *National Jewish Conference Policy Studies,* January. Mimeo.

Scholl, Kathleen K. 1986. "Contributions and Gifts in Cash." *Family Economic Review*. 1986 (4): 12–16.

Winter, J. Alan. 1985. "An Estimate of the Affordability of Living Jewishly." *Journal of Jewish Communal Living* 61: 247–256.

Response to J. Alan Winter

DEBORAH E. LIPSTADT

As a historian—not an economist or sociologist—I was intrigued by the different ways one can calculate the costs of Jewish life that are enumerated in Dr. Winter's paper.

However, since we have been charged with the responsibility of helping the Wilstein Institute set its policy agenda, I believe that it is crucial that we think in a very coherent fashion about the best allocation of our resources—and it is particularly fitting that we do so when the topic at hand is, as it is in this session, the resources of the Jewish community.

Dr. Winter makes certain observations which are beyond dispute. There are a wide variety of income levels in the Jewish community. So, too, there are many varied levels of affiliation and identification. Most importantly, the cost of belonging to the Jewish community and its institutions can be significant. While "belonging" can mean different things to different people, it generally includes certain basics, such as synagogue membership, charitable contributions, and Jewish education (day school, religious school, and/or camps). The cost rises higher for those who follow the dietary laws and other traditions, such as buying a lulav and etrog and strict observance of the laws of Passover.

While I agree wholeheartedly with Dr. Winter's contentions that we must find ways of both keeping this cost as low as possible and convincing more people to participate in Jewish life, I seriously doubt whether we need sophisticated calculations to prove what we already know: the cost is high and places a real burden on certain families.

There is, however, a certain irony here which cannot be ignored. It sheds some doubts on the contention that it is solely cost which keeps people from belonging and actively participating. Why is it that the Orthodox community, which is the "poorest" segment of the Jewish community, has the highest rate of affiliation and identification? Their strict adherence to Jewish law renders the costs that they must bear even higher than those faced by others in the community. Why is it that Orthodox schools rarely, if ever, turn a child away because of financial constraints? Is it because they are the only ones who truly understand the meaning of *talmud torah k'neged kulam* ("the study of Torah takes precedence over all the other mitzvot")?

If the poorest sector among us, which faces even higher Jewish living costs and which tends to have more children, has the strongest rate of affiliation, does that not shed some doubt on the argument that it is cost that is driving people away?

Nonetheless, I agree that we should explore avenues to alleviate the financial burden placed on certain families. Jewish endowment funds—both communal and private—could play a significant role in this arena, as the Gruss Fund has in New York City. One of the policies that might be tried is an endowed trip to Israel for every Jewish youngster, on graduating from high school. The trip would be preceded by certain classes on the history and meaning of Israel. Another policy might be for every synagogue to provide a year's "grace" in membership dues to newlyweds and to families during a year when a new child is born. There are many other ideas and policies which might be and, in certain communities, are already being pursued.

They should have as their goal:

- Enhancing Jewish identity so that increasing numbers of Jews will believe that the "sacrifice" that they must make in order to belong to the Jewish community is not a sacrifice but an investment.
- Convincing Jewish institutions that they must reach out to members of the Jewish community and make them feel wanted.
- Finding a way to *graciously* make room in these institutions for those who cannot afford it.
- Instilling a sensitivity among Jewish educational and religious institutions as to the great financial strain Jewish life places on families.

A prime example of the kind of insensitivity reference to in the last item was recently demonstrated in my own community by a synagogue in a very wealthy neighborhood which has a school which caters to both very wealthy and middle-class families. The synagogue board—which has ultimate power over policies in the school—decided to introduce a new policy. Parents of children in the school had to now belong to that synagogue irrespective of whether they already belonged to another synagogue, even one of the same denomination. (The school is denominationally affiliated.) In addition they were to be taxed for the building fund. This was all done simultaneously with the raising of school tuition.

A parent confronted a long-time member of the board on this issue. The parent, who had already decided to keep his children in the school, was concerned about another family. He raised the issue about the cost of maintaining two synagogue memberships. The board member's response was, "If they cannot afford to come, let them leave. We have other children on the waiting list whose parents will pay."

In another synagogue a different but related kind of insensitivity was demonstrated recently when a young couple appealed for a reduction of the fee charged for holding a wedding in the sanctuary. The couple, neither of whom earned a significant salary, had no parents and were paying for the wedding themselves with help from their siblings. The woman had belonged to the synagogue for many years, as had other members of her family. Her husband was new to organized Jewish life, had no Jewish education, but was willing to have a traditional wedding with kosher food. The synagogue administrator informed them that if they couldn't afford to pay, they should get married someplace else. Discussions with other members of the synagogue administration, including the rabbi, yielded nothing despite the fact that they all knew of the family's financial limitations.

To add insult to injury, when they asked about the synagogue's *stated* policy of not charging newlyweds membership dues, they were made to feel as if they were asking for a special dispensation. They were told that despite the fact that it was a policy, the issue would have to be discussed by the synagogue board because she was already a member. (This latter situation was resolved when the board was reminded that two years earlier the son and daughter-in-law of prominent and wealthy synagogue members had been automatically granted free membership even though the son was already a member.)

In both these cases the lay and professional leadership of these institutions demonstrated a decided insensitivity to the needs of people who were genuinely strapped by financial demands. There was a little—if any—sympathy for their situation. Naturally, synagogues and Jewish institutions face malingerers all the time, e.g., people who "cannot afford" to pay tuition because they are building a new addition to their home or planning a trip to Europe. But there are many—including some in the solid middle class—who must stretch and strain to participate. The painful irony here is that it is often Jewish communal professionals who find the cost of Jewish living a real burden. Insensitive behavior such as the two cases described here is far too frequent in the Jewish community and certainly makes those who are less committed reevaluate the cost of belonging.

Maybe J. Alan Winter says it best in his paper as he begins and ends at the same point: *es ist shver tzu sein a yid* (it is hard to be a Jew). Let us be careful of policy explorations that take us full circle back to where we began and back to what we already know. Instead, let us commit our resources to effecting change and moving forward.

Response to J. Alan Winter

RUSSELL D. ROBERTS

Professor Winter's paper tries to measure the cost of living Jewishly. It is hard to measure. Words like "need," "necessity," "affordable," and "discretionary income" are difficult to define. One person's necessity is another's luxury. In a fundamental sense, all income is discretionary.

Rather than assuming a fixed amount of discretionary income available to spend on Jewish activities, I will take the perspective of the economist and assume that the amount of money and effort people spend on Jewish activities varies in response to monetary and nonmonetary incentives. How can Jewish institutions and the Jewish community affect those incentives to improve the quality of Jewish life?

People have limited income to spend on numerous wants and desires. Because income is not infinite, you must make choices. Your desires include mezuzahs, Dodger baseball games, cars, VCRs, kosher food, helping the State of Israel, and so on. Some of your choices are irrelevant to leading a Jewish life, while others may have a positive or negative influence. Many of your choices are irrelevant to me as a Jew or a fellow citizen. For example, I don't care whether you spend a lot of money on apples instead of pears. But as a Jew, I may care deeply about your choices on items related to Jewishness. As Jews, we wish there were more money going to Israel, more money going to Jewish institutions at home, more money to help Jewish elderly, more time spent participating in Jewish activities, and so on.

For Jews, these Jewish activities have a characteristic that apples do not. The people who spend money on these activities, benefit others as well as themselves. So when I give money to Israel, you feel good because Israel has more security or more resources. When I keep kosher, if that is important to you, you feel good because it reinforces your feeling part of a community. When I marry a Jewish woman, you are happier than if I do not.

A fundamental result of economics is that we tend to spend too little of our resources on these types of goods where our actions benefit others as well as ourselves. Each individual feels he or she is spending the right amount. But as a community, we would all be better off if every individual spent more. The reason is that when I, as an individual, allocate my scarce income between my competing wants and desires, I weigh the costs and benefits to me. But unless I am sufficiently altruistic, I will ignore or undervalue the contribution my spending makes to the happiness of others.

Here is a simple example. You are deciding whether to volunteer in some area of Jewish service, say in spending part of your Sunday at the Jewish old-age home. If you volunteer, you get the satisfaction of helping the elderly. To do so, you must give up whatever pleasure you would have received from using your time in an activity other than volunteering, say watching a football game. You weigh these factors, perhaps unconsciously, and you make your decision about whether to volunteer. Even with your altruism toward the elderly, you are likely to ignore in this decision the benefits other *nonelderly* Jews receive from seeing more help go to the elderly in the old-age home. Unless you are sufficiently altruistic, you will ignore these benefits. You may still volunteer—your personal pleasure from helping the elderly may be great enough. But some people will not volunteer who would have if they had been able to capture some of the good feelings of the other nonelderly members of the community. There are likely to be too few volunteers helping the elderly.

Successful communities use a variety of mechanisms to get people to spend more time and energy than they might on their own, on activities that benefit the entire community. They can raise the cost of an action that harms others or fails to help others. Or they can raise the psychological or monetary benefit from helping others. I would like to spend the rest of the time discussing what tools are available and how they can be used to improve the quality of Jewish life.

One legendary technique is guilt. In all societies, guilt plays a major role in getting people to do things they might not wish to do on their own, but where the net benefit to the community is positive. When communities raise money for Israel or for their synagogues, they may publicly reveal the donations of individuals in order to shame and embarrass people who might give very little. The question is, how much guilt is necessary? Making people feel guilty has direct and indirect costs. It makes some people unhappy, and it uses up time and energy that could be freed up to use elsewhere in the community. You want to apply guilt to the things that have the widest community impact.

A dramatic example is intermarriage. Intermarriage imposes lots of costs on the Jewish community, and so the community reacts by making those who intermarry feel guilty. Application of this guilt may even continue after the marriage takes place. This seems irrational, but it raises the cost of future intermarriages by other members of the community.

Institutions use guilt, dunning phone calls, and the raised eyebrows of their members to encourage generosity. These methods raise the cost of being selfish. Alternative approaches raise the benefits from being generous. One way to get individuals to consider the benefits to others when they make individual decisions is to incorporate the idea of a matching grant. Typically, matching grants are used by large donors to raise the return on giving for small donors. But the principle behind matching grants can be used more widely.

First, consider the minyan. The concept of a minyan is a very clever way to get people to do something for the community they might not do on their own. The mitzvah of prayer could be only that it is good to pray with more Jews than fewer—it is better to pray in shul than at home. Each morning, I will have to decide whether it is worth fulfilling this mitzvah or whether I should stay at home. I will compare my sleepiness to the satisfaction I will receive from the mitzvah of praying with others. If I am altruistic, I may also get the satisfaction of helping others pray in a larger crowd because my attendance makes the crowd bigger by one. Some mornings, my sleepiness will win out because the benefits accruing to the other Jews at shul from my attendance (because I will have made the crowd a little bit larger) are not large enough where the crowd will be a little bit smaller without me.

A minyan is an all-or-nothing project. You can't say seven-tenths of the Kaddish when you only have seven people. Many times I have heard nonobservant Jews tell me that the restriction of the minyan is foolish. They say you should say Kaddish even without a minyan because God can hear you anyway. I'm sure God can. But it wasn't set up that way. By not saying Kaddish when you do not have a minyan, you greatly raise the costs of not having a minyan, and increase the benefits of having one. This induces people to show up for shul when their private calculation might lead them to stay at home.

How do you apply this in a practical way to fundraising? One way is to turn fundraising into an all-or-nothing project. You say, "We are either going to raise $10,000 for the scholarship fund (or the bond drive or whatever), or we're going to spend zero. If we collect $7,000, we're not going to spend it, we're going to give it back." This seems destructive on the face of it. Isn't a $7,000 fund better than nothing? It may be in the short run. But in the long run, if you can keep your all-or-nothing promise, you will have a much higher chance of collecting the $10,000.

The all-or-nothing project says to the potential donor, your gift no longer adds $100 or $200 to the scholarship fund—it may add $10,000. Without you we have nothing. With you, we have the scholarship fund. The key is to pick the right level for the project, in the same way that the size of the minyan is crucial. A minyan of five, ten, or twenty would lead to different behavior and probably a different size of community.

The potential power of the all-or-nothing threat can be seen by comparing it to a standard fund project. Suppose you are raising money for a synagogue improvement and you have $8000 raised so far. The more money you raise, the nicer the improvement will turn out. If you ask a donor to contribute $500, the donor considers the increase in the quality of the improvement if there is $8,500 to spend instead of $8,000, and compares this increase to the personal use of the $500. Again, in the absence of social pressure or guilt, the donor ignores the enjoyment of the other synagogue members from his $500 contribution. He may decide to keep the $500 and not make a contribution—he will get to enjoy an $8,000 improvement instead of an $8,500 one, but he will have the $500 to spend on himself. In the all-or-nothing project, if the total does not exceed the minimum level set in advance, the donor who holds back his $500 for personal enjoyment gets none of the benefits of the spending of others. At the same time, his contribution may pack much more of a wallop than just $500.

The all-or-nothing approach is a way of implicitly getting people to cooperate. They almost have to take into account the effect of their spending on others. A way to achieve this directly is to create matching-grant situations among donors. Suppose there are two donors who last year gave $100 to Israel. They each like the idea of giving $200 instead of $100, but they each decided to keep that second hundred for themselves. It wasn't worth giving up $100 of one's own spending to increase Israel's by $100. But suppose you call each of these donors independently and ask them if they would be willing to give an additional $100 if at the same time their contribution was matched by another donor. If they both agree, their extra $100 of spending yields $200 extra dollars. In this way, each individual's return to donating goes up in a way that is related to the benefits going to others. The likelihood of an increased donation also goes up.

A community is a group of people with a set of shared interests. Individual decisions may not always take account of the full effects on the community. When a community is small enough, as it is in the case of a family, for example, the members can sit down together and make sure that individual actions are taken cooperatively to ensure that individual decisions take account of community interests. Such cooperation can make each individual better off. Fortunately, the Jewish community is too large to sit at a single table to ensure cooperation. I have tried to suggest some ways that this can be done implicitly through guilt and matching grants to improve the quality of Jewish life.

PART VI

CREATING A POLICY RESEARCH AGENDA

Jewish Identity and Policy Research

DAVID ROSENHAN

Roy Feldman and I have decided that what we want to do is speak relatively briefly. Of course that promise is always more conservative at the outset than it is at the end. We're going to try to run a group dog-and-pony show, meaning that we'll both speak for no more than ten minutes, we hope, and then open it up to wider discussion.

It has been an interesting meeting. As others have done before me, I take this opportunity to thank Susan and David Wilstein for enabling an Institute of this sort where issues that are central to the Jewish agenda can be explored. And I thank—we thank—the Institute's director, David Gordis, whose collaborative imagination brought forth this conference on Jewish identity. It has been a meeting wherein I have not only been informed but have made some good friends. I learned, for example, that my father, during the depression, spent more than an occasional Shabbos with Roy's grandfather in Lynchberg, West Virginia. It's been a meeting I've really enjoyed.

The obvious task—to summarize this conference and to focus its content on policy research—is clearly more than can be done in so short a time. Consider the array of information that has been made available in the past three days. We have heard in this short time historical analyses of Jewish identity; examinations of the role of myth and popular culture in Jewish identity; adjurations regarding the content, and especially the oral content, of Jewish identity; and sociological and psychological examinations of the structure, development, and substance of Jewish identity. The papers and observations by Professors Cohen, Phillips, and London; the elegant and controversial historical analysis by Professor Feingold, and the enormously thoughtful response it evoked from Howard Friedman; the contributions of the rabbis—the striking observations of Chaim Seidler-Feller and the competing and complementary visions expressed by Rabbis Levy, Schulweis, and Landes; and the remarkable research foray designed by Daniel Steinmetz; the examination of popular identity as it appears in modern popular culture by Arnold Band and Alan Berger; and this brief overview omits some very important papers on the operation, durability, faults, and economics of the Jewish identity. I shall not, I *cannot* summarize these observations in so short a time and on so small a platform. But my own thinking has been much informed and inspired by these deliberations.

First, regarding the methods of research. There have been moments when our discussions of method in social science have been silly if not worse, and I want to make clear why this is the case. Unless you are willing to settle for *bubbemaises* and for rabbinic war stories, there is no way to assess Jewish identity without using the methods of social science. To paraphrase Thurstone, if Jewish identity exists, it exists in some quantity. And if it exists in some quantity, it can be measured. The available methods of measurement are quite sophisticated—let no one make any mistake about that. They are by no means limited to simple questionnaires by any means. We can, with modern social science techniques, approximate interior states of mind and experience. We can conduct as many and as penetrating in-depth interviews as anyone requires. We can survey, scientifically and well.

Choice of method is no longer determined by emotional allegiance, as it was in the fifties and sixties. Rather, it is determined by the more mundane issues of time, cost, skill, and the nature of the problem. Again, make no mistake about it—the methods for the scientific study of Jewish identity range from the very simple to the very complex, and in cost from the rather inexpensive to the very costly. They have limitations—all methods do. But these limitations have not been broached at these meetings. To argue for the use of sophisticated social scientific methods is not to argue, as Henry Feingold and I discussed this morning, that humanists and humanist thought should be left out of these issues. Quite the contrary. If what is insisted upon here is evidence beyond mere expert opinion, you have no alternative but to measure, carefully and well. We should not attend to the *nahrishkeit* that somehow diminishes the enormous strides in methodology that have been made over the past twenty-five or thirty years.

Second, I should like to propose a shortcut in the research agenda, one that will save both time and money and holds a good deal of promise to boot. Rather than examine the various elements of Jewish identity that we've discussed at this time, we ought to examine, I believe, ideal types: the people and institutions that have successfully transmitted Jewish identity across, say, the past fifty years. We should concentrate upon the values, beliefs, allegiances, moral commitments, community supports, and ideologies that we think are important and especially useful. For present purposes, the Institute might convene a small panel to nominate such people and institutions and to stipulate why they are of such interest and what values and contents they have been successful in transmitting.

Let me give just a few examples. Rabbi Landes is absolutely certain that despite the pressure and changes in the cultural envelope in which all of us exist, despite the fact that the end result of Jewish fecundity has been assimilation, his own children will remain Orthodox Jews. That's worth examining. There are families who have indeed resisted the pressures of intermarriage and assimilation across several generations. Study them. There are institutions that have been especially successful in conveying the contents, often the specific contents, of Jewish identity. I've heard some very special things said about Valley Beth Shalom, about Camp Ramah, about Summer in Israel programs, to name just a few without at all presuming to narrow the agenda. Study them.

Finally, there are people who seem particularly adept at transmitting the contents of Jewish identity. Whether we call them charismatic figures or influential teachers, these are people who are much more adept than the rest of us at getting across the things that we value, the things that we think are important. Study them.

Response

ROY FELDMAN

The papers presented at this Wilstein Institute Conference on Jewish Identity in America illustrate the multifaceted nature of the concept of American Jewish identity. They also show that the dimensions of American Jewish identity vary substantially, depending upon whose needs the concept serves. This paper is a research proposal derived from one viewpoint of these presentations. The purpose of the proposal is not to select or prefer any particular definition of American Jewish identity, but rather to take what we have learned from the humanistic perspectives of historical and literary analyses and from the social science perspectives of psychology, sociology, economics, anthropology, and policy analysis, and suggest *research which can be used to promote Jewish identity regardless of the preferred definition.*

This overview of a research agenda has three goals:

1. Identify a number of basic research areas which provide policy-relevant data.
2. Suggest a way of categorizing policy research areas and indicate applied research questions which should be pursued.
3. Suggest a number of demonstration projects which could determine what works and the associated costs, as well as what doesn't seem to work and the benefits and costs of eliminating or scaling back ineffective programs.[1]

Social research on Jewish identity should utilize the insights and perspectives of literary and historical analyses in formulating research questions. One of the most important results of the conference papers and discussion was the stimulating interaction of humanistic and social science approaches to the study of Jewish identity. Multiple research methods ought to be used to assess the meaning of Jewish identity for different sectors of the American Jewish community. Research ought to examine differences in the conception of Jewish identity by gender, age, socioeconomic status, region, and other characteristics, as well as for different sectors of the Jewish community, such as UJA Young Leadership Cabinet, federation allocation committees, etc.

Conference participants agreed that no single research method provides an ideal measurement of Jewish identity. The research community builds confidence in its assessments of Jewish identity when a variety of methods and approaches point in a similar direction. The choice of methods in any given project should be based upon an assessment of the likely benefits and estimated costs of those methods in conjunction with the questions we are asking. If attitudes are a central part of an investigator's preferred definition of identity, survey research may be particularly attractive. If deeply held values are central, in-depth interviews and/ or ethnographic analysis may be utilized. If a project focuses upon observance of custom or ritual, ethnographic and survey research may be selected. As a policy studies organization, the Wilstein Institute aims to "explore ways of strengthening Jewish identity and addressing existing barriers to Jewish identity, affiliation and participation."[2] With the resources planned for the next five years in the area of Jewish identity studies, I think it makes sense for the Wilstein Institute for Jewish Policy Studies to place its primary focus upon applied policy research rather than basic research.[3] The institute ought to be a consumer of basic research and a generator of policy-relevant studies informed by basic research.

Policy research areas related to the development and strengthening of American Jewish identity can be grouped as follows:

1. The role of the family in Jewish identity formation.
   A. How to strengthen positive affect toward Jewish culture, practices and learning.
   B. How to develop the earliest linkages between the child('s family) and Jewish institutions and agencies outside of the home, e.g., Jewish-sponsored infant care and day care with Jewish content.
2. How to promote the strongest possible *formal Jewish education*, of whichever persuasion the parents prefer.
   A. How to help schools improve their outreach.
   B. How to increase the pay and status of teachers in Jewish day schools and thereby sustain and increase their quality.
   C. How to provide increased knowledge and positive affect between the bat/bar mitzvah years and college years.
   D. How to develop an Israel-related curriculum that meets the objectives of the sponsoring groups whether their orientation is cultural, religious, or political.

3. How to use *informal Jewish education to increase identification during the critical college/graduate and professional school years?* How to assist Hillel Foundations at all universities. How to increase resources and quality programing.
4. How to promote Jewish programing and social activities for Jewish singles, both young adults, especially female-headed families, and older adults.
5. How to bridge the gaps in the understanding of American and Israel Jews about the ways in which they are similar and differ (see Steven M. Cohen's paper in this volume). How to address the decline in commitment to Israel among younger Jews. (See Cohen's conclusion that "every ten years' decline in age is associated with about a five percentage point decrease in pro-Israel answers to each of several questions" in the survey data. In addition, "The decline in Israel attachment is . . . not a function of any hypothetical decline in overall Jewish attachment.")
6. How to assess the role of different Jewish organizations in sustaining and promoting growth of Jewish identity, e.g., the synagogue, the Jewish school, the federation, the Jewish community center, etc., and relate these assessments of organizational impact to the allocation of community resources.
7. How can secular and unaffiliated Jews transmit *their* conception of Jewishness to their children and reduce the risk of total alienation from the Jewish people.
   A. How to find out what values "just Jewish" or self-oriented Jews would like to transmit to their children.
   B. There is a need to solicit their advice regarding secular social services that can be offered to this sector of the Jewish population. Seek an understanding of "hooks" that will allow provision of desired social services, and broaden their exposure to the diversity of the Jewish community. Here is Roy Feldman's list of "Priority Areas for Policy Research and *Demonstration Research Projects* Related to Promotion of Jewish Identity":

1. Set up model demonstration projects in Jewish-sponsored infant care and day care. Set aside slots for community outreach beyond the "committed." *Do funded baseline and follow-up research on the participating families as contrasted with appropriate comparison groups.*
2. Assess perceptions of perceived Jewish and general social needs of Jewish students in college, graduate, and professional schools.

Through competitive grant funding *set up demonstration research projects on college campus—outreach through Hillel Foundations*. Require appropriate baseline and follow-up data on participants as contrasted with appropriate comparison groups.

3. Develop measurements of the community status of Jewish studies educators. Develop and fund demonstration research projects which aim to *upgrade the status and quality of Jewish studies educators* and which upgrade the quality of teachers recruited. Give priority to funding and public relations for endowed chairs in Jewish day school education. Begin funding chairs at the highest-quality schools in a number of major Jewish communities.

Notes

1. Budgets ought to be developed to estimate the costs of the research agenda, but this is beyond the scope of this presentation.

2. First brochure of the Susan and David Wilstein Institute of Jewish Policy Studies, Los Angeles, Fall 1988.

3. Basic research is likely to be more expensive, higher-risk, and, in my judgment, best undertaken in large university settings.

Reflections on the Establishment of the Wilstein Institute

MARSHALL SKLARE

Birth is a time for rejoicing and congratulations. A new life, or a new institution, suggests exciting new possibilities. A new life has the attraction that it can open up new and as yet undreamt-of vistas. A new life has the further attraction that it is as yet untouched by the compromises which must be made by every human being, and by every institution.

We wish the Susan and David Wilstein Institute of Jewish Policy Studies well. We hope it will have a long and fulfilling life. We trust that it will realize the hopes of the academicians who guide it and the supporters who have made its establishment possible. This volume is a record of the papers and discussions which took place at the Institute's inaugural conference, held at the University of Judaism on June 4–7, 1989.

The inauguration of the Wilstein Institute calls for more than routine congratulations. The establishment of a center dedicated to the study of contemporary Jewish life, with a particular emphasis on questions of social policy, is a very special event. Since those of us who participated in the opening conference of the Institute were aware that very few similar centers exist, hopes for the growth and success of the Wilstein Institute were greater than the present modest size of the venture would suggest.

To be sure, the Wilstein Institute is not a singular institution—there are several other research institutes located in the United States and in Israel which are devoted to the study of contemporary Jewish life and to questions of Jewish social policy. But institutions of this type are few in number and suffer from financial constraints. Thus the establishment of a new center is not only a sign of new resources but it reinforces our belief in the potential of contemporary Jewish studies.

The situation in contemporary Jewish studies is quite different than that found in certain other fields, where one could say at times that there has been an overabundance of research institutes. Thus, several decades ago many major universities, and even some smaller institutions of higher learning, established Russian research centers. Their numbers proliferated so rapidly that it became difficult to justify all of these new centers. However, the multiplication of such centers ceased when government funds were cut back. Some Russian research institutes became defunct while others sharply reduced their operations. And even when money was in good supply for such enterprises, there was a constant shortage of scholar-administrators having a record of accomplishment in the field of Russian or Slavic studies and capable of managing such institutions.

When news of the establishment of the Wilstein Institute reached me, I wrote a letter of congratulations to Dr. Gordis. I applauded this new initiative and made the point that the very establishment of the Wilstein Institute would render a service to the handful of already existing institutes which had the same general objectives.

I believe in competition as well as in cooperation. Life has taught me that it is inadvisable for research centers to have a monopoly, and to do their work entirely free from the competition of rival institutions. Special circumstances may dictate that work on a given problem be concentrated entirely in a single research center, but scholars as well as businessmen generally do their best work when they are forced to compete with others. Thus I believe that one of the contributions of the Wilstein Institute can be to introduce more competition into the field of contemporary Jewish studies.

In analyzing its prospects we must consider that the Wilstein Institute is associated with the University of Judaism, which is the West Coast affiliate of the Jewish Theological Seminary of America. A seminary is a special type of academic institution. Although dedicated to the search for truth, difficulties can arise when that search casts doubt on the religious affirmations of its sponsors. On a more prosaic level, seminaries not only have theological affirmations but they generally require students to take on certain obligations of a religious nature. Thus, rabbinical seminaries require that students (particularly those being trained as "pulpit rabbis") make commitments which would be considered either superfluous or objectionable in the usual university setting. This situation is, of course, not unique to Jews. Many Protestant institutions require seminarians to conform to a given way of life; Catholic institutions are even more specific in detailing a way of life which seminarians are required to follow.

The question thus arises as to the extent to which the Wilstein Institute will require conformity on the part of its staff and its researchers. Historically the Seminary does not have a reputation for stressing ideological conformity. Furthermore, judging from a distance it appears that the University of Judaism has latitude in matters of ideology as well as in questions of personal style.

In reviewing the papers in this volume I looked for examples of partisanship, of special pleading, of narrowing the research agenda to issues which are unique to "our kind of Jew," and especially to conclusions "adjusted" to please the administration of the Institute, the University of Judaism, and the Seminary. I did not detect such tendencies. I was unable to discern any difference between our Wilstein meeting and gatherings held under "nonsectarian" sponsorship.

I trust that the Wilstein Institute will tolerate, and even encourage, freedom of research. To be sure, the test will occur when the Institute becomes more firmly established, and when trustees and administrators of the University of Judaism and the Seminary may begin to conceive of the Institute in terms of a service being rendered to the Jewish community rather than as an intellectual enterprise free to decide its own agenda. A related issue is whether the Institute will see fit to employ individuals whose ideological position and personal behavior do not conform to the general understanding of Conservative Judaism and to the way of life of Conservative Jews.

The phrase "a service being rendered to the Jewish community" suggests a highly worthwhile endeavor. Institutions of higher learning generally consider such service to be a responsibility which they owe to society. In addition, service to the community has a practical advantage. Through the instrumentality of "contract research" it supplies a research institute with a source of funding. Service to the community cannot be done without resources, and it is clear that those who expect services from a research center are obliged to supply the required funds. Thus, a research center which renders direct and unambiguous service to the community may be in the happy position of ensuring its financial stability.

Is serving the community and the arrangement of contract research a feasible option for a Jewish research institute? On first glance it would appear to be so. In recent years research needs of the Jewish community have become increasingly apparent. Organizations on the national level which are involved in raising funds need to know who their contributors are, as well as the social characteristics of noncontributors. The attractiveness of different fundraising appeals requires evaluation. Furthermore, the analysis of the long-range prognosis for Jewish fundraising is a constant preoccupation of fundraising organizations and thus a subject requiring repeated analysis.

Local bodies, most notably the federations, require Jewish population studies. The first priority in such studies are questions of a demographic nature. But population studies also inquire into the need for services which members of a local community feel. Jewish population studies also collect data on the Jewish identity of respondents. Such data generally include information on behavioral as well as attitudinal questions. Finally, Jewish population studies gather data on the philanthropic behavior of respondents.

In addition to studies commissioned by the national fundraising bodies and by the local federations, Jewish intergroup agencies have sponsored large-scale studies of anti-Semitism. Most studies in this area focus on the attitudes of non-Jews. In recent years more modest projects have been in vogue, in contrast to the very ambitious projects of the 1940s, 1950s, and 1960s. Many of the current studies do not focus on domestic anti-Semitism. Rather they seek to assess attitudes toward Israel and toward Israeli policy. In addition they seek to measure how respondents feel about U.S. assistance to Israel.

In the general research field, contract research is the central core of the work done by profit-making research centers. Most clients of the larger profit-making centers are sizable corporations engaged in the production of consumer goods. In addition to such clients, profit-making centers are interested in "noncommercial" clients. Work for such clients suggests that the center has interests which are wider than assisting companies to achieve larger sales and higher profits. Noncommercial clients run a wide gamut. They may be membership organizations concerned about the appeal of their programs to those segments of the population from which their support has traditionally come. Other clients may be organizations concerned with public issues. They may, for example, wish to test responses to pending legislation. Then there are professional organizations that wish to assess the image which the public has of their profession and its practitioners.

In addition to the private companies which do research there are the nonprofit research centers. Such centers are frequently connected with universities. Their focus is generally on the study of significant public issues. While they do contract research, they tend to rely upon research grants, many of which come from governmental agencies. Some of these centers specialize in a single problem, such as crime or poverty.

Contract research has its attractions. Usually the request for research is initiated by the client. Thus it is not difficult to convince those who will supply the funds of the worthwhileness of the research. Furthermore, the effort is targeted at a well-defined public who may derive a distinct benefit from the investigation. Negotiations about the research take place with a staff of experts rather than with philanthropists or with their representatives. And even if the client conceives of the project in limited terms, there is generally no overriding objection to the researchers gathering data which they believe will have larger implications. The researchers expect to return to such data sometime after they render a report which deals with the client's immediate concerns. Thus the researchers aim to design and carry out a project which will be satisfactory to the client and at the same time will gather data which, if properly analyzed, can constitute a significant addition to knowledge.

But the goal of making a significant addition to knowledge is rarely attained by the profit-making centers. Even the nonprofits do not always achieve this goal. The demands of new projects frequently preclude returning to unanalyzed data. Since returning to "old" data is not chargeable to the original client, costs must be covered by the center's resources. It is difficult to find a sponsor who is attracted to a study based on analysis of old data. A project that does not have a sponsor will necessarily be run at a deficit, no matter how modest the study design and how devoted the staff.

We would expect that Jewish research institutes would be attracted to contract research designed to meet the needs of Jewish agencies. However, contracts with Jewish agencies are not frequent enough or large enough to support even a modest institute on a continuing basis. Furthermore, competition for contracts is not restricted to research institutes, individual academicians are free to enter bids.

The most frequent type of contract for a Jewish research institute is a population study, sometimes called either a demographic or a community study. Increasingly such contracts are awarded through competitive bidding. Bidders may include research agencies both of the profit and nonprofit type. Nonprofit agencies may include those whose focus is general as well as those with a specifically Jewish focus. However, the majority of Jewish population studies are conducted not by research agencies but by academicians who sign a contract with a federation and work on a free-lance basis. Since a professor's overhead is minimal, he or she can usually underbid a not-for-profit research agency as well as a for-profit firm. Another advantage which the professor enjoys is that unless a leave of absence is taken, the professorial salary continues. Thus the professor is not dependent upon a research project for basic income.

It has long been recognized that the scientific contribution of Jewish population-study reports is severely limited. Part of the reason for this is that federations are generally satisfied with a very simple study report. Like research companies and research institutes, the academician who free-lances hopes that at some future time he will have an opportunity to return to the data and prepare an exhaustive analysis of the demographic, attitudinal, and behavioral material which has been collected. But such good intentions are seldom realized. A study in a different community is announced and bidders soon turn their attention to obtaining a new contract. The data tapes are placed in storage in the hope that they will be used at some future time. And if the academician does not win a new contract for a Jewish population study immediately, he may turn his attention to other issues: the study of methodological questions, the study of another ethnic group, or problems in social theory, demography, or in one or another specialization in which he is qualified. Such shifts are particularly common among academicians who are not full-time professors of Jewish studies.

The not-for-profit general research institutes have two significant sources of research funds. One is made up of federal or state programs which are specifically allocated for rescarch or deal with issues where research is required. The very large public-service foundations are the other source. Such foundations have programs, or seek to inaugurate programs, that deal with social problems of national or international scope. Frequent areas of concern are crime and delinquency, minority groups, family life, health, and poverty. Since such social problems defy easy solution, researchers are called in for consultation. Consultation generally leads to an assessment of what is known and to an analysis of what needs to be known-that is, an analysis of research needs. The objectives of the giant foundations are generally "practical," but the best such foundations recognize that "pure" research on the issues they confront may be as helpful as "applied" research.

In theory a not-for-profit Jewish research institute should be able to follow the path of the general research institute. But in actuality this is not possible. Given their income, their educational level, and their occupational profile, Jews are not thought of as constituting a significant social problem or even a minority group. The social theorist may consider Jews to be the perfect minority group, but when the yardstick applied is the extent to which Jews constitute a social problem, it is obvious that Jews will be given a low ranking, and hence a low priority. In sum, the situation of Jews lacks appeal to those who use the usual measuring rod in assessing either the pain of deprivation or the threat which a group poses to societal cohesion.

There is a further reason why it is difficult to obtain money for Jewish research from either governmental sources or from the large public-interest type of foundation. Jews are thought of as a religious group;

public agencies avoid research which deals with religion. The same is true, to a somewhat lesser extent, in the case of the very large public-interest foundations. Ironically, the desire of Jews and of Jewish inter-group-relations agencies to represent the Jews as a religious group works to their disadvantage in the area of research support.

This leaves the Jewish family foundations as a resource. Such foundations pose problems. They generally do not have the resources of the giant foundations. In some cases they may lack substantial uncommitted funds inasmuch as the family may continue to have a sense of obligation to institutions which they have helped to support over many decades. There are also cases where personal rifts between family members may limit the foundation to the support of causes which are of a neutral kind and thus acceptable to family members who have very different patterns of Jewish identity.

Under these circumstances the administrators and staff of a Jewish research institute are generally not free of financial concerns; an operation which is supported in whole or in part by philanthropic funds from the smaller foundations may involve an uncomfortable amount of continual fundraising. However, a research center supported by this type of patronage has advantages which are so important as to override the disadvantages. It does not have to service clients. It does not have to depend upon grants from government or from giant foundations—grants which are so difficult to achieve by a Jewish research operation. It is free to select those problems and concerns which it—rather than clients—judges to be crucial. The advantage of setting one's own agenda rather than conforming to the needs of a client is so significant that I believe that the potential of research institutes of the Wilstein type is much more significant than that of institutes designed along different principles.

Some decades ago, when the Jewish population of the nation was still concentrated in the Middle Atlantic and New England states, Dr. Louis Finkelstein, then the head of the Seminary, made the following comment to a meeting of the Rabbinical Assembly, the national organization of Conservative rabbis:

> Some years ago, I undertook to prepare a comprehensive work describing the whole phenomenon of Judaism. It was to include a history of the Jews, a description of their present condition, a discussion of their contribution to civilization . . . and an outline of their beliefs and practices as Jews. . . . What surprised me . . . was the dearth of information about Jews today. There are probably a hundred people, and more, whose profession it is to discover all that can be known about the Jews in Jerusalem in the first

century; there does not seem to be one who has the same duty for the Jews of New York in the twentieth century. So it comes about that we understand Judaism in the first century better than we understand Judaism in the twentieth.

Surely the Wilstein Institute will accept this challenge. In doing so it should contribute significantly to the understanding of Jews and Judaism in the twentieth century, as well as beyond.

Contributors

Hanan Alexander is Dean of Academic Affairs and Associate Professor in Philosophy and Education at the University of Judaism

Arnold J. Band is Professor of Comparative Literature at the University of California, Los Angeles

Steven Bayme is Director of Jewish Communal Affairs of the American Jewish Committee

Yoav Ben-Horin is Associate Director of the Wilstein Institute

Alan L. Berger is Professor and Director of Jewish Studies at Syracuse University

Stephen M. Cohen is Professor of Sociology at Queens College of the City University of New York

Bernard D. Cooperman is Professor of Jewish History at the University of Maryland

William Cutter is Professor of Education and Modern Hebrew Literature at Hebrew Union College in Los Angeles.

Stuart E. Eizenstat is an Attorney at Powell, Goldstein, Frazer & Murphy in Washington and was Domestic Policy Advisor to President Jimmy Carter

David Ellenson is Professor of Jewish Religious Thought at Hebrew Union College in Los Angeles

Henry Feingold is Professor of History at Baruch College of the City University of New York

Roy Feldman is a political scientist and President of Behavior Analysis, Inc. in Cambridge

Howard I. Friedman, an Attorney at Loeb & Loeb in Los Angeles, is Chairman of the Board of Directors of the Wilstein Institute and Honorary President of the American Jewish Committee

David Gordis is Director of the Wilstein Institute and Vice-President of the University of Judaism

Allissa Hirshfeld is a graduate student in Clinical Psychology at Teachers College at Columbia University

Daniel Landes, Rabbi, is Director of National Education at the Wiesenthal Center in Los Angeles

Richard N. Levy, Rabbi, lectures on Rabbinic literature at Hebrew Union College and directs the Los Angeles Hillel Council

Seymour Martin Lipset is Caroline S. G. Munro Professor of Political

Science and Sociology, Senior Fellow of the Hoover Institute, Stanford University, and Senior Scholar at the Wilstein Institute

Deborah E. Lipstadt is Adjunct Professor of Religious Studies at Occidental College and Director of Research of the Skirball Institute of American Values

Perry London is Dean of the Graduate School of Applied and Professional Psychology at Rutgers University

Howard Miller is an attorney-at-law in Los Angeles and served as President of the Board of Education of Los Angeles

Bruce A. Phillips is Associate Professor of Jewish Communal Studies at Hebrew Union College in Los Angeles

Russell D. Roberts is visiting Professor of Business & Economics at the University of California, Los Angeles

David Rosenhan is Professor of Law and Psychology at Stanford University

Jonathan D. Sarna is Professor of American Jewish History at Brandeis University

Harold M. Schulweis is Rabbi at Valley Beth Shalom, founded the Foundation for Christian Rescuers, and teaches at the University of Judaism and Hebrew Union College in Los Angeles

Chaim Seidler-Feller, Rabbi, is Director of the Hillel Foundation at UCLA

Marshall Sklare is Professor of Contemporary Jewish Studies and Sociology at Brandeis University

Daniel Steinmetz is Associate Director of Project STAR at the University of Michigan School of Social Work

Irving White is a clinical psychologist and is President of CRA, Inc. in Los Angeles

J. Alan Winter is Professor of Sociology at Connecticut College

Steven J. Zipperstein is Associate Professor of History at the University of California, Los Angeles